𝕯𝖆𝖓𝖟𝖎𝖌 1939: TREASURES OF A DESTROYED COMMUNITY

Published by Wayne State University Press for The Jewish Museum / New York
Detroit, 1980

Danzig 1939: TREASURES OF A DESTROYED COMMUNITY

Preface

JOY UNGERLEIDER-MAYERSON

Essays

GÜNTER GRASS

GERSHON C. BACON

JOSEPH GUTMANN

ELIZABETH CATS

Catalogue

VIVIAN B. MANN

JOSEPH GUTMANN

THE JEWISH MUSEUM / NEW YORK

This exhibition and catalogue were made possible by a grant from the National Endowment for the Humanities.

Further assistance was received from The Joe and Emily Lowe Foundation, Inc., Ruth and Henry Herzog in memory of Trude Plaut, and The Peter Cats Foundation.

Editor: Sheila Schwartz
Catalogue Designer: Leon Auerbach
Typography: Unbekant Typo Inc. and Jafa Typographers, N.Y.
Printing: Thomson-Shore Inc. Dexter, Michigan

Copyright © 1980 by The Jewish Museum, 1109 Fifth Avenue, New York, N.Y. 10028, under the auspices of The Jewish Theological Seminary of America.

Published by Wayne State University Press, Detroit 48202.

LCC 79-92643
ISBN 0-8143-1661-1 (clothbound)
ISBN 0-8143-1662-X (paperbound)

The quotations from Heine's "The Rabbi of Bacherach" in the essay by Günter Grass are reprinted by permission of Schocken Books Inc. from "The Rabbi of Bacherach" by Heinrich Heine, translated by E. B. Ashton copyright 1947 renewed © 1975 by Schocken Books Inc.

Exhibition Coordinator: Eileen Krest
Research Associates: Naomi Strumpf, Elizabeth Cats, Anita Friedman
Exhibition Designers: Stuart Silver, Peter Felperin

Participating Institutions:

AMT FÜR WISSENSCHAFT UND KUNST IN DER PAULSKIRCHE
Frankfurt am Main

BETH HATEFUTSOTH MUSEUM OF THE JEWISH DIASPORA
Tel Aviv

B'NAI BRITH MUSEUM
Washington, D.C.

BRAUNSCHWEIGISCHES LANDESMUSEUM
Braunschweig

HEBREW UNION COLLEGE SKIRBALL MUSEUM
Los Angeles

JOSLYN ART MUSEUM
Omaha

THE MAURICE SPERTUS MUSEUM OF JUDAICA
Chicago

MUSEUM OF ART UNIVERSITY OF OREGON
Eugene

RHEINISCHES LANDESMUSEUM
Bonn

SCHATTEN GALLERY ROBERT W. WOODRUFF LIBRARY EMORY UNIVERSITY
Atlanta

SEMITIC MUSEUM HARVARD UNIVERSITY
Cambridge

UNIVERSITY ART MUSEUM UNIVERSITY OF CALIFORNIA, BERKELEY, in association with the JUDAH L. MAGNES MEMORIAL MUSEUM
Berkeley

THE WICHITA ART MUSEUM
Wichita

Table of Contents

Danzig 1939:

The Great Synagogue of Danzig marked for destruction.
The placards read: "The Synagogue will be torn down" and "Come dear May and free us of the Jews."

Preface

JOY UNGERLEIDER-MAYERSON

On July 26, 1939, ten huge crates, weighing over two tons, were delivered to 122nd Street and Broadway, New York City—the home of The Jewish Theological Seminary of America. These crates contained ceremonial objects, books, scrolls, tapestries, textiles and memorabilia—the precious possessions of a community that was about to be destroyed, the Jewish community of the Free City of Danzig. In the early spring of 1939, the elders of the Jewish community, realizing that life in Danzig was becoming increasingly restricted by the Nazis, undertook a heartbreaking project. By agreement with the Nazi officials, who had been elected to the Danzig government in growing numbers from 1930 on, the elders negotiated the sale of Jewish communal property, including the historic Danzig Synagogue and the Jewish cemetery. The proceeds of these sales were put into a special bank account to finance the emigration of those members of the community who were still permitted to leave. This dispersal would, in effect, make Danzig "a city without Jews" (p. 8).

There remained the disposition of the religious ceremonial objects used daily in the Great Synagogue, as well as the exceptional Lesser Gieldzinski Collection that was housed in a special room of the same synagogue. The collection, a gift of Lesser Gieldzinski, art collector, connoisseur, and art adviser to Kaiser Wilhelm II, had been donated to the community in 1904 and contained outstanding examples of silver Torah headpieces, breastplates, crowns and pointers; of spice boxes and *Kiddush* cups; of silver and brass *menorot*; and many other ritual objects. The American Jewish Joint Distribution Committee, in cooperation with leaders from the Danzig Jewish community, managed to negotiate the complicated arrangements for the shipment of these precious objects to The Jewish Theological Seminary of America for safekeeping. For a certain sum of money—which presumably would also help expedite the emigration of Jews from Danzig—the Police Department of Danzig permitted the export of these objects to the United States. (The original police permit is on display in the present exhibition (see p. 19).) The community stipulated that The Jewish Theological Seminary was to house the collection for a period of fifteen years; and if the Danzig Jewish community were to be re-established before that time, the collection would be returned to the Free City. If, after fifteen years, there would be no safe and free Jews in Danzig, the collection would remain in America for the education and inspiration of the rest of the world. Shortly after permission was granted by the police, the collection was hastily packed in crates. It arrived at The Jewish Theological Seminary on July 26, 1939. One month later, on August 31, the German army marched into Danzig.

Forty years have passed. In those early years, The Jewish Museum was housed in the library of The Jewish Theological Seminary and only a few objects from the Danzig collection could be exhibited. In 1947, the collections of The Jewish Museum were transferred to its new home at 1109 Fifth Avenue, New York City, the former Warburg mansion. But a major exhibition of the Danzig material could only be mounted after the collection was properly researched and catalogued, and its objects conserved and restored.

Over a period of years, through the cooperative efforts of many individuals and agencies, the Danzig objects have been intensively researched, and historical documents, including important photographs, have been dug out of dusty archives. The result of these combined efforts is the present exhibition, *Danzig 1939: Treasures of a Destroyed Community*. The Jewish Museum believes that this exhibition of the personal and communal objects of a single Jewish community brings us closer to those millions throughout Europe who died in the crematoria of concentration camps and whose possessions were appropriated by the Nazis. The Danzig community, more fortunate than others, had the opportunity and foresight to retain some part of its heritage by sending its material culture to America for preservation.

We have also been brought closer to the experience of the Danzig community through interviews with those who escaped "the final solution." Advertisements and press coverage announcing the forthcoming exhibition produced many letters and visits from former Danzigers, mainly from Israel and the United States. I was privileged to interview a number of these former residents, such as Dr. Erwin Lichtenstein, who was an executive director of the *Synagogen-Gemeinde,* the Jewish community organization, from 1932 to 1938; Moshe Landau, currently a judge in the Israel Supreme Court; and Dr. Ruth Rosenbaum-Spiro. When it was no longer possible for Jewish children to attend public schools in Danzig, Dr. Spiro organized a unique education facility in her parents' home. Jewish children were there able to continue their academic studies, while at the same time they were provided with vocational training to prepare them for a new life elsewhere. The staff of three—Ruth, her father, and her mother—rapidly grew in number and stature through the addition of distinguished scholars who had been dismissed from prestigious German universities because they were Jewish. Pictures and records of *Die Höhere Jüdische Privatschule,* as well as other archival documents, are included in our exhibition.

The organization of this exhibition has been a complex task. On behalf of The Jewish Museum, I would like to acknowledge many individuals and institutions for their assistance. Our special thanks and appreciation to the National Endowment for the Humanities, a Federal agency, for providing us with planning and implementation grants to mount this exhibition. I would also like to thank the Samuel H. Kress Foundation for funding the conservation of the Danzig textiles. Thanks for generous financial support are also due to the Joe and Emily Lowe Foundation, to the Peter Cats Foundation, and to Mr. and Mrs. Henry H. Herzog, whose gift was made in memory of Trude Plaut. To Elizabeth Cats and Naomi Strumpf, Research Associates, I owe a deep debt of gratitude for their unstinting dedication and devotion over many years to their work as researchers of the collection. Cissy Grossman, formerly Assistant Curator of Judaica, was deeply involved at the inception of this project. Stuart Silver, design adviser of the exhibition, was more than a designer: he shared with The Jewish Museum its commitment to the perpetuation of the Danzig legacy. For his personal involvement my wholehearted thanks. To Peter Felperin for his creative design I am most appreciative. Thanks also to the Leo Baeck Institute for making available research personnel, especially Dr. Steven Lowenstein. Special acknowledgement is due Dr. Vivian Mann, Curator of Judaica. She has worked behind the scenes, helping to coordinate wherever necessary, and has done particularly valuable research on the objects in the exhibition, as well as having written all the catalogue entries. She was ably assisted by Emily Bilski of the Judaica department. I am grateful to Professor Joseph Gutmann for his expertise in the selection and research of objects and for his scholarly essay. I further wish to acknowledge the following people for their assistance and support in this project: Professor Ismar Schorsch, Professor Bezalel Narkiss, Dr. Gershon Bacon, Dr. Menahem Schmelzer, Eileen Krest, Coordinator of the Exhibition, Dr. Sheila Schwartz, Leon Auerbach, Anita Friedman, and Anne Danzig. My personal thanks are extended to Susan Goodman, Chief Curator at The Jewish Museum, for her availability and perceptiveness during the long course of planning and implementation of this exhibition. And finally, it was a memorable moment for me when Günter Grass, a native of Danzig, visited with us, and after seeing the collection and learning how it came to the Museum, agreed to write an essay for this book. My appreciation to Mr. Grass for his personal thoughts on a subject that means so much to him.

The dismantling of the Great Synagogue of Danzig.

Rosenbaum School students costumed for a play.

What Shall We Tell Our Children?

GÜNTER GRASS

"When at the end of March it became necessary to evacuate the Central Synagogue on Reitbahn (as per contract), Doubt and his remaining pupils helped to pack the ritual objects, which were soon sent to New York, where they became the Gieldzinski Collection in The Jewish Museum. (In 1966 the scrolls of the Torah were destroyed when fire broke out in the library.)" This passage in my book, *From the Diary of a Snail,* relates how the Jewish community of Danzig was dispersed in the spring of 1939 and how it had to finance the emigration of its members by selling the synagogues and Jewish cemeteries. "After the contract was signed, the aged synagogue directors and Leopold Schufftan, the cantor of the Central Synagogue, were said to have wept."

Now, forty-one years later, the treasures of the Danzig synagogue are being exhibited in New York. My reflections on the subject cannot relate to their cultural or historical significance, but must inevitably follow from the consequences of the German crime and from the nature of my literary activity. For the past can never cease to be present to us, and we are still asking ourselves: How could such a thing happen?

We are still without an answer. Thirty-five years after Auschwitz the problem confronting Germans is once more: What shall we tell our children? Or more precisely: How are parents born after the war, parents who in their childhood were fobbed off with lies, evasions and half-answers to their questions, to explain to their own children what was done "in the name of the German people" in Auschwitz, Treblinka and Majdanek? What are they to say of the German guilt that has lived on from generation to generation and must remain forever indelible?

Other peoples have been more fortunate in a dubious sort of way, that is, more forgetful. No one thinks of holding the Russian people responsible for the mass murder committed in the name of the Revolution under Stalin. Relatively few citizens of the United States feel responsible today for the American war crimes committed in Vietnam. England, France and Holland have successfully forgotten the injustice

(whose consequences are still with us) of their colonial regimes. All that is water under the bridge, ancient history, and history goes on.

The Germans alone cannot evade their responsibility. The more inoffensive they try to seem, the greater the dread they inspire in their neighbors. Their economic success cannot conceal the moral vacuum engendered by their incomparable guilt. No amount of talk about the innocence of the Germans who had not yet been born or about the crimes of other peoples can relieve them of their guilt. Others point at them, and they point at themselves. With the same merciless pedantry that tolerated, planned and carried out the genocide of six million Jews, they go on asking themselves why it happened, and being asked (more urgently from generation to generation) by their children. As in the Hebrew Bible, guilt lives on and is inherited. In the late 1960s, I, who for years had questioned others—people of my parents' generation—was questioned by my children, then four, eight, and (the twins) twelve years of age. Being children, they asked: What about the children, were they gassed too? Or: Why children? Or they bogged down in technical details: What kind of gas was it? The numbers, the millions, were beyond their understanding. When my older sons asked about the reasons for such horror, their parents lost themselves in talk of complicated historical, social or religious developments, cited dozens of causes, which when taken together seemed simply absurd. The children's interest shifted to other questions, relating to daily life, the golden hamster, a television program, the next vacation.

Only when I spoke of individual destinies—a flight into death, a flight to Palestine, for example—did I hold the children's attention, though I could not be sure that they heard anything more than an adventure story. I began to write down their questions and my uncertain answers. And since I was kept busy from March 1969 to the following fall with the forthcoming Bundestag elections, my children's questions mingled in my diary with notes on the election campaign to form the basis of the book, *From the*

Diary of a Snail, that I was to write some time later. In my book the story of the persecution, expulsion and destruction of the Danzig Jews runs parallel to a record of present-day political events. It seemed to me that my perception of my native city of Danzig was still clear and vivid enough to provide me with a credible setting for an account of the onset and slow development of the German crime. What happened in Berlin, Leipzig, Nuremberg, Frankfurt and Düsseldorf also happened in Danzig, though somewhat delayed by Danzig's status as a free city. And all in broad daylight. The same limitless hatred was proclaimed in posters and in shouted slogans. The same cowardly silence on the part of the Christian churches. There, too, the citizenry adapted to the new situation. There, too, the people deliberately disenfranchised themselves.

My decision to approach the horror of the "final solution" from the periphery, to follow its development in a place well known to me, derived from an old project of mine, undertaken years before and abandoned as a failure, namely, to complete Heinrich Heine's fragment, "The Rabbi of Bacherach."* Heine's romantic irony had provoked me; I wanted to contradict him. His defeat by so overwhelming a subject had aroused my ambition. Today I know that without the detour through Heine's "Bacherach" I would not have found my way to the Jews of Danzig, through whom I hoped to bring the Jewish community of a medieval Rhenish town back to life and uncover threads of destiny that lay buried beneath the sands of time. Three chapters totaling less than sixty pages are all we possess of "The Rabbi of Bacherach." The tale seems to end in mid-sentence. The author assures his readers in parentheses that the ensuing chapters and the end of the tale were lost through no fault of his. And yet, so often was his work on the manuscript interrupted, so unwieldy and unmanageable did the material become, and so compelling were the arguments against publishing the story as a whole or even the fragment at the time, that Heine busied himself with the material for a full fifteen years. The story of the writing of "The Rabbi" reads like a chronicle of failure.

In the summer of 1824, a year after the Napole-

onic Edict of Tolerance was partly revoked in Prussia (whereupon it became possible to deprive Jews of teaching positions in schools and universities), the law student (and author of *Die Harzreise—Travels in the Harz Mountains*), began his preliminary work at the Göttingen Library. He who as a poet subscribed as a matter of principle to "indifferentism," who scorned all positive religion, who looked upon Judaism and Christianity alike as expressions of contempt for humanity, whose sole attachment to his origins consisted in an occasional sentimental impulse (and this in exasperation at the dominance of Christianity), he, the liberal, who believed only in reason, began to delve into the history of the Jewish people's millennial sufferings. To his friend Johann Jakob Moser he wrote: "I am also immersed in the study of chronicles and especially in historia judaica. The latter because of its connection with the Rabbi and perhaps also out of inner need. Very special feelings move me when I leaf through those sorrowful annals; in them I find an abundance of instruction and grief."

At the start of the very first chapter, after the small town of Bacherach is presented in a romantic light and the small Jewish community within its walls introduced, the theme is struck in historical retrospect: "The Great Persecution of the Jews began with the Crusades and raged most grimly about the middle of the fourteenth century, at the end of the Great Plague which, like any other public disaster, was blamed on the Jews. It was asserted that they had brought down the wrath of God, and that they had poisoned the wells with the aid of the lepers."

Heine tells of hordes of medieval flagellants, who, "chanting a mad song to the Virgin Mary," passed through the Rhineland on their way to southern Germany, murdering Jews by the thousands. He points to the source of the centuries-old lie: ". . . that the Jews would steal the consecrated wafer, stabbing it with knives until the blood ran from it, and that they would slay Christian children at their Feast of Passover, in order to use the blood for their nocturnal rite."

With this the tragic theme is announced. For with the Feast of Passover, at which the small Jewish community of Bacherach gathers around Rabbi Abraham, the plot of the still unfinished story begins. While the Rabbi (then a young man, who had studied in Toledo in Spain, where he had come to take a sympathetic view of Christianity) is conducting the old rites in the

---

*The unfinished story by Heinrich Heine (1797–1856) is available in English translation in *Great Jewish Short Stories,* ed. Saul Bellow, Dell Publishing Co., Inc. New York. The quotations that follow are from this translation.—Ed.

great hall of his home, while the silver Sabbath lamp "casts its most festive light on the devoutly merry faces of old and young," while, in other words, the liberation of the people of Israel from Egyptian bondage is being peacefully commemorated, adorned with legends, documented from Scripture, and celebrated with the words of the *Haggadah*—"Behold, this is the food our fathers ate in Egypt! Let any who is hungry come and partake!"—two strange men in wide cloaks enter the hall and present themselves as traveling co-religionists who wish to join in the Passover service.

As grandly as the celebration is described— ". . . the men sat in their black cloaks and black, flat hats and white ruffs; the women in strangely glittering garments made of cloths from Lombardy, wore their diadems and necklaces of gold and pearls . . ."—the reader is left with a foreboding of doom. A little later, Rabbi Abraham discovers that one of the stangers had brought in the bloody corpse of a child and deposited it under the table—the pretext for the massacre to come. But Heine spares his delicate readers the details of the pogrom, and the story takes a romantic turn. In obedience to the ancient injunction to live and bear witness, the rabbi leaves his congregation, over whom "the Angel of Death" is hovering, and manages to escape with his young wife Sarah. They board a boat on the River Rhine, and during the night "Silent Wilhelm who, although a deaf-mute, was a handsome lad," rows them to Frankfurt on the Main. The two remaining chapters are set in the Frankfurt ghetto. There is no pronounced climax as in the first chapter.

Of the second part of the tale, which was to take place in Spain, as we learn from Heine's letters, we know nothing. He probably chose Spain as the goal of Rabbi Abraham's flight because of the opportunity it would provide to develop his ideal of a tolerance embracing all religions (and his critique of all orthodox doctrines).

Shortly before his graduation in June 1825, Heinrich Heine was baptized as a Protestant. He wished to lecture on philosophy and history in Berlin and also had social ambitions. Yet, though he adapted himself to the servitudes of the day, he continued to work on "The Rabbi of Bacherach" until new interruptions relieved him of a task that was becoming increasingly burdensome. For a time he planned to publish a short version in the second part of his *Reisebilder* (*Travel Scenes*), but that too was abandoned. In 1833, when a fire in his mother's house in Hamburg destroyed a

large part of the manuscripts stored there, the manuscript of "The Rabbi," which in the meantime had swollen to two volumes, was lost. All that remained were fragmentary rough drafts, with which the author, then an exile in Paris, planned to go on working.

But it was not until 1840 that a current happening—a Passover ending in a pogrom—led Heine to resume work on his book: a group of Damascus Jews, accused of murdering a Capuchin priest and drinking his blood at their Passover celebration, were tortured by order of Count Ratti-Menton, the French consul. What in Heine's tale had resulted from the superstitious madness of the Middle Ages, had been reenacted in Heine's own time, in defiance of all enlightenment and the humanitarian principles of the French Revolution.

Heine stated his views in a series of articles, some of which appeared in the *Augsburger Allgemeine Zeitung*. In one article suppressed by the editors, he directly attacked the French prime minister: "At his morning audience Monsieur Thiers . . . with an air of total conviction, declares it to be an acknowledged fact that the Jews drink Christian blood at their Feast of Passover. . . ."

This series of articles, later collected in the first part of his *Lutetia*, were among Heine's journalistic masterpieces. Tempering the earnestness and passion of his attacks with irony, concealing his grief and shame with wit, digressing to report the latest gossip of the Opéra and drawing a picture of contemporary Paris (in expectation of the return of Napoleon's body), he nevertheless keeps hold of his central theme. He proves that the martyrdom of the Jews in Damascus was not an isolated reversion to the Dark Ages, but might well be the forerunner of a new and more terrible form of persecution, fomented by Christian hatred. True, there had been protests against Consul Ratti-Menton, who had instigated the pogrom in Damascus and promoted it with rabble-rousing pamphlets, but the prejudice remained. Heine clearly saw and analyzed the explosive situation in the Near East and the false view taken of it in Europe. In this instance the "indifferentism" often deplored by his Jewish friends helped him to keep cool and (as elsewhere with regard to Marxism) to foresee the crimes of the 20th century: the shift of the traditional Christian hatred of the Jews into organized racism and anti-Semitism.

16

As if the events in Damascus had given him new impetus, Heine now reworked his tale. But though he dedicated "Das Paschafest" ("The Feast of Passover") as he now called it, to Baroness Betty Rothschild, he soon withdrew it in favor of his earlier version. Possibly to free himself from the theme, undoubtedly to give more weight to the volume containing his so-called "Salon," he included the three now extant chapters of his fragment, which fulfills its high literary aspiration only in the account of the Passover and otherwise loses itself in flowery descriptions and strained wit.

After fifteen years, Heine tore himself away from the subject that had become an obligation and a burden to him. In his work as a journalist, he gained and communicated clearer insights into the theme. Possibly the failure of the fragment was due to the romantic style of the day which, even when tempered with irony, was not equal to the terrible reality that Heine was trying, in retrospect and with foreboding, to deal with. In resignation he wrote to Campe, his publisher: "I wrote this picture of medieval life fifteen years ago, and what I am publishing here is only the exposition of the book that was burned in my mother's house—perhaps fortunately for me, since in the latter chapters I reveal heretical views that would have provoked an uproar among Jews and Christians alike."

In a letter to his friend Moser, written before starting work on "The Rabbi," Heine had shown in advance a better appreciation of the provocative quality inherent in the work as it now stands: "I admit that I shall come out vigorously for the rights and civic equality of the Jews, and in the hard times that are sure to come the Germanic mob will hear my voice and responses will be roared in German beer halls and mansions."

There has been a good deal of controversy about Heine, who has usually been approached from the wrong direction. As an enlightened patriot, yet critic, of his country, he was unexcelled. The accuracy of his reporting was termed subversive, his wit denigrated as alien to the German people; still, his flattest rhymes and his self-imitating sentimentalities were numbered among the treasures of German literature, and found quotable at all times. Heine remains a stumbling block to the Germans. His witty seriousness and laughing despair are beyond them. I do not except myself, for when soon after the end of the war, young and hungry

for hitherto forbidden literature, I read Heine's "Rabbi of Bacherach" for the first time, my initial brief impression was one of annoyance; after that, and for much longer, I saw it as a challenge to embark on a presumptuous venture. I decided to continue the fragment and played (experimentally) with imitations of the style. I wanted the Rhine boatman to carry the fugitive Abraham and Sarah, not to medieval Frankfurt, but to the Frankfurt of the 1930s. A detail at the beginning of the second chapter gave me the idea of continuing the tale in the present. As they approach there destination, Abraham cries out to Sarah: "Over there, those houses beckoning amidst green hills, that's Sachsenhausen, where Lame Gumpertz goes to get the fine myrrh for us at the time of the Feast of Tabernacles. . . ." My leap in time was suggested by this incidental mention of a place that was to give its name to a concentration camp.

An obstinate notion, which kept reviving of its own accord everytime I abandoned it as hopeless. But nothing was ever committed to writing, for in the meantime I was pursuing my own ideas. The setting of my story could not be Bacherach, Frankfurt on the Main (Sachsenhausen), or Toledo. I clung to my roots, and in pursuing my question—How shall I tell my children?—I could only take Danzig as my starting point. The challenge of Heine's fragment was still with me, but it had ceased to be a literary inspiration.

In the mid-1960s, when I went to Israel for the first time, I made the acquaintance in Tel Aviv of Erwin Lichtenstein, who as a lawyer and former syndic of the Danzig *Synagogen-Gemeinde* was now busying himself with so-called reparations claims. As a young man, he had been obliged to deal with the Nazi authorities and preside over the sale of Jewish religious buildings and cemeteries. He had collected copious material bearing witness to the persecution, expulsion, and destruction of the Danzig Jews. Although he had been working for years on the manuscript of his book, which was to appear in the early 1970s,* no literary ambition deterred him from putting copies of his documents at my disposal. Through him I was able, on a later trip to Israel, to visit several survivors of the Danzig Jewish community, among them Ruth Rosenbaum, who as a young teacher had

*Dr. Lichtenstein's book appeared in 1973 as *Die Juden der Freien Stadt Danzig unter der Herrschaft des Nationalsozialismus*, Tübingen.—Ed.

Sam Echt's Jewish school (primary school equivalent to Ruth Rosenbaum's High School)

Dr. Ruth Rosenbaum, seated front row center, with the fifth grade class of her Private Jewish High School, March 1937.

A classroom in the Rosenbaum School displays students' work on Judaism and Palestine.

founded and directed the Jewish private school which continued in operation from 1935 to spring 1939, in the midst of the rising Nazi terror. Shortly before the "Departure of the Five Hundred" (a shipment of Danzig Jews who, after adventurous wanderings, reached Palestine aboard the freighter *Astir*), the Rosenbaum school was closed because the number of pupils had fallen from over two hundred to thirty-six. "At the end of February eight students (the last) had managed to obtain their secondary diplomas (which were certified by the Senate). (When in Jerusalem I asked Eva Gerson for details, she said: 'The Nazis on the examining commission, including Schramm and other bigwigs, were rather impressed by our performance.')"

Although I had grown up next door to the martyrdom of the Jews, it was then that I gained the knowledge that enabled me to speak with precision. Through countless affidavits, diary entries, documents and newspaper reports that I found at Erwin Lichtenstein's, I became aware of the crime that then, during my childhood, was slowly taking on more and more monstrous proportions. Yet I would not have been the right author for a linear chronicle. To expose the many layers of the German trauma I required a present constellation as a counter-theme, for the generations of those who had participated and of those who knew and kept silent, was not only inconspicuously present, but was reaching out for new political responsibility as though nothing had happened.

In the late 1960s, when the Cold War and the Adenauer era of internal restoration had drawn to a close, there was a possibility, for the first time in the Federal Republic, of a democratic transfer of power. But by letting the parliamentary opposition dwindle to nothing, the government of the Great Coalition, formed of Christian Democrats and Social Democrats, confronted the still insecure democratic consciousness of the West German people with its first real challenge. On the left, the student protest movement gave rise to an "Extraparliamentary Opposition"; on the right, the growth of a neo-fascist party, the NPD, was encouraged by the choice, as chancellor of the Great Coalition, of a man with the political past of Kurt Georg Kiesinger. This seemed to invalidate the arguments of the government parties against the Neo-Nazis. As a long-time member of the National Socialist Party, Kiesinger had held important positions under the Third Reich, undeterred to the last by the crimes that were well known to him. His chancellorship was an insult to all those who had resisted Nazism. The political revaluation of his past called into question everything the West Germans, those model students of school democracy, had been teaching one another: political responsibility, return to a liberal system of justice—not merely colorless good behavior, but also shame and grief rooted in knowledge of German crimes that cannot be wished away.

The fact that the Social Democrat and one-time

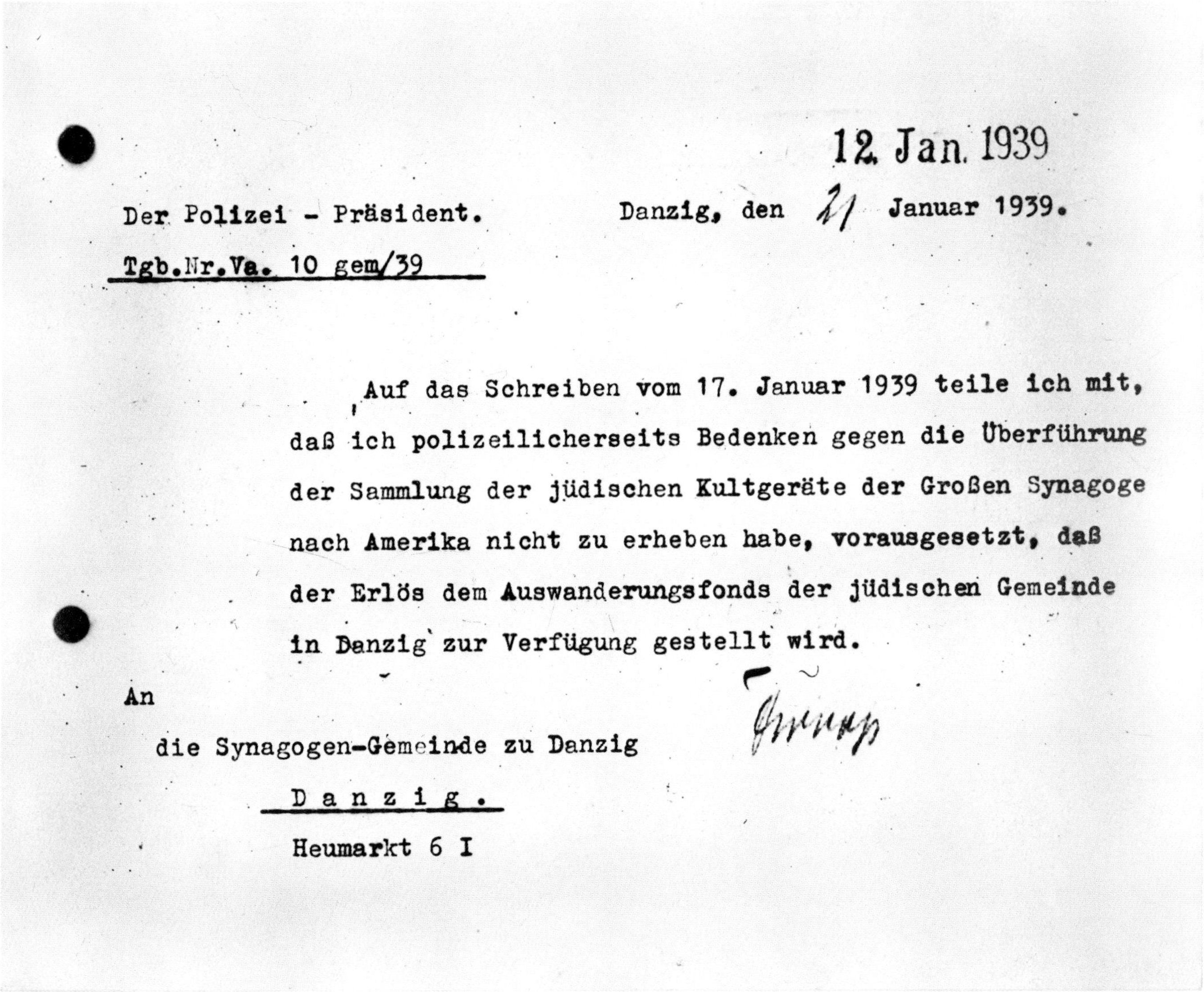

12. Jan. 1939

Der Polizei - Präsident.   Danzig, den 2/ Januar 1939.

Tgb.Nr.Va. 10 gem/39

　　　　　Auf das Schreiben vom 17. Januar 1939 teile ich mit,

daß ich polizeilicherseits Bedenken gegen die Überführung

der Sammlung der jüdischen Kultgeräte der Großen Synagoge

nach Amerika nicht zu erheben habe, vorausgesetzt, daß

der Erlös dem Auswanderungsfonds der jüdischen Gemeinde

in Danzig zur Verfügung gestellt wird.

An

die Synagogen-Gemeinde zu Danzig

　　　D a n z i g .

　　　Heumarkt 6 I

The 12 Jan. 1939 Police permit reads: "Regarding your letter of 17 Jan. 1939, I would like to inform you that from the point of view of the Police, I have nothing against your sending the Jewish ritual objects from the Great Synagogue to America, provided that the proceeds be used for the purposes of the emigration of the Jewish Community of Danzig."

Wir erklären hiermit an eidesstatt, dass nachstehende aufgefü
Gegenstände gebrauchtes Eigentum der Synagogen-Gemeinde Danzig si
Die Gegenstände werden nach New York U.S.A. versandt.

Inhaltsverzeichnis der 10 Kisten S.1-10.

2 Vorbeterpulte
9 Amulette
2 Beschneidungsmesser
2 Beschneidungstabletts
11 Geruchsbüchsen
16 Leuchter
5 Fruchtdosen
8 Gebetbücher
23 Handzeiger
11 Kronen
1 Ehevertrag
8 Weinbecher
1 geschriebene Tafel
1 Kamm
12 Lichtgestelle
2 Mäntel
7 kleine Gebetrollen
2 Medaillen
11 Segenssprüche
3 Oelbilder
11 Mäntel
12 Vorhänge
5 Behänge
2 Sabbathlampen
6 Schüsseln
1 Sabbathschüssel
4 Widderhörner
1 Gebettafel
1 Schleier
1 Sofa
———
181

Transport 181
13 Torabehänge
1 Paar Gebetriemen
52 Torarollen
3 Paar Wandarme
6 Stück Wandarme
6 Waschgeräte
2 Becher
1 Handtuch
2 Wasserbehälter mit Becke
6 Wimpeln
25 Sammelteller-und Büchsen
2 Stück Blaker
1 Messingtafel
1 Adler
2 Löwen mit Gesetzestafeln
1 Marmortafel
1 Bibal
14 Altardecken
12 Vorhänge
8 Toramäntel
2 Fahnen
———
342 Stück

Dreihundertundzweiundvierzig Stück

Danzig, den 8. Februar 1939

der Synagogengemeinde in Danzig
New York
U.S.A. verladen werden.
Dr. Kurt Itzig u. E. Lichtenstein
Danzig 8. 2. 39

The contents of the ten crates destined for New York City are enumerated in a packing list of 8 Feb. 1939, signed by members of the Danzig Jewish Community.

refugee Willi Brandt served as Kiesinger's vice-chancellor and foreign minister could not sweeten the unsavory compromise. Especially the postwar generation, sensitized by the movement of protest against the Vietnam war, rejected the "government of national reconciliation" as lacking in credibility. No amount of street demonstrations or moral appeals could shake the new power cartel, but there was reason to hope that the Bundestag elections, scheduled for autumn 1969, might replace Kiesinger and his Great Coalition with a Socialist-Liberal Democrat coalition headed by Willi Brandt.

I took an active part in the ensuing election campaign. With a group of friends, I helped to organize a Socialist Voters' Drive. For seven months I was on the road, leaving my home in Berlin on Monday and returning at the end of the week. Coming and going, I was confronted with my children's questions: What are you doing? Who are you doing it for? How come Kiesinger was a Nazi? Why did Willi Brandt have to leave Germany when he was young? Exactly what happened to the Jews? And what were you doing then?

For the first time I was confronted by the question: What explanation shall we give our children? It was easy enough to tell them what I was doing: I was a Hitler Youth, aged seventeen at the end of the war and called up with the last draft, too young to acquire guilt. But when asked: What if you had been older?—it was hard to answer. How could I know for sure what I would have done? The belated anti-Nazism of my generation was never subjected to the danger test. I could not swear that if I had been six or seven years older, I would not have participated in the great crime. My doubts were such that I was plagued (more and more often as time passed) by nightmares in which I felt myself to be guilty. The dividing line between real and potential action was blurred. My dubious relief at belonging to the "right age group" expressed itself in the stammerings that followed my children's questions in my diary. Interspersed with entries about the election campaign, jottings from the provinces. The present ailing with the past. The demonic idyll. The speed-crazed Today overtaken by Yesterday. German time dislocations. The future postdated. Snail tracks that could be read forward or backward. *From the Diary of a Snail.*

That was to be the title of the book, in which I would tell my children and other children the story of the Danzig Jewish community, mingled with daily items from the present election campaign, shot through with the interaction between melancholia and utopia, and roofed over by the principle of Doubt. I wanted to convey to the rising generation the workings of a slow, phase-delayed development of the gradual processes which no leap could accelerate, which on the one hand have held back social progress and, on the other, first piled up small quantities of guilt that then grew into a monstrous crime: the burden that could no longer be thrown off. I wanted to teach the children that the history which is now taking place in Germany began hundreds of years ago, that these German histories, with the rubble they leave behind them, with their ever new debits of guilt, cannot become obsolete, cannot die away. My unsuccessful attempt to have Heine's Rabbi Abraham escape from 15th-century Bacherach to 20th-century Frankfurt found a sort of counterpart when I suspended chronology, made the 1930s catch up with the 1960s, and denied the leveling power of time.

That the treasure of the Danzig Central Synagogue, the Gieldzinski Collection, is being exhibited in New York today, is much more than an artistic event. Many things that cannot be displayed in showcases or on pedestals should at the same time be said and heard. Let us free our time sense from the servitudes of historical correlation. While viewing the collection, let us ponder Heine's medieval Bacherach with its Passover ending in a pogrom, the Danzig of my childhood with its Jewish community established there for centuries and persecuted out of racist madness, the still endangered existence of Israel, and the two German states that are sick with the sickness of Heine's century and its ideologies, which are still enslaving humankind. To the question: "What are you writing?" my answer was: "A writer, children, is someone who writes against the passage of time."

When my book was finished, all the children had grown older. By then they could have read it. But they didn't want any old stories. Only the present counted. A revolutionary future was being talked into existence. The great leaps that always end in regression were in vogue.

Since then the past has again (once again) caught up with us. Growing children, children who have grown up in the meantime, their several times stunned parents and still bewildered grandparents sit viewing the *Holocaust* series on their family television screens. Public opinion institutes have published the first reactions: confessions, horror, rejection, protestations of innocence. Some discover a false historical detail and hasten to condemn the whole series as untrue, some claim to be shattered, as if they had never heard, seen, or read anything of the kind: We didn't know! We were never shown anything like that. Why weren't we told sooner!

Thirty-five years after Auschwitz the mass media are celebrating their triumph. Nothing counts but mass effect, large numbers. The documents, reportages, analyses that have been available for the past thirty years are meaningless, beside the point, they have failed to reach the masses. Clearly, the written word is too difficult. The catch phrase "mass enlightenment" (the counterpart of "mass destruction") has been used to quash all criticism of the no less questionable than successful television series. And writers, that rare, incurably old-fashioned species, no doubt threatened with extinction, who still expect the individual and the masses to read, are urgently advised to throw their elitist aesthetics overboard, to abandon their subtleties and complexities, and devote themselves to mass enlightenment. In this view the question—What shall we tell our children?—should find its answer (between commercials) on television, where no one else can fail to see and hear it.

I wish to disagree. The success of "popular" enlightenment has never been more than skin deep. Demonstrably as television series (as shown by public opinion polls) shatter, touch, or horrify the masses, much as they move them to pity or even shame—and this was the effect of *Holocaust*—they are quite incapable of disclosing the complex "modernity" of genocide and the many-layered responsibilities at the root of it. Basically, Auschwitz was not a manifestation of common human bestiality; it was a repeatable consequence of a network of responsibilities so organized and so subdivided that the individual was conscious of no responsibility at all. The action of every individual who participated or did not participate in the crime was determined knowingly or unknowingly by a narrow conception of duty. Only the active agents—Kaduk or Eichmann, for instance—have been condemned, but those who sat dutifully at their desks and all those who suppressed their own powers of speech, who did nothing for but also nothing against, who knew but stood aside—they were not judged, they had not (visibly) soiled their hands.

Up until now the grave guilt of the Catholic and Protestant churches has not been aired. Yet it has been proved that by their passive acceptance they shared in the responsibility for Auschwitz. Attempts of churchmen to justify their actions by adducing reasons of state make it clear that clerically organized Christians took refuge in irresponsibility unless they themselves were endangered, with the exception of certain courageous individuals who acted in disregard of their church's instructions, and of the thus far isolated case of the Evangelical Church's "Stuttgart Confession of Guilt." Since Auschwitz, Christian institutions (in Germany at least) have forfeited their claim to ethical leadership.

The medieval persecutions of the Jews and the deep-rooted Christian hatred of the Jews have been taken over by modern anti-Semitism abetted in recent years by the passive irresponsibility of the churches. Not barbarians or beasts in human form, but cultivated representatives of the religion of human brotherhood allowed the crime to happen: they are more responsible than the criminal in the spotlight, be his name Kaduk or Eichmann.

In Danzig, too, the bishops of both churches looked on, or stood indifferently aside, when in November 1938 the synagogues in Langfuhr and Zoppot were set on fire and the shrunken Jewish community was terrorized by SA Sturm 96. At that time I was eleven years old and both a Hitler Youth and a practicing Catholic. In the Langfuhr Church of the Sacred Heart, which was ten minutes walk from the Langfuhr Synagogue, I never up to the beginning of the war, heard a single prayer on behalf of the persecuted Jews, but I joined in babbling a good many prayers for the victory of the German armies and the health of the Führer Adolf Hitler. Individual Christians and Christian groups shared the utmost bravery in resisting Nazism, but the cowardice of the Catholic and Protestant churches in Germany made the churches inactive accomplices.

No television series says a word about that. The many-faceted moral bankruptcy of the Christian West would not lend itself to gripping, shattering, horror-inspiring action. What shall we tell our children? Take a good look at the hypocrites. Distrust their gentle smiles. Fear their blessing.

—Translated by Ralph Manheim

The Hitler Youth being addressed by their leader.

Rabbi Dr. Robert Kaelter (1874-1926).

Danzig Jewry: A Short History GERSHON C. BACON

To the emotionally uninvolved observer, the history of Danzig (Gdańsk) Jewry presents an anomalous picture of a community at times so average as to escape one's notice entirely and at other times so different in its make-up and historical fate as to give it a special place in the annals of European Jewry. This anomalous situation stems in large part from the unusual position of the city of Danzig itself, a city of mixed cultural, ethnic and political allegiances, which in its long history has lived under Polish and German rule. It was a city ever conscious of its dual position as an outpost of German culture on the borders of Slavic Eastern Europe and as an economic outlet for the products of the Polish interior.

The history of Danzig Jewry reflects these conditions. Unwelcome in Danzig for many centuries, Jews eventually created an active and vibrant community in the 19th century, similar to the scores of Liberal Jewish communities throughout Germany. Nevertheless, Danzig Jews had frequent contact with their Eastern European brethren and made their mark on the commerce of the city through their dealings with the Polish interior. Alongside the German Jews, a number of Russian and Polish Jews lived in Danzig, despite occasional harassment on the part of Prussian authorities. After World War I, this small enclave within Danzig Jewry swelled to many times the size of the native community as would-be emigrants crowded into the newly constituted Free City on their way to foreign shores. Community leadership remained in the hands of the German Jews, who tried to deal with both the new political framework of Danzig and the new demographic make-up of the Jewish community. Even during the first Nazi years, the unique political status of Danzig gave the Jews special opportunities to secure their rights. Eventually, however, they found their position no different from that of Jews in Germany. But, as we shall see, even in the Nazi era, the fate of Danzig Jewry took an unusual turn: under some duress, the community dissolved itself and most of the local Jews left the city before the outbreak of war. A long and colorful history came to an end in the horrors of the Holocaust.

In the earliest period of its history, from about the 10th century to the 15th century, Danzig proper had no Jewish community and allowed no Jewish settlement whatsoever. The rulers of adjoining territories, however, did grant trading rights to foreign merchants, including Jews. In these areas, which became the suburbs of Altschottland and Hoppenbruch, Jews probably had some contact with Danzig merchants, although no documentary evidence of such contact exists.[1]

The local tradition of intolerance continued during the period of Polish rule over Danzig (1454–1793). Danzig received a semi-autonomous status which included, among other privileges, the authority to refuse citizenship rights and trading rights to foreigners, whether Nurembergers, Lombards, Englishmen, Flemings or Jews.[2] Thus, although the kings of Poland granted extensive rights to Jews, these rights did not apply in Danzig. At best, Jews could enter the city for a few days to trade during the major fairs in August and November.[3] Even this fairly standard break from the normally exclusivist economic policies of medieval cities was granted only grudgingly to Jewish merchants by the city fathers of Danzig; indeed, they made several attempts to curtail the entrance of Jews into the city. In the 16th century, under pressure from local storekeepers, Jews were forbidden to engage in retail trade within the city limits.[4] When Jews began to remain in town after the fair and on occasion even carried on regular prayer services, the city council took action to expel all those who had stayed (1616).[5] The Jews sought the intervention of the Polish king, who responded with an order to the city council to restore the trading rights of the Jews. When the council failed to respond, the Council of Four Lands, the consultative body for all Polish Jewry, sent a delegation to negotiate with the Danzig council, but the negotiations proved futile.[6] Only after two or three years did Jews receive permission for abbreviated visits during the August fair. As time passed, the city council, despite great public pressure to the contrary, allowed longer sojourns for Jewish merchants.[7] Although the wealthier merchants might have preferred to be even more permissive, the representatives of merchants and artisans in the so-called Third Committee (Ordnung)[8] maintained their stiff opposition. Thus the city council granted neither free trading privileges nor extended residence rights to Jews.[9]

Despite all these restrictions, Jews continued to travel to Danzig for the fairs. Community documents from Poznań (Posen) reveal intense economic activity revolving around Danzig trade. The kehilla* authorities ordered Jewish merchants to travel together for mutual defense on the way. For the preservation of chastity, they forbade Jewish women to go to the fairs. The same documents reveal that Danzig merchants lent money to Jewish communities and traded in notes issued by various kehillot.[10] On one occasion in 1664, we know that the leaders of Polish Jewry were assembled at the Danzig fair because a document records their resolution of a legal dispute between two Jewish communities in Germany.[11] Thus Danzig, as a key Baltic port and export center for Polish goods, may have remained closed to Jewish settlement, but Jews used whatever opportunities they had to participate in its commercial activities.

From the late 17th century and on into the 18th, Danzig entered a period of decline due to the political decline of the Polish state and the interruptions of Baltic trade caused by the Swedish wars.[12] These economic reverses intensified the intolerant attitudes of Danzig citizens towards religious dissenters and Jews, particularly since these groups often competed with local artisans and merchants. This helps explain the increased restrictions against Jews in this period, as attested by local ordinances of 1719, 1740, 1745, 1752, 1763 and others. Jews could stay for limited sojourns, and only with a special pass issued by the Danzig authorities at a price proportionate to the length of the stay and the stature of the individual.[13] For example, the 1752 law stipulated a 12-florin tax for a month-long stay by a Jewish merchant, an 8-florin tax for an assistant, and a 4-florin tax for a servant.[14]

Although Danzig remained closed to Jewish settlement, a modest number of Jewish families did settle in the surrounding suburbs. By the 18th century, there existed organized communities in Altschottland and Weinberg, which employed rabbis and other functionaries, built a hospital and ritual bath, and provided for the poor.[15] These communities, along with the younger community in Langfuhr, provided the nucleus for the modern Danzig Jewish community.[16]

The transition to the modern Danzig Jewish community came with the shift to Prussian rule. After the first partition of Poland (1772), Prussian troops entered the suburban areas, and there began a period of political and economic intimidation of Danzig which culminated in the annexation of the city by Prussia in 1793.[17] The Jews of the Danzig suburbs, though temporarily of use to the Prussian regime in its struggle with Danzig, could not be sure of their status until they received a General-Privilege in August 1773 which regularized their legal status. Thus 240 families with 1257 souls—three kehillot—now became Prussian subjects.[18] This was the beginning of the association of Danzig Jewry with Germany, the German economy and German culture which lasted until the dissolution of the community in the Nazi era.

Prussian Danzig was no longer the key Baltic port it had once been, although it continued its role as an outlet for Polish goods and the port remained central to the city's economy. And as the provincial capital of West Prussia, Danzig became the home of administration, customs and taxation officials. The development of civilian and naval shipbuilding added a further source of income. In addition, the climate and location of Danzig and the growing seaside resort of Zoppot attracted vacationers and pensioners alike. Throughout this period of growth and change, the city of Danzig retained its distinctive architecture, which bespoke its days of glory as the major Baltic port. In those days, the wealthy merchants brought in Flemish and Italian architects to design and decorate their homes. Nineteenth-century buildings imitated the style of the older homes. Prussian Danzig was an attractive, provincial city, overwhelmingly German in population, language and culture, involved in the political concerns of the German state.[19]

In this atmosphere of slow economic growth and German nationalism, the Jews of Danzig tried to build a community. Although their legal status as Prussian subjects had been recognized for some time, Jews still faced legalistic maneuvers by local officials which called their rights into question.[20] They finally

*kehilla, kehillot—Hebrew term that signifies a local Jewish community organization.

achieved full legal equality in 1869 along with the rest of the Jews of northern Germany. But even before the achievement of full equality, the improvement in their political situation and the potential for ultimate equality helped bring about significant changes in the attitudes of many Jews. Already in the first half of the 19th century Jews participated in the cultural life of the city and fulfilled various tasks in the city administration and the merchants' associations.[21]

In this hopeful new atmosphere, the five communities that now comprised Danzig Jewry went through some of the Liberal-versus-orthodox tensions that existed in many German-Jewish communities. Unlike other Jewish communities, however, Danzig is unique because not until well into the modern period did its Jewry unite. Instead, Danzig Jews continued to exist as five separate communities hardly different from the communities of many a small Prussian town. It appears, nevertheless, that matters of class and prestige rather than of ritual stood in the way of *kehilla* unification. Thus, well into the 19th century, the communities of Altschottland, Weinberg, Langfuhr, Danzig-Breitgasse and Danzig-Mattenbuden elected their own officers, built synagogues, ran charitable institutions and chose their own rabbis. In some cases, one rabbi served as spiritual leader for as many as three of the five *kehillot,* even though the *kehillot* remained separate. Most notable among those was Rabbi Israel Lipschütz, rabbi of one or another of the five communities from 1837 to 1860. Lipschütz became renowned in all of Jewry for his commentary on the Mishna, known collectively as *Tiferet Yisrael,* parts of which were first published in Danzig.[22] The first Liberal rabbi in Danzig was Dr. Abraham Stein, elected rabbi of the more modernist Altschottland community in 1850. In addition to introducing moderate reforms in the synagogue service, Stein authored the first history of Danzig Jewry.[23]

Despite a Prussian law of 1847 which mandated a single Jewish community in each city, the five-community set-up persisted. But the pressures of raising funds for charity and providing Jewish education eventually helped push the *kehillot* towards unity. The lack of a unified *kehilla* enabled some Jews to avoid paying community taxes, thereby increasing the economic burden on the rest of the Jews. The first steps towards unity came through the efforts of the leadership of the Altschottland community under Gustav Davidson and their newly elected rabbi Dr.

Cossman Werner (1878). They convinced the leaders of the other communities to organize a committee to make plans to carry out unification (December 1880). In February 1883, elections were held for a unified *kehilla* board.

By this time, Danzig Jewry was in the main a Liberal community. The minority of orthodox Jews was concentrated in the Mattenbuden Synagogue. As a sign of unity, the leaders of the community resolved to close the synagogues of the old *kehillot* and build a modern house of worship for the entire community, which would be the headquarters of the newly constituted *Synagogen-Gemeinde.* The Danzig *Synagogen-Gemeinde* was a modern-style *kehilla*—a kind of community organization centered around the synagogue, which had already become common in German Jewish communities. Completed in 1887, the Danzig temple symbolized more than the unity of Danzig Jewry: it aimed to show the Jews as part of the life of the city. The very design of the temple was intended to fit into the architecture of Danzig yet retain the Arab-Byzantine lines characteristic of major German synagogues.[24] This impressive house of worship became the center of Jewish communal activity in Danzig until the tragic end of the community. Community leaders did allow the Mattenbuden Synagogue to remain open for the mainly Eastern European orthodox minority, so long as a minimum of twenty tax-paying members worshipped there.

In many ways, Danzig was a typical German Jewish community which identified with what it perceived to be the universal, humanitarian aspects of German nationalism. Most Danzig Jews considered themselves "Germans of the Mosaic persuasion" and rejected political Zionism, which regarded the Jews as a nation. Not surprisingly, the first Zionist group in Danzig consisted of Russian Jews.[25] In the last decades of the 19th century and the first decade of the 20th, the panoply of religious, fraternal and defense organizations that characterized German Jewry also existed in Danzig. Leading Jews of Danzig played important roles in the development of the local economy in trade and banking. A local Jew, Paul Simson, wrote the standard history of Danzig.[26]

In the decade preceding World War I, however, German nationalism and anti-Semitism grew apace, and the social isolation of Jews increased, but the liberal, Germanic orientation of Danzig Jews did not change. With the outbreak of World War I, Danzig

Jews, along with other German Jews, volunteered in large numbers for military service. Ever conscious of the anti-Semitic canard that Jews evaded army service, Jewish organizations compiled detailed statistics showing Jewish participation in the war effort. Of the 12,000 German Jewish war dead, perhaps as many as ninety-five were from Danzig.[27] Their names were inscribed on a special memorial plaque displayed in a place of honor in the Danzig temple. Years later, the plaque was evidently considered of such importance that it too was shipped to America with the ritual objects of the community, a mute testimony to Jewish allegiance to Germany in bygone days.[28]

It should be noted in passing that until World War I, the Jewish community of Danzig remained small, and had even shrunk in both absolute and relative terms:[29]

1816	3,798 Jews	
1880	2,736	= 2.4% of total population
1885	2,859	
1895	2,367	
1900	2,553	
1905	2,546	
1910	2,390	= 1.4% of total population

This rather small community, so typical in many respects, differed from other German Jewish communities in certain aspects of its historical experience. As a center of the German Liberal party which opposed anti-Semitism, Danzig offered Jews a ready political outlet for the fight against anti-Semitism. Many local Jews, including Rabbi Dr. Werner, played active roles in the Liberal Party. The party leader, Heinrich Rickert, was one of the founders of the Organization for Combatting Anti-Semitism (1891). At least until the turn of the century, Danzig Jewry refrained from joining the Centralverein, the major Jewish defense organization, and instead employed older methods of quiet intervention and apologetics against manifestations of anti-Semitism. Only when nationalistic and anti-Semitic sentiment grew in the early 1900s did Danzig Jews form a Centralverein chapter of their own.[30]

Many German Jewish communities made considerable efforts to aid and protect Eastern European Jews living in or passing through Germany. Because of its port and its close economic connections with Poland and Russia, Danzig always had a resident nucleus of Eastern European Jews. Danzig Jews had a distinguished record in protecting these Jews from the harassment of Prussian officials.[31] Particularly noteworthy are the actions of Rabbi Dr. Robert Kaelter in this regard. During World War I, he personally secured the release of Russian Jewish prisoners of war. He also helped prevent the expulsion of civilian Russian Jews from Danzig. These Russians, mostly merchants, greatly aided the German war effort by helping to secure supplies from occupied areas of Russia.[32] But although they aided their Eastern European brethren, Danzig Jews also wanted to maintain their German-Liberal style community. Because Eastern European Jews often sympathized with Zionism, the leadership of Danzig Jewry made several attempts to limit non-citizen participation in *Synagogen-Gemeinde* elections.[33] These incidents left a residue of bitterness between the two groups that exacerbated the social and cultural differences which were never totally overcome even in the final days of the community.

We have noted several times how the special nature of Danzig had profound effects on the development of its Jewish community. At no time was this relationship more evident than during the period of the Free City (1920–39). During the peace conference after World War I, Danzig became a major point of contention between defeated Germany and the newly independent Polish state. The Allies had declared as one of their war aims the establishment of an independent Poland with access to the sea. As Poland's traditional outlet to the sea, Danzig seemed destined to become part of Poland. Yet another principle clashed with the desire for an independent Poland, namely the principle of national self-determination. Danzig was overwhelmingly German, and the local citizenry, including the Jewish community, had publicly stated their opposition to inclusion of Danzig in the Polish state. The solution that the peace conference eventually came up with, the creation of a Free City of Danzig under the supervision of the League of Nations, satisfied none of the parties most directly concerned. Despite significant concessions to them regarding the operations of the port, the Poles felt that a city administration antagonistic to Poland could render these concessions worthless. The Germans regarded the Danzig settlement as another distasteful part of an imposed peace. The Danzigers had no desire for an independent "national" existence, even though in earlier eras Danzig had had just such a semi-autonomous

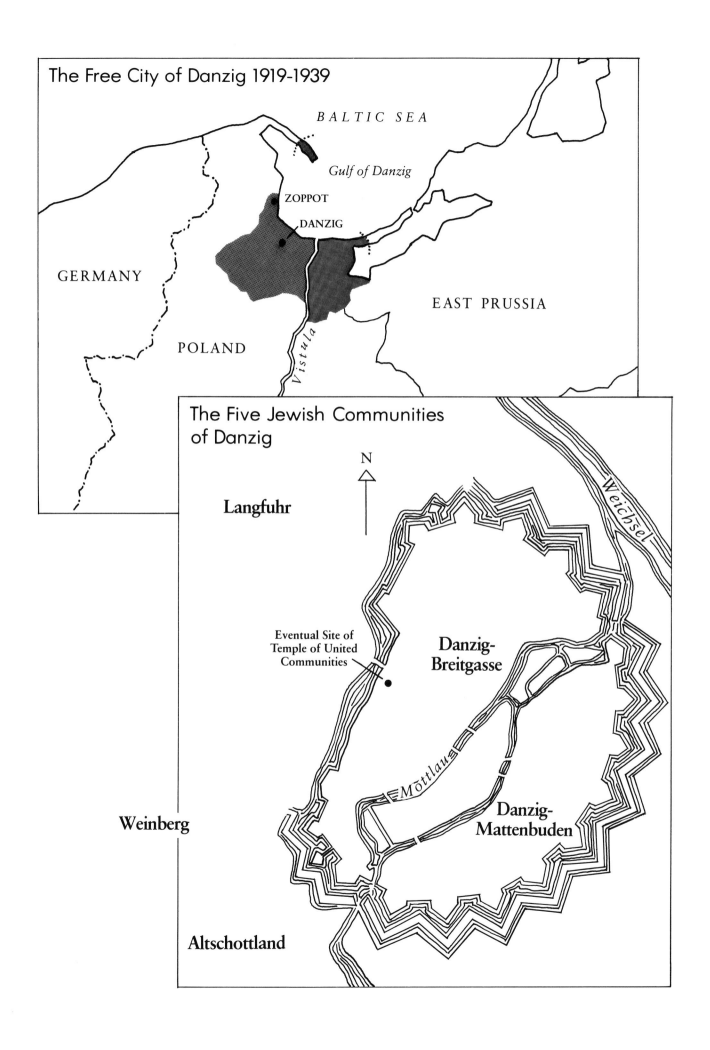

The Free City of Danzig 1919-1939

BALTIC SEA

Gulf of Danzig

ZOPPOT

DANZIG

GERMANY

EAST PRUSSIA

POLAND

Vistula

The Five Jewish Communities
of Danzig

N

Langfuhr

Weichsel

Eventual Site of
Temple of United
Communities

Danzig-
Breitgasse

Möttlau

Danzig-
Mattenbuden

Weinberg

Altschottland

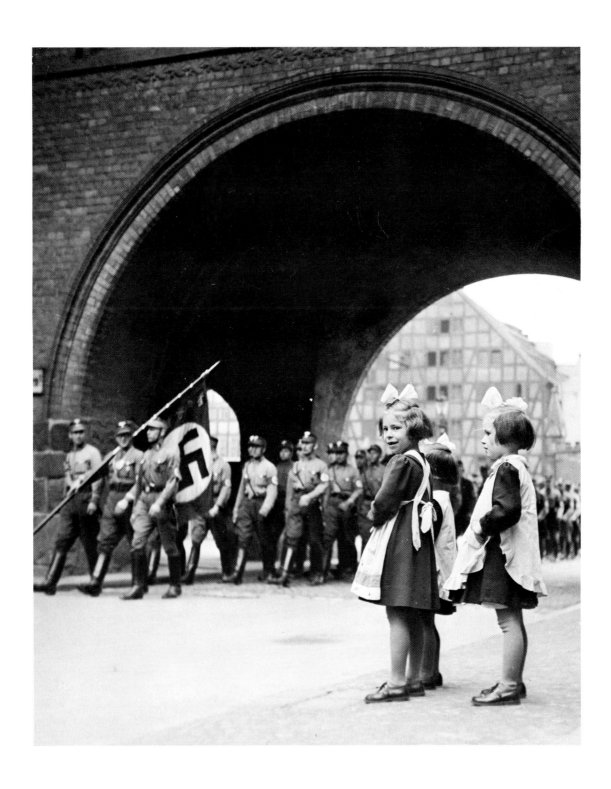

Little Polish girls watching German storm troopers

existence. However undesirable the new situation was to them, the Danzigers quickly took up the tasks of running the city and maintaining order, lest the Poles find some pretext for intervention.[34] The Free City as constituted included Danzig proper, the resort of Zoppot and three rural districts with a total area of 1,951 square kilometers and 357,000 inhabitants.[35]

The Liberal German Jews of Danzig had many important adjustments to make. In the post-Versailles Free City, the right wing of German politics had great strength, much more than in Germany, and anti-Semitic incidents increased. Danzig Jews faced a dilemma. In Germany, Jews could at least justify their fight against anti-Semitism as a fight to secure democracy. But publicizing anti-Semitic activity in Danzig might serve the interest of Poland and hence was "unpatriotic." Similarly, at least until 1932, the German Jews in Danzig did not appeal to the League High Commissioners. To meet anti-Semitic threats, which even included blood libel accusations, Jewish leaders used traditional apologetics and quiet intervention, as well as their not inconsiderable economic clout. Often local police officials cooperated with Jewish leaders because they feared Polish intervention in the city's internal affairs.[36]

As a city under international protection and a free port without visa restrictions, Danzig became the goal of thousands of Jewish refugees from Russia and Poland. Suddenly, the small Danzig community found itself confronting the monumental task of temporary care for people awaiting visas for America or Canada. Danzig Jewry, at first on its own, under the leadership of Rabbi Kaelter, and later aided by the Joint Distribution Committee and Hias, cared for these refugees, many of whom arrived penniless. Refugees stayed in a special transit camp in Troyl, an island in the port area. In the period 1920–25, some sixty thousand Jews passed through Danzig. This immense task exacted a heavy toll on Rabbi Kaelter, who died in 1926 at the age of fifty-two, mourned by young and old, German and Eastern European Jews alike.[37]

The easy entry into Danzig brought about fundamental changes in the demographic make-up of Danzig Jewry. In the space of a few short years, the size of the community increased to three times and then four times the pre-World War I figure:[38]

December 1910	2,717
November 1923	7,282*
August 1924	9,239
August 1929	10,448

Some of these Jews had left smaller West Prussian communities which had come under Polish rule, but the majority of them came from Russia and Poland.[39] The Liberal leadership of the community regarded this change with mixed emotions. A great social and cultural gap separated the two communities, and some German Jews believed the *Ostjuden* had to become "civilized" through the acquisition of German culture. Yet others took pride in the great variety of Jewish expression in the Free City, and, in some circles, there was a feeling that in this meeting place of East and West, some new synthesis of Jewish national and religious identity might arise.[40]

In the short run, the influx of Eastern European Jews brought about the development of a new satellite community in Zoppot and of many new Jewish youth and political organizations. It also meant a rebirth of orthodox Jewry in Danzig. For the first time since the death of Rabbi Lipschütz in 1860, the community elected an orthodox rabbi to care for the religious needs of the orthodox Mattenbuden Synagogue. Rabbi Jakob Sagalowitsch, who took office in 1923, provided Danzig Jewry with the unfamiliar spectacle of an Eastern European style rabbi in its midst. He reorganized *kashrut* supervision in the city, and thus gained new markets in Poland for Danzig food products. He worked to regularize the marital status of many women who, in a period of great emigration and wandering, had lost contact with their husbands. But he also aroused the ire of the very proper German Jews by performing marriages solely for the sake of circumventing entry restrictions to Palestine (he was associated with the Zionist Mizrachi movement) and by his involvement as an arbitrator in business disputes among Jewish merchants. By 1932, dissatisfaction with Sagalowitsch and political infighting in the community grew to the point that his contract was not renewed. A year later, he left Danzig and accepted a new post in Brussels.[41]

The struggle over renewing the contract of Rabbi Sagalowitsch reflected a larger, ongoing struggle within the community between the Liberal leadership and the Zionists. Even with a series of restrictions on voting designed to frustrate Zionist advancement, by

---

*2,500 Danzig nationals, 4,782 non-citizens.

Herr Löbsack, advisor to Nazi District Leader of Danzig, addressing visitors from Berlin in Town Hall of Danzig.

1928 the Zionists polled thirty-nine percent of the votes in the community elections and in 1931 forty-seven percent. The debate between the two groups focused on a fundamental difference in viewpoints on the nature of Judaism, the proper structure and function of the *Synagogen-Gemeinde,* and the best way to combat anti-Semitism. At one point or another, both the Liberals and Zionists weighed the possibility of breaking away from the unified community and forming a separate *kehilla.* The Liberals finally gave up on the idea when government officials determined that, in the event of a split, the property of the *Synagogen-Gemeinde* would go to the more numerous group. As for the Zionists, the dismissal of Rabbi Sagalowitsch seemed to them an overt political challenge and an affront to the orthodox segment of the community. After several unsuccessful attempts at a compromise with the Liberals, Dr. Isaac Landau, a Zionist member of the community council, announced the formation of *Kehillat Yisrael,* a religious-national organization which had the earmarks of a separate *kehilla* in the making. This group set up its own *kashrut* supervision under Rabbi Sagalowitsch (early 1933). The city authorities recognized the legitimacy of ritual slaughter supervised by the new group, thus lending

further probability to a split. But the growing Nazi threat and the need to create a common front to meet that threat put an end to the secession attempt. In addition, the two leading figures in the struggle, Dr. Landau and Rabbi Sagalowitsch, left Danzig.[42]

The Nazi victory in the May 1933 elections signaled the beginning of the tragic final era of Danzig Jewry. Once again, the special nature of the Free City gave Nazi policies a slightly different direction from those in the Reich. At least at first, the Germans adhered on paper to the Danzig constitution and tried to minimize any offense to the League or to Poland. For the first few years of the Nazi era, the government in Danzig even had to play by the rules of democracy and allow the existence of opposition parties.[43]

Regarding the Jews, the new Nazi administration kept a publicly restrained posture which fit into its general policy of moderation. The document on Polish rights signed in August 1933 included a stipulation that Polish Jewish merchants in Danzig could freely carry on their business.[44] In a meeting with Jewish community leaders, Arthur Greiser, the Nazi vice-president of the Danzig Senate, declared that no Aryanization laws or boycott actions would take place in Danzig. All inhabitants of Danzig would be treated equally, without regard to religion or nationality.[45] The new Senate president, Hermann Rauschning, both before and after his election, declared that anti-Jewish policies would harm Danzig. He even maintained that Nazi anti-Semitism was not really racial in nature—one example of many attempts by Rausch-ning to put a more moderate face on Nazi policies and ideology.[46] Nazi party officials in Danzig, however, used public pressure and executive actions to remove Jews from public office and from professional associations, even in the absence of anti-Jewish legislation.[47] Physical assaults against Jews and Poles also occurred, which party officials piously denounced as "breaches of party discipline."[48] The departure of Rauschning from office in 1934 removed an important restraining influence on local Nazi policy. Officially, the new president Greiser promised to uphold the constitution, but in practice the government permitted the continuation of boycott actions, public display of the anti-Semitic newspaper *Der Stürmer* and the public singing of songs calling for the spilling of Jewish blood.[49]

Danzig Jewry used both traditional and innovative methods to meet the pressures of the new era. First and foremost, the factionalism among German Jewish leaders of the *Synagogen-Gemeinde* came to an end. Several years before similar actions in Germany, the Danzig Jews decided to set up the executive body of the *Synagogen-Gemeinde* with an equal representation of Liberals and Zionists.[50] Danzig Jewry also pioneered in setting up an independent Jewish winter relief effort, since the general relief campaign offered no aid to non-citizens and thus excluded the majority of local Jews most in need of help.[51] To represent the interests of Jewish professionals, merchants and artisans excluded from the Nazified unions and professional associations, local Jews set up a series of Jewish professional groups.[52] Perhaps the most significant change for the old-line Liberal Jews of Danzig was the decision to open a private Jewish school to spare Jewish students the increasingly hostile atmosphere of the public schools. The elementary school headed by Samuel Echt and the high school headed by Dr. Ruth Rosenbaum compared favorably with the best of the public schools.[53] In addition to the schools, the community developed a whole series of Jewish and general cultural programs, which provided work for Jewish performers and helped raise the spirits of the community as a whole.[54] A sign of the new spirit in the

community was a more positive attitude toward the Yiddish theater and the Yiddish language.[55]

As their situation worsened, the Jews of Danzig used various means of defense to protect their rights. They used the local courts as long as these showed some signs of independence. Along with other citizen groups, they appealed to the League of Nations (May 1935) when further intervention with local authorities appeared useless. The League did indeed find that the increasingly totalitarian regime in Danzig violated the constitution, and reminded the Senate of its obligations. But Greiser had no intention of carrying out the recommendations of the League.[56] Ironically, it took pressure from within the Nazi party to put a stop to public harassment of Jewish tourists in 1935–36. A large drop in tourism would hurt an already suffering Danzig economy.[57]

By 1937, however, economic considerations began to play a secondary role in determining the Danzig regime's policy towards Jews. The only moderating force was a German desire to avoid any direct confrontation with Poland over Danzig. Thus the party officially disassociated itself from a mob assault on Jewish businesses and homes (October 23, 1937) and even imposed prison terms on some of the rioters.[58] Yet the anti-Semitic agitation continued and the regime introduced new anti-Jewish measures. By 1937, some three thousand of the more than ten thousand resident Jews had already left Danzig, and for the first time some community leaders began considering an at least partial evacuation of Jews from the city.[59] Administrative pressure for the Aryanization of businesses coupled with stormtrooper-enforced boycott activity made things harder and harder for Jews. From November 1937 to the summer of 1938, another two thousand Jews left the city.[60]

The culmination of all this pressure came in the pogroms of Kristallnacht on November 12–13, 1938 (November 9 in the Reich). Besides mass arrests and destruction of Jewish property, stormtroopers razed the synagogues in Langfuhr and Zoppot. Only timely intervention by community leaders with the police saved the Great Synagogue from a similar fate. A group of Jewish war veterans mounted a guard around the synagogue. In the course of these nights of terror, and over the next few days, some fifteen hundred Jews fled over the Polish border.[61] From then on, the Jews of Danzig regarded emigration as a matter of highest priority. Further pressure on the Jews came with the introduction of the Nuremberg Laws into Danzig, making Nazi race theories the law of the land (November 1938).[62]

Community officials invited back to Danzig Zvi Hermann Segall, a local Revisionist Zionist figure who one year earlier had first broached to them an evacuation plan for Danzig Jewry. Segall also had good connections with the local police. There began a series of meetings with local officials to develop an "orderly" plan for Jewish emigration. Some six thousand Jews left in Danzig needed places to go, and only about half could easily find places of refuge (these latter being the two thousand Jews who were Polish citizens and the one thousand with wealth or personal connections). In these desperate times, Segall's plans no longer seemed outlandish.[63]

The local Danzig authorities wanted the Jews to leave, but still insisted on the legalistic formality of having the Jews "agree" to leave. For this purpose, a community-wide meeting was convened in the Great Synagogue on December 17, 1938. Two thousand people filled the synagogue, where they heard Segall and others speak of the painful decision they had to make. Those assembled rose from their seats to show their agreement with the emigration plan and their willingness to allow the community leaders to make all necessary arrangements. The Danzig officials further insisted that each Jew sign a document in which he promised to follow the directives of the Jewish community officials. According to the plan proposed by Segall, Polish Jews in Danzig would return to Poland, other Jews who could get visas to various countries would do so, and the remainder (the majority) would go in illegal transports to Palestine. The Danzig Senate gave the Jews until May 1939 (later extended until the fall of 1939) to evacuate all but the elderly and infirm Jews. In fact, even the elderly tried to leave.[64]

To finance their emigration, Danzig Jews needed large sums in foreign currency. Little aid came from Western Jewry. Some organizations opposed any project run by the right-wing Revisionists, while British Jews considered aiding illegal immigration to Palestine a "disloyal" act. Finally, the American Joint Distribution Committee provided aid in a roundabout way: it sent dollars to Danzig as the "purchase price" for the collection of ritual objects belonging to the community.[65] (These are the objects sent to The Jewish Theological Seminary in New York that constitute the present exhibition.) The community also sold off all the real estate it owned, including the Great Synagogue, for a fraction of its actual value. A tragic scene unfolded when Danzig Jewry gathered for the last time in the Great Synagogue on April 15, 1939. The event symbolized for all the beginning of the end of their community. They consoled themselves with the thought that the sale of their beloved synagogue would help finance the emigration of some community members, so that Danzig Jewry might live on somewhere else.[66]

The exodus of Danzig Jewry continued until October–November 1941, when the Nazis stopped all emigration. Before that time, some Jewish children found refuge in England. Several hundred Jews went on various illegal transports to Palestine. Some were successful. Others were on the *Patria,* a ship the British were using to deport illegal immigrants, which was blown up in Haifa harbor on November 25, 1940. Those Danzig Jews who survived the *Patria* disaster were the only ones allowed to stay in Palestine. Danzig refugees who had not yet been transferred to the *Patria* were sent to distant exile in Mauritius. Jews still in Danzig received "special treatment" by the Nazis. Whereas the mass deportation of Jews in the Reich only began in the fall of 1941,[67] the deportation of Danzig Jews began the previous February—to the Polish ghettos and to Theresienstadt, from where they were sent to their extermination.[68] By the end of the war, only a handful of people the Nazis defined as Jews remained alive in Danzig.

For all practical purposes, the Danzig Jewish community was no more. But Danzig Jewry lives on in the memories of survivors scattered across the globe, several of whom have written about their community. Danzig Jewry lives on in the community archives, which the community leaders decided to entrust to the Jewish community of Jerusalem.[69] Present and future Jewish historians can examine in minute detail the inner workings, ideals and frustrations of this community as it faced the challenges of modernity and ultimately the horrors of this century. Finally, Danzig Jewry lives on in the collection of ritual objects from its Judaica museum and its houses of worship. They are a silent reminder of a living, vibrant community and a silent cry of anguish lamenting the tragic end of that community.

Footnotes

1. Samuel Echt, *Die Geschichte der Juden in Danzig,* Leer and Ostfriesland, 1972, pp. 13–14.
2. Echt, p. 14.
3. Israel Halpern, ed., *Pinkas Vaad Arba Aratzot,* Jerusalem, 1945, p. 543.
4. Edmund Cieślak and Czeslaw Biernat, *Dzieje Gdańska,* Gdańsk, 1969, p. 1974.
5. Echt, p. 15.
6. Halpern, pp. 30–31.
7. Echt, p. 16.
8. See Simon Askenazy, *Dantzig and Poland,* London, 1921, p. 16.
9. Echt, p. 16.
10. Bernard Weinryb, *Texts and Studies in the Communal History of Polish Jewry,* New York, 1950, pp. 23, 34, 100, 145 (Hebrew pagination).
11. Halpern, pp. 99–101.
12. Herbert S. Levine, *Hitler's Free City—A History of the Nazi Party in Danzig, 1925–39,* Chicago, 1973, p. 7.
13. Cieślak and Biernat, p. 300.
14. Text in Echt, pp. 32–33.
15. Echt, pp. 17–19.
16. There is, however, some evidence that a few Jews stayed in Danzig proper under various pretexts; see Echt, p. 27.
17. Askenazy, pp. 32–54.
18. Echt, pp. 21–25.
19. Christoph M. Kimmich, *The Free City—Danzig and German Foreign Policy 1919–34,* New Haven, 1968, pp. 1–3.
20. Echt, pp. 42–44.
21. Elijahu Stern, *Korotehem shel Yehudei Danzig me'az ha'emantsipatsiya ve'ad ha'gerush be'yemei ha'shilton ha'Nazi,* unpublished doctoral dissertation, Hebrew University, Jerusalem, 1978, p. 3.
22. Echt, p. 251.
23. "Die Geschichte der Juden zu Danzig," *Monatsschrift für Geschichte und Wissenschaft des Judentums* 6 (1857); see Echt, p. 49.
24. Stern, pp. 6–10.
25. Stern, p. 33.
26. Echt, p. 58.
27. Stern, pp. 69–70.
28. Echt, p. 203.
29. Echt, p. 60.
30. Stern, pp. 11–12.
31. Stern, pp. 20–21.
32. Stern, pp. 44, 67, 71.
33. Stern, pp. 60–62.
34. Kimmich, pp. 4–22; Levine, pp. 10–11.
35. Kimmich, p. 3.
36. Stern, pp. 96ff. and 208.
37. Erwin Lichtenstein, *Die Juden der Freien Stadt Danzig unter der Herrschaft des Nationalsozialismus,* Tübingen, 1973, p. 9.
38. Lichtenstein, p. 10; Echt, p. 99.
39. Echt, p. 94.
40. Stern, pp. 218, 230, 148–49.
41. Echt, p. 102; Stern, pp. 298–304.
42. Stern, pp. 318–22.
43. Levine, pp. 54–56.
44. Levine, p. 62.
45. Lichtenstein, p. 13.
46. Levine, pp. 51–52.
47. Lichtenstein, pp. 15–16.
48. Levine, p. 65.
49. Lichtenstein, pp. 34–35; Stern, pp. 350–52.
50. Lichtenstein, pp. 18–19; Stern, p. 342.
51. Stern, p. 356.
52. Echt, pp. 146–48.
53. Lichtenstein, pp. 22–25; Echt, pp. 149–53.
54. Echt, pp. 148–49.
55. Stern, p. 404.
56. Stern, p. 354.
57. Levine, p. 129.
58. Levine, pp. 131–32; Lichtenstein, pp. 56–58.
59. Levine, p. 130; Stern, p. 424.
60. Stern, p. 440.
61. Lichtenstein, pp. 76–77.
62. Levine, p. 134.
63. Levine, p. 135.
64. Stern, pp. 450–52.
65. Stern, p. 456; Echt, pp. 201–3.
66. Echt, p. 212; Stern, p. 457.
67. Lichtenstein, pp. 232–34.
68. Stern, p. 469.
69. Stern, p. 459.

225. Pair of Rimmonim, Danzig, 1829-31.

The Danzig Treasures

JOSEPH GUTMANN

The Danzig treasures, comprising more than three hundred Jewish ceremonial objects, constitute a distinctive collection, one which testifies "eloquently to the place of art in the life of the Danzig Jew" and is "expressive of all manifold phases of [Danzig] Jewish life."[1] The Danzig collection is one of the very few Jewish communal collections to have survived the Nazi Holocaust. Unlike the Prague State Jewish Museum, whose collections from Bohemian and Moravian communities bear witness to Nazi diabolism —they were assembled by the Nazis to celebrate their success in destroying European Jewry—the Danzig collection reflects the wisdom of the leaders of Danzig Jewry. Conscious of the imminent destruction of their community at Nazi hands in 1939, they shipped their treasures to The Jewish Theological Seminary in New York for safekeeping.

The collection from Danzig consists of three parts: objects from the private collection of Lesser Gieldzinski; objects from the Great Synagogue of Danzig (including those once in the older synagogues of Danzig-Breitgasse, Mattenbuden, Langfuhr and Schottland); and objects never listed or described before 1939, probably heirlooms donated and added by individuals anxious to send them to safety in the United States. Printed catalogues for the Gieldzinski and Great Synagogue collections had been issued in earlier years.[2] Most of the Danzig objects date from the 18th and 19th centuries, although a few in the Gieldzinski collection can be ascribed to the 17th century. For the most part, the Danzig treasures can be authenticated and should serve as a model study collection.[3] Judaica museums—inundated ever since World War II with spurious objects—can now look to the Danzig collection for secure guidance in scientifically evaluating similar objects.

The Danzig objects have the additional advantage of coming from the same general geographic area; hence they offer a rare opportunity to study the donors of the objects and local Jewish customs. They also permit examination of the local Christian craftsmen commissioned to make these objects and of the way they appropriated the motifs and forms of contemporary art for Jewish purposes. Only one Jewish artist can be identified among the craftsmen of the Danzig objects —a 17th-century engraver, Salom Italia (1619–55?). Born in Italy, he studied drawing and engraving there and then settled in Amsterdam in 1641 (no. 48, *megillah*). Because Jews were excluded from Christian guilds, Jewish ceremonial art had to be made by Christian craftsmen.[4] Hence, many of the pieces in the Danzig collection were fashioned by Christian silversmiths from Danzig and nearby cities in Poland and Prussia. Such 18th-century Danzig Christian masters as Johann Gottlieb Stegmann (no. 68, Torah shield; no. 33, spice box) and Wilhelm Raths (no. 92, pointer) are identifiable, in addition to the 19th-century masters Carl Moritz Stumpf (no. 25, *Kiddush* cup) and Johann Gottlieb Ulrich (no. 81, *rimmonim; no.* 119, alms box). The Danzig collection boasts of works by the 18th-century Berlin craftsman August Ferdinand Gentzmer (nos. 64 and 198, Torah shields; no. 80, *rimmonim*) and Joachim Hübner (no. 87, Torah pointer; no. 74, Torah crown; nos. 62-63, Torah shields) and the 19th-century craftsmen Johann August Gebhardt (no. 65, Torah shield) and Johann Christian Samuel Kessner (no. 66, Torah shield). A. Riedel, who probably worked in Warsaw during the second half of the 19th century, may have been commissioned to do several objects (no. 72, Torah shield; no. 86, *rimmonim*). Wolfgang Schubert of 18th-century Nuremberg (no. 59, Torah shield), and Carl Friedrich Korok of 19th-century Breslau (no. 85, *rimmonim*), are also represented.

Stylistically, the objects in the Danzig exhibition conform to the accepted artistic modes of their day. The 17th-century pieces exemplify the flamboyant, dramatic baroque style, while the 18th-century ones reflect the picturesque and more delicate rococo style with its penchant for whimsical asymmetry. The late 18th- and early 19th-century objects often evince the cold, severe, yet majestic neo-classical style; and many of the 19th-century works testify to the general stylistic eclecticism then so much in vogue.

The Danzig collection includes objects rarely seen in Judaica museums. Among them are a handsome Biedermeier elmwood sofa, carved, gilded and painted (no. 10), which may have been made in Danzig and was donated to the Synagogue in 1838 by Salomon Friedländer and his wife. It was on this sofa that the bride sat, prior to the wedding, and had the veil placed over her head. Two embroidered 18th-century curtains (nos. 6, 138) are certainly worthy of further study. They are circumcision curtains, which were hung in the synagogue when the ceremony was performed there. The silk mirror in the center of the curtain contains the text of the circumcision ceremony.[5]

Torah pointers (yaddaim) are not uncommon in Judaica collections, but the Danzig group has four unusual ones (nos. 91-94). Their rectangular tapered shafts terminate in a curious motif—two clasped hands emerging from a dolphin's(?) mouth. The meaning and origin of the motif have yet to be established; the earliest pointer of this type dates from the 18th century. Rare, too, is the placing of the Eternal Light in a cupboard, as in the openwork brass example from the 19th century (no. 98).[6] In Ashkenazi communities, the Eternal Light is typically suspended in front of and above the Torah ark curtain in commemoration of the biblical light set up "to burn continually" outside the Tent veil (Ex. 27:20–21; Levit. 24:2–3). Further substantiation of this practice, common enough in some Eastern European Jewish communities, is found in a drawing of such an Eternal Light in a cupboard (no. 131, the 1833 Membership Book of the Eternal Light Society of Mattenbuden).

Although many objects in public Judaica museums have been labeled pidyon ha-ben plates, the Danzig plate (no. 7) is one of the few to be properly identified. These plates were used when the first-born son, at the age of one month, was presented to the kohen (descendent of Aaron, the priest) and redeemed from the priesthood through a ritual in which the priest is given five shekels by the father. In the concave molding of the Danzig plate, probably dating from the late 18th or early 19th century, a baby is depicted in swaddling cloths surmounted by hands giving the priestly benediction; around the rim is the abbreviated blessing for the redemption of the first-born son.

Along with the rarity of the objects in the Danzig collection, the quality and historic value of many of the items are notable. The Prague State Jewish Museum has the richest array of objects associated with Jewish Burial Societies—a subject not yet adequately studied by Jewish scholars.[7] However, the Danzig collection displays some fine tankards used at annual banquets and has many synagogue furnishings donated by the Burial Societies (e.g. nos. 133 and 263).

Two brass sheviti tablets, probably made in the late 18th or early 19th century, are unusual for their elaborate decoration (nos. 109-10). These plaques stood over the cantor's lectern as he faced the Torah ark to chant the public prayers. Called sheviti because of the opening word "I have set the Lord always before me" (Ps. 16:8), this verse and such quotations as "Know before whom you are standing" (Babylonian Talmud, Berakhot 28b) were perhaps intended to remind the cantor to conduct himself in a spirit of humility. Whether such brass plaques also served as sounding boards for cantors—a frequent claim—has not been established. From the 18th century on, it was common practice to decorate Jewish ceremonial objects with designs and figures reminiscent of the biblical Tabernacle / Temple, as on no. 109, the sheviti tablet donated in 1804. In the center before the parted Tabernacle curtains are the Ten Commandments, flanked by the seven-branched lampstand, the bronze laver, the table of showbread and the altar for burnt offerings. Whether the spiral columns on the sheviti tablet no. 110, which also appear in frontispieces of Jewish books from the 16th century on and in later Jewish ceremonial objects (cf. no. 54), are symbolic of the columns of Solomon's Temple, as assumed in many scholarly books, needs further research. Some spiral columns are known in Christian Spain, for instance, as columnas salomónicas, but it is not certain that Judaism adopted this Christian symbolism.[8]

The work of the 17th-century Italian Jewish engraver Salom Italia is represented by a megillah (Scroll of Esther), which he probably made prior to his departure for Amsterdam in 1641 (no. 48). Italia employs the popular arched portals with broken pediments topped by lions and finials of vases and flowers. In niches between the arches he depicts the main characters of the Esther story, standing on socles which are decorated with narrative scenes from the biblical Book of Esther, the book read in the synagogue at Purim.[9]

Large silver Kiddush goblets for the sanctification prayer over wine on Sabbaths and holidays were

DANZIG JEWS IN THE SYNAGOGUE (1869) / Wilhelm Stryjowski

meant for synagogal use only. Such 19th-century Danzig goblets as nos. 26 and 27, replete with lid and finials, feature repoussé and engraved work. Especially noteworthy on no. 26 is the engraved scene of the interior of the Mattenbuden synagogue—an invaluable sketch for students of synagogue architecture. The rediscovery by Vivian Mann of an 1869 drawing, "Danzig Jews in the Synagogue" by Wilhelm Stryjowski (p. 39), proves that the large vessels (no. 112a, b) once thought to have been used in the ritual purification of the dead, were water dispensers for washing the hands before prayer. Pewter Seder plates (nos. 49-50), for use during the Passover holiday and dating from the 18th century, carry in the cavetto the usual pictorial scenes and, on the rim, the text giving the prescribed order of the Passover Seder service. More unusual is the three-tiered, openwork Seder container for the required *matzot* (no. 51). The upper part has holders for the ritual foods used during the meal. Around the circumference are three pairs of rampant lions holding up cartouches with inscriptions which, in turn, are surmounted by a central crown. The earliest such containers date from the 18th century; our Biedermeier-style specimen may date from the early 19th century.

The cast brass Hanukkah lamp (no. 46) is one of several extant examples and probably dates from the early 19th century. Its round, raised base has a center shaft supporting three arms with foliate designs on each side. A bar running across the top of the arms is fitted with prickets for the candles. A large lamp of this sort was intended for wayfarers and others who could not kindle the prescribed lights at home, so that when all were assembled "the miracle might be spread and proclaimed" in the synagogue. Such lamps, resembling in shape the ancient Temple *menorah,* first make their appearance in Jewish communities during the 17th century.[10]

Without question, the Torah ornaments form the most significant part of the Danzig collection—the Torah shield *(tas),* Torah pointer *(yad),* Torah crown *(keter)* and Torah finials *(rimmonim),* used in the synagogal worship service. Also found in the collection are Torah mantles *(me'ilim)* and Torah binders *(mappot sefer-Torah),* also known as *Wimpeln.* These binders (cf. nos. 55-56), it should be noted, are not indigenous to Eastern Europe or to Prussia, but are found primarily in western and southern Germany. Around 1500, the custom seems to have arisen of

making the *Wimpel* from the linen cloth upon which a boy was circumcised; the cloth would be cut into three or four pieces and stitched together. The boy's name, the date of his birth, and the standard formula "May the Lord raise him up to the study of Torah, to the *huppah,* and to good deeds" were embroidered on the *Wimpel;* in later centuries, the inscriptions were painted on. The *Wimpel* was usually presented to the synagogue in a special ceremony on the child's first visit there.[11]

As for Torah shields, many in the Danzig exhibition bear the hallmarks of well-known Christian masters. Two of the shields (nos. 64 and 198), by the Berlin craftsman August Friedrich Gentzmer, are rectangular in shape and have two columns, scroll designs, and Tablets of the Law surmounted by a crown held by rampant lions. Notwithstanding the strenuous objections of the rabbis, there began in the 16th century the practice of placing the Ten Commandments in the synagogue and on its ceremonial objects.[12] Gentzmer also designed a pair of *rimmonim* (no. 80).

Another prominent Berlin craftsman, Joachim Hübner, designed two Torah shields (nos. 62-63). Rectangular in shape, with elongated tops, they have two columns topped by buds. Two rampant lions support the Tablets of the Law. The same artist also made a Torah pointer (no. 87; and cf. the closely related pointers, nos. 88-89), and a Torah crown (no.74).

It is difficult to determine whether Gentzmer (no. 80) or some other master craftsman was the first to fashion *rimmonim* in the shape of a turret with three graduated cut-out tiers holding bells and topped by a crown and acorn finials. The influence of this form can be seen in no. 81 and, with variations, in nos. 225 (p. 36) and 79. One aspect of the designs of these *rimmonim*—the direct inspiration of local buildings, such as churches and town halls—deserves further study.[13]

Torah crowns are more common in Italy than in Germany and Eastern Europe, but the Danzig collection has examples from both areas (no. 73, Italy; nos. 74-75, German; no. 77, Eastern Europe). Along with similar crowns in the Prague State Jewish Museum, the regional variations of these 18th- and 19th-century Torah crowns—frequently modeled after crowns of the Madonna and royal diadems—would make a fascinating study. Indeed, such an investigation should also be undertaken for Torah shields, Torah finials, and Torah pointers.[14]

The treasures of Danzig, one hopes, will encourage art historians to research further the works of Christian silversmiths in Europe and inspire Jewish scholars to study the remarkable customs and ceremonies which shaped this collection.

Footnotes

*. For full references to works cited in abbreviated form, see the bibliography on p. 138.

1. J. Kirschbaum, "A Museum of Jewish Art, Danzig," *Menorah Journal* 10(1924), pp. 171-73.

2. Danzig, 1904; Danzig, 1933.

3. Such objects as the 1614 Italian majolica Seder plate (no. 52) and similar ones, presumably dating from the 16th and 17th centuries, are considered spurious by some scholars. Vivian Mann has found evidence to date this piece in the second half of the 19th century. She is preparing a more extensive treatment of the problem for forthcoming publication. Similarly questionable is the early date and country assigned no. 164, a Hanukkah lamp. Such Hanukkah lamps in other collections are variously attributed to Italy, Germany, France and Spain and dated between the 13th and 15th centuries because of the supposed Gothic motifs employed.

4. Cf. *Beauty in Holiness*, pp. 15ff. Vivian Mann graciously pointed out to me that Gerhard Hintz, a Christian craftsman, was dismissed from the Danzig guild in 1702 because he employed Jews. For Hintz, see Czihak², no. 392, and p. 69 for the dismissal.

5. Cf. D. Davidovitch, "A Rare Parokhet for the Circumcision Ceremony," *Museum Haaretz Yearbook* 15-16(1974), pp. 112–18.

6. Cf. L. Loeb-Larocque, "Ewig-Licht Ampel (jüdisch)," *Reallexikon zur deutschen Kunstgeschichte*, VI, Stuttgart, 1966, pp. 643ff.

7. Cf. the fine article by I. Shachar, "Burial Society Glass," *Bezalel* (Bulletin of the Bezalel National Museum, Jerusalem) 2(1963), unpaginated (in Hebrew with English summary).

8. Cf. J. Gutmann, ed., *The Temple of Solomon: Archaeological Fact and Medieval Tradition in Jewish, Christian and Islamic Art*, Missoula, 1976.

9. Cf. J. Gutmann, "Estherrolle," *Reallexikon zur deutschen Kunstgeschichte*, VI, Stuttgart, 1966, pp. 88–103.

10. Cf. J. Gutmann, "Hanukkah in Art," *The Hanukkah Anthology*, P. Goodman, ed., Philadelphia, 1976, pp. 126–31.

11. R. Hagan, D. Davidovitch and R. Busch, *Tora Wimpel: Zeugnisse jüdischer Volkskunst aus dem Braunschweigisches Landesmuseum*, Braunschweig, 1978, pp. 7ff.

12. Cf. J. Gutmann, "How Traditional are our Traditions?" *Beauty in Holiness*, pp. 417ff.

13. Only a few preliminary studies have been published. Cf., for instance, D. L. Bemporad, "Arte ceremoniale ebraica in Italia," *Commentari* 25(1974), pp. 258–70; J. Stone, "English Silver Rimmonim and their Makers," *Quest* 1(1965), pp. 20–23, and G. Schoenberger, "The Ritual Silver made by Myer Myers," *Beauty in Holiness*, pp. 66ff.

14. Some statements in J. Gutmann, "Torah Ornaments, Priestly Vestments and the King James Bible," *Beauty in Holiness*, pp. 122ff., should be emended. The designation *tas* was known before the 18th century, as an inventory from Zirndorf, 1696, already mentions a silver *Das (tas)*; see E. Zimmer, *Aspects of Jewish Life in the Principality of Ansbach during the Seventeenth and Eighteenth Centuries*, Ramat Gan, 1975, p. 73 (in Hebrew). The assertion that the Torah shield has no association with priestly vestments should also be corrected. Apparently such links were made in the 19th century, as we can see on the Torah shield no. 207, which in the right-hand column inscription has the word *tzitz* (Ex. 28:36); a Torah shield in the London Jewish Museum mentions *hoshen mishpat* (Ex. 28:15); see Barnett, no. 146. It should be noted that many Italian Jewish communities placed the crown over the *rimmonim*. In Ashkenazi communities, the crown often takes the place of the *rimmonim* and is put directly on the Torah staves.

L. GIELDZINSKI

Lesser Gieldzinski/Art Collector, Humanitarian and citizen of Danzig

Lesser Gieldzinski (1830-1910) ELIZABETH CATS

When visitors enter the "Danzig" storeroom at The Jewish Museum, they are dazzled by the splendor of the brass, silver and pewter objects that once adorned the Great Synagogue of Danzig. Seeing this "treasure house," they always ask the same question: "Who was Lesser Gieldzinski, the man who gave so many of these objects?"

For many years, we gave a brief answer that was based on the introduction of the 1933 catalogue of the Danzig Judaica collection: "The collection was greatly enriched by a gift of a member of the Danzig community, Lesser Gieldzinski, who selected the Jewish ceremonial objects from the treasures of his art collection and presented them to the community on his seventy-fifth birthday, January 10, 1904." With this donation, he sent the following statement: "I, Lesser Gieldzinski, bequeath my collection of ancient and ceremonial objects to the Synagogue and Jewish community of Danzig as their property for all time. The collection shall be known as the Gieldzinski Donation, always to be exhibited in a separate and appropriate room, carefully preserved and open free to all. This document shall remain forever in this room with the collection as an eternal remembrance."

As our research into the Danzig Judaica collection progressed, it became quite clear that the objects donated by Gieldzinski were the most unusual, valuable, and sentimental ones in the whole collection. Attached to the velvet stand of a copper and gilded Italian Torah crown from Bolzano, dated 1699 (no. 73) was a note in Gieldzinski's handwriting, stating that "this Crown was lost in a pogrom in Russia and found again." We admired the splendid group of silver alms boxes, engraved with inscriptions from the old Danzig synagogues and made by well-known 18th-century Danzig silversmiths (e.g., nos. 117, 118). A Scroll of Esther, engraved by Salom Italia about 1641 (no. 48), a faïence Seder plate from Pesaro (no. 52), a miniature Torah scroll with its own silver breastplate and pointer (nos. 15, 17, 95)—these are but a few of the fascinating objects.

But for a long time, our investigation revealed little more about Lesser Gieldzinski than had appeared in the 1933 catalogue. We questioned many former residents of Danzig about him, and searched through libraries and archives, but all that we could learn was that he was a wealthy grain merchant who served on the Board of Directors of the *Synagogen-Gemeinde* from 1884 until his death in 1910. From his collection, we saw that he was a man of great aesthetic taste, who had a deep love and respect for his religion and its customs; a man of filial piety and sentiment, who lovingly preserved his father's white silk Yom Kippur *yarmulke,* (no. 38), and collected photographs of 19th-century European synagogues.

And then one day, in the summer of 1976, the "Gieldzinski mystery" was solved. A woman knocked at the door of The Jewish Museum, one hour before opening time. When she was turned away, she became quite persistent, and in halting English explained that her grandfather's collection from Danzig was at The Jewish Museum. Fortunately, Rita Gieldzinski Palester, granddaughter of Lesser Gieldzinski, was allowed to enter. She told us that she and her family lived in Buenos Aires, and that she was on a short vacation in New York. As a farewell gift, a friend had given her Günter Grass' book *From the Diary of a Snail,* in which it is mentioned that the Gieldzinski collection was saved, and was at The Jewish Museum in New York. It was the last day of Mrs. Palester's trip, and she rushed to the Museum. For all who were present, it was an unforgettable moment when she came face to face with the treasures collected by her grandfather almost one hundred years ago.

Rita Palester talked about her father and her uncle, the two sons of Lesser Gieldzinski, and most important of all, she told us what a well-known art collector and connoisseur her grandfather had been, and of the existence of a catalogue of his entire collection (excepting the 1904 Danzig donation), which was auctioned in Berlin after his death in 1910. She also promised to send us her grandfather's scrapbook of newspaper articles about himself, clipped from Danzig newspapers during the years 1900 to 1912. We

Memorial plaques for the death dates of the parents of Lesser Gieldzinski.

studied the enormous sales catalogue (2381 items) and read all the newspaper articles, and soon a picture of Lesser Gieldzinski as art collector, humanitarian, and citizen of Danzig emerged.

Lesser Gieldzinski was born in Włocławek, Poland, in 1830. His father Michael (1796–1878) was a merchant, and the son followed in his father's footsteps. In 1860, Lesser settled in Danzig, and soon became a very successful grain merchant. As his business prospered, he began to take an active part in Danzig's civic life. His travels took him all over Europe, and he became an avid collector of antique furniture, porcelain objets d'art, paintings, and Jewish ceremonial objects. He moved into a great patrician house at Langgasse 29, which had belonged to the well-known Freder family in the 17th century. There, in seven large rooms, he exhibited his collection, and Langgasse 29 became one of the sights of Danzig. To visit Gieldzinski's collection, and to admire his taste and connoisseurship was part of every visitor's itinerary. The German Emperor Wilhelm II and Empress Augusta were frequent guests. There is a charming newspaper article (dated May 1901) describing an afternoon visit of the empress and her four children to his home. In gratitude, she presented him with a hand-painted and gilded tea service and a signed photograph. The royal couple also sent Gieldzinski a stream of important visitors and dignitaries, to whom he gladly showed his collection.

By looking at the 1912 sales catalogue, we can almost reconstruct the seven rooms at Langgasse 29. What becomes quite obvious is that Gieldzinski had a passion for collecting what today would be called "Danzigiana." We can see this from the many examples of finely carved armoirs, tables and chests from the early 17th century, attributed to such Danzig master woodcarvers as Abraham von dem Block and Simon Hoerl. Gieldzinski also loved to collect objects from the 17th- and 18th-century Danzig guilds. There are tankards and goblets, tobacco plates and alms boxes, all decorated with the emblems and insignias of the butchers, the bakers, and the weavers, to name but a few of the guilds. These objects were particularly popular because they nostalgically recalled a bygone era, when Danzig was an important Hanseatic port—the "Venice of the North." Also much admired was Gieldzinski's collection of china—Sèvres, Meissen and Delft—as well as his miniatures, engravings and oil paintings. He also collected objects in gold, silver and pewter, made by the great Danzig silversmiths, many of whom worked for the Jewish community. Their names appear on secular works of art, as well as on Jewish ceremonial objects in the Gieldzinski collection.

During his lifetime, Lesser Gieldzinski was much admired for his boundless generosity. In 1901, a historical room, devoted to the ancient decorative arts of Danzig, was opened in a patrician house at Langen Markt 43. This was known as the "Danzig Diele" (the "Danzig Hall") and Lesser Gieldzinski was one of the main donors. He wrote the following refrain, which hung over the entrance door:

> Der Alten Kunst, gar lang' versteckt
> Hab' ich hier wieder aufgedeckt.
> Das sie nun lacht in alter Pracht,
> Und mir und Andern Freude macht.

> (Art of the Ancients, hidden for so long,
> I have uncovered once again.
> May she laugh decked in old glory,
> And give pleasure to me and others.)

This last line—"and give pleasure to me and others"—may indeed be called Gieldzinski's motto. He gave freely to the Danzig he loved. Furniture to the Artushof (which housed the stock exchange), embroidered tapestries to the Franciscan monastery, a set of medals from the time of Frederick the Great to the Emperor's Hussars, a newly carved portal for the Stockturm (a 16th-century Danzig landmark)—these are just a few examples of his generosity. In 1901, the empress expressed her appreciation and satisfaction that ". . . Mr. Gieldzinski had donated such great treasures during his lifetime and had dedicated himself to the public good." It was for this reason that in 1905 Emperor Wilhelm II decorated him with the Order of the Red Eagle and the Order of the Crown.

As one reads of all the honors accorded Lesser Gieldzinski, one marvels at his ability to keep a balance between being a German and being a Jew, especially at a time when anti-Semitism was widespread in Germany and in Danzig. But he did retain a strong sense of identity as a Jew, and it was this that led him to collect Jewish ceremonial objects. He thus became one of the earliest Judaica collectors. According to his wishes, the collection was housed in a separate room of the Danzig Synagogue, known as the "Gieldzinski Zimmer," and, in 1904, this room became one of the first Jewish museums in the world.

Despite his high position in the community, Lesser Gieldzinski was also a man of great humility, a man who did not forget his origins. Amidst the many signed photographs of statesmen and royalty that stood on his writing desk, there was also a photograph of a grey-haired lady, incribed with the simple phrase, "meine liebe Mutter" ("my dear mother"). At Gieldzinski's funeral in May, 1910, a few months after his eightieth birthday, Rabbi Dr. Robert Kaelter, beloved Rabbi of Danzig from 1909 to 1926, spoke these words: "His humanity and his Jewishness made him a true Jew, so that the high honors accorded to him did honor to all Jews, and helped to halt the prevailing prejudices."

In 1912, Lesser Gieldzinski's entire art collection, except for the Jewish ceremonial objects which remained in the Danzig Synagogue, was sent to Berlin and auctioned on six consecutive days. Some twenty-seven years later, the Danzig Synagogue was dismantled by the Nazis, and Jewish life in Danzig came to an end. In 1945, Danzig was razed to the ground, and with it, most of the monuments that Lesser Gieldzinski had helped to beautify. By a great miracle, the Danzig Judaica collection survived, and the spirit of Lesser Gieldzinski lives on.

Catalogue of the Exhibition

Notes to the Catalogue

VIVIAN B. MANN

JOSEPH GUTMANN

Ceremonial objects connected with private life and worship appear first in the catalogue; then appear those used on the Sabbath and holy days, followed by those used in communal life. Within these broad groupings, the works are listed according to their place of origin, beginning with those made in Western Europe, and ending with those from Russia or the European East.

In the entries, all dimensions are cited in order of height, width, depth; for circular objects, height is followed by diameter, designated dm. Unless otherwise noted, measurements are maximum. The D numbers (e.g. D 61) which follow the measurements are Jewish Museum accession numbers. A glossary of the Hebrew terms used in the entries begins on p. 48 and a list of bibliographical abbreviations appears on p. 142.

Special note has been made of Judeo-German inscriptions; the remainder are Hebrew. All transcriptions are complete. However, standard Hebrew honorifics were omitted from the English translations and such elisions are indicated by ellipses. The only notable exception is the term *z.l.* which significantly contributes to the meaning of the inscriptions. Another interesting feature of Hebrew inscriptions is the use of chronograms that are based on the numerical value traditionally assigned to each letter. All of the chronograms used on Danzig objects omit the first digit of the Hebrew year. (It should be noted that the Hebrew lunar year and the Gregorian calendar do not exactly correspond.) The remaining numbers are sometimes incorporated within a quotation from Scripture or the liturgy, with the relevant letters marked by accents. (It should be noted that the Hebrew lunar year and the Gregorian calendar do not exactly correspond.) Due to printing limitations, the range of diacritical marks used in the inscriptions could not be reproduced exactly, yet an attempt has been made to suggest their variety. The Hebrew translations are largely the work of Malka Reisner; others were written in consultation with Menahem Schmelzer and Werner Weinberg.

We also wish to acknowledge the help of Jessie McNab and Helmut Nickel of The Metropolitan Museum of Art, Gert Schiff of the Institute of Fine Arts and Joe Rothstein of the American Museum of Natural History, whom we consulted on particular aspects of some of the objects. Rafi Grafman, Jerusalem, contributed many editorial and scholarly comments which were incorporated into the Revised Edition.

Finally, a word on Danzig silver marks. In 1730, the guild of Danzig silversmiths established a three mark system: city, master and control marks. The city mark of two crosses and a crown changed shape over the years, but since earlier forms were later reused, these marks are not reliable indications of date. Danzig silversmiths generally used their last names, initials or abbreviations as their master mark. Symbols were rarely used. The third mark, that of the assay master for a particular year or series of years, nearly always consists of one or more initials. Since the names and terms of office of the assay masters are known, their marks are the most specific indication of the date of an object's manufacture. Unless otherwise indicated, the dating of silver and pewter pieces are based on their hallmarks.

Glossary

denotes words defined in the glossary

amulet—an object believed to serve a protective function. The efficacy of Jewish amulets is considered to depend on the inscription thereon of one or more names of God or those of his angels.

atarah—a decorative collar sewn to a prayer shawl *(tallit)*.

etrog—citron, a fruit resembling a lemon, that is one of the four species of plant used during the liturgy of the Sukkot holiday (Feast of Tabernacles). When not in use, the *etrog* is stored in a protective box.

Eternal Light—a continuously burning lamp that hangs before the Torah ark* in a synagogue.

Gabbai—an officer of a communal organization who was responsible for the collection and distribution of funds.

Haggadah—book containing the service read during the Seder*.

Hanukkah—lit. dedication [of the Temple]; a Jewish holiday commemorating the victory of the Hasmoneans over their Greco-Syrian overlords in 165 B.C.E. and the establishment of religious freedom in ancient Israel.

havdalah—lit. separation; ceremony held Saturday evening to mark the end of the Sabbath and the beginning of the new week.

Hevrah Kaddisha—lit. holy society. Burial Society responsible for the cleansing and burial of the dead according to Jewish law.

huppah—canopy under which the bride and groom stand during their wedding ceremony.

Kaddish—a prayer glorifying God customarily recited by a mourner in memory of the dead.

ketubbah—Jewish marriage contract. The signing of the *ketubbah* is an integral part of the wedding ceremony.

Kiddush—prayer of sanctification over wine recited on Sabbaths and Festivals.

kohen—a descendant of Aaron, the Biblical high priest.

matzot—unleavened bread eaten during Passover*.

megillah—a scroll, e.g. *Megillat Esther*, the Book of Esther written on a scroll.

menorah—seven-branched lampstand once found in the Tabernacle*; a similar lampstand found in synagogues; a lamp with eight lights used during the Hanukkah* festival.

mezuzah—lit. doorpost; a parchment scroll inscribed with Biblical passages (Deut. 6:4-9; 11:13-21) that is affixed to the doorposts of Jewish homes, usually encased in a protective cover.

mirror—central panel of an Ashkenazi Torah curtain*.

Passover—spring festival commemorating the Exodus from Egypt.

rimmon(im)—lit. pomegranate; an adornment for the staves of a Torah scroll.

Rosh Hashanah—the New Year, holy days occurring on the first and second days of the Hebrew month of Tishri.

Seder—lit. order; liturgical home service for the first two nights of Passover* at which the history of the Exodus from Egypt is recounted and symbolic foods are eaten.

Shaddai—name of God usually written on the back of a *mezuzah**.

shammash—servitor, the light used to kindle the lights of a Hanukkah* *menorah**.

Shavuot—Feast of Weeks, a two day festival commemorating the Giving of the Torah at Sinai, which occurs seven weeks after the second day of Passover*.

sheviti—plaque hung in a synagogue inscribed with the verse *sheviti hashem lenegdi tamid*, "I have set the Lord always before me" (Ps. 16:8).

shofar—a ram's horn sounded during services on Rosh Hashanah* and Yom Kippur* as a call to repentence.

spice box—a container for the spices used during the *havdalah** service.

Tabernacle—portable sanctuary built by the Israelites.

Tablets of the Law—tablets inscribed with the Ten Commandments.

Ten Days of Penitence—the first ten days of the Hebrew month of Tishri. The period begins with Rosh Hashanah and ends with Yom Kippur and is a time of introspection and prayer for the Jew.

Torah—a scroll inscribed with the first five books of the Hebrew Bible.

Torah ark—a cabinet set in or against one wall of a synagogue that holds the Torah scrolls and is a focus of prayer.

Torah ark curtain—an embroidered curtain hung on the Torah ark*. It generally consists of a curtain, *parokhet,* and a valance, *kapporet*.

Torah binder—band that holds the two staves of a Torah scroll together when the Torah is not being read.

Torah mantle—cover of silk or other precious fabric that encases the Torah scroll and is removed for reading.

Torah pointer—small rod of wood or precious metal used by the reader of a Torah to follow the text.

Torah shield—an ornamental metal plaque hung from the staves of a Torah*, sometimes having small interchangeable plates, each of which indicates a specific reading.

Wimpel—the Ashkenazi name for a Torah binder*.

yarmulke—small cap worn by Jewish men as a reminder of God's presence.

Yom Kippur—lit. Day of Atonement; a day of fasting and prayer that falls on the tenth day of the Hebrew month of Tishri.

z.l.—z[*iḥrono*] l[*ivraḥah*] lit. "may his remembrance be for a blessing"; Hebrew honorific used after the name of a deceased male. (Fem., *ziḥronah livraḥah*.)

54. Torah Curtain, Danzig, 1795

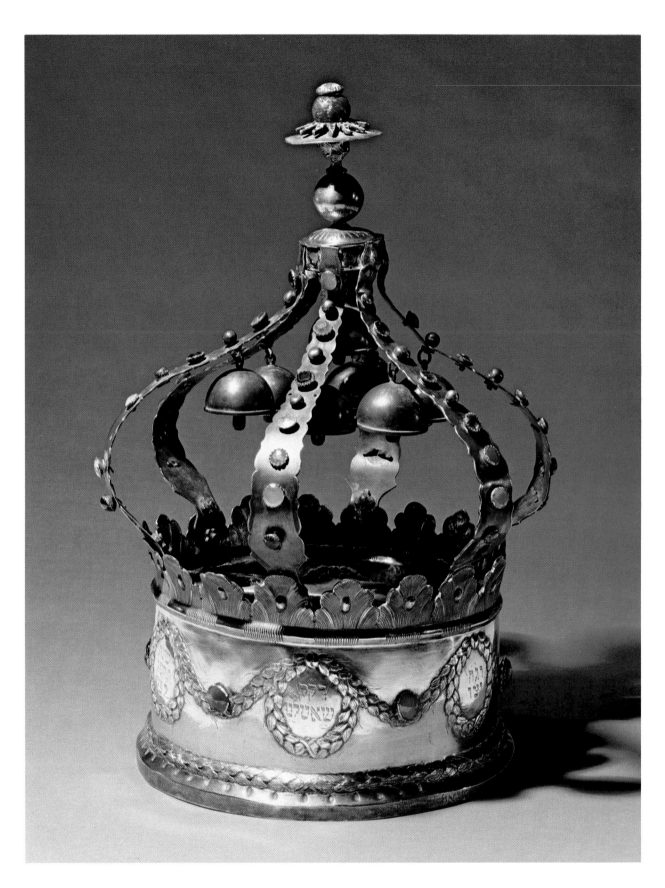

74. *Torah Crown, Joachim Hübner, Berlin, 1779*

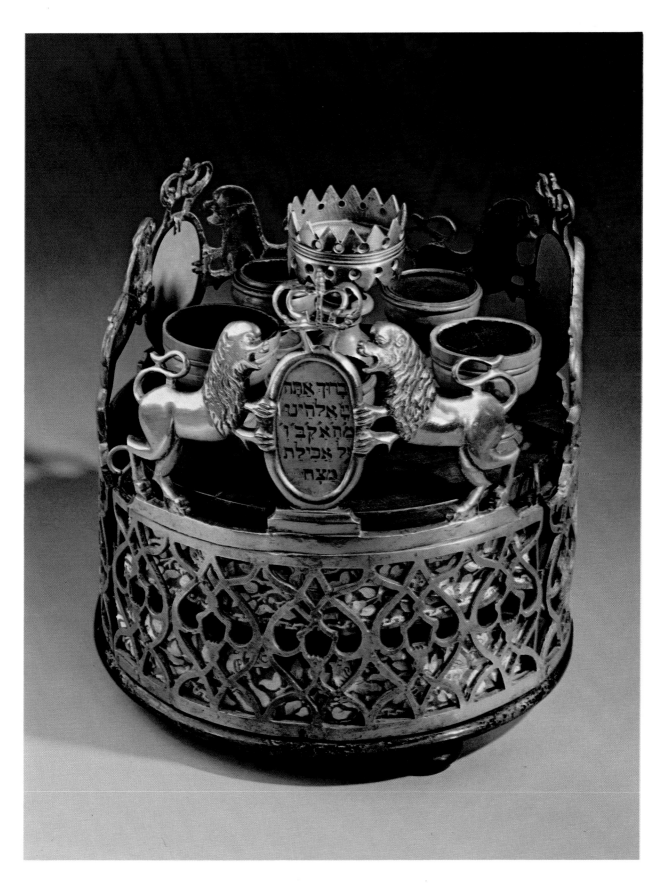

51. Tiered Seder Plate, Poland, 18th century

57/79/91. Torah Mantle, Prussia, first half of the 18th century; Pair of Rimmonim, *Berlin, 1788-1802; Torah Pointer, Danzig, 1766-1812*

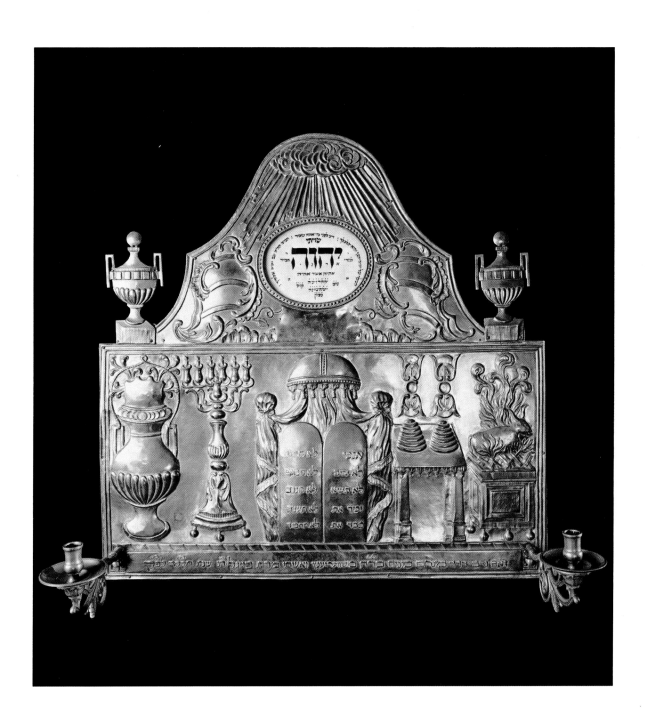

109. *Sheviti Tablet, Poland, 1804*

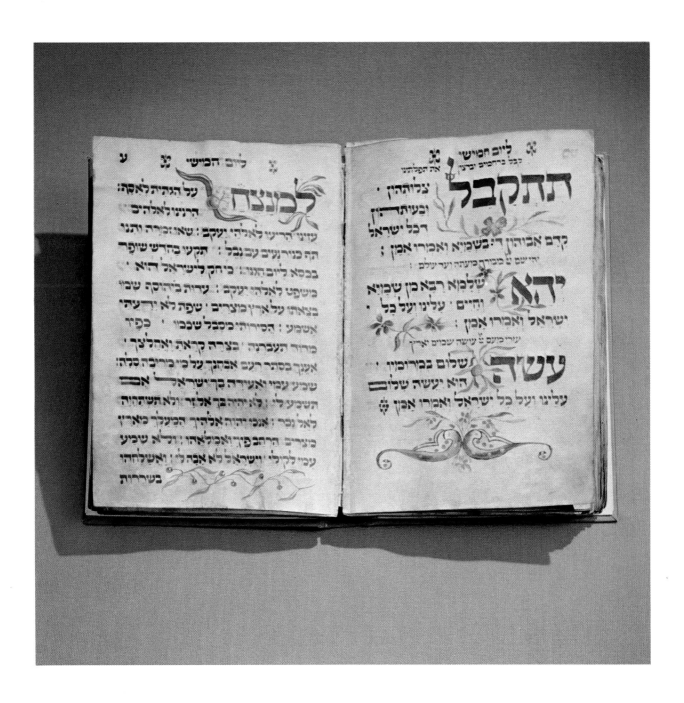

99. *Prayer Book, Ashkenazi Europe, 1725*

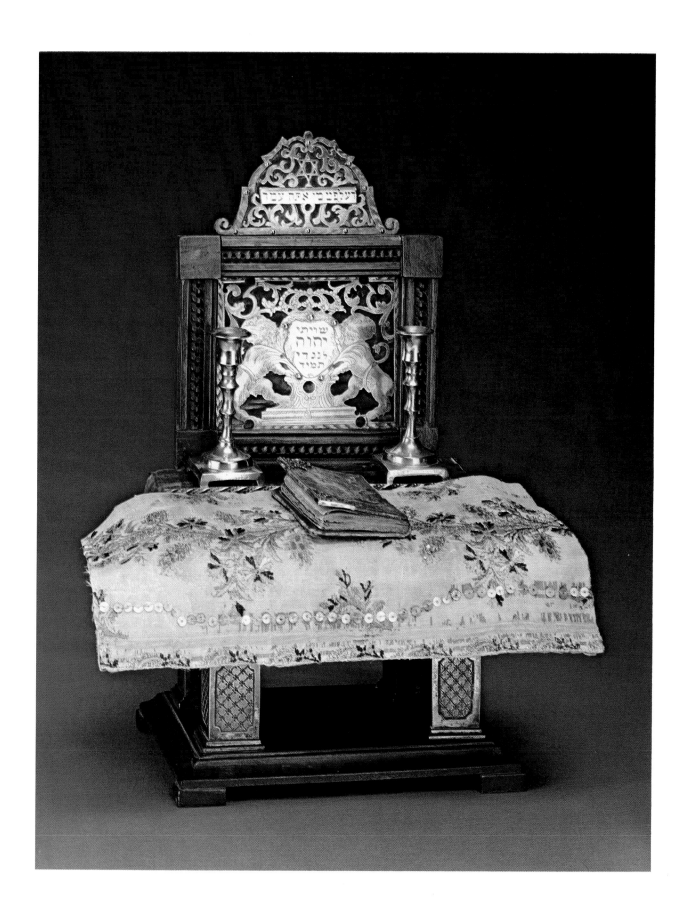

19 a-c/101. Miniature Reader's Desk and Furnishings, Danzig, 19th century; Prayer Book, Dyhernfurth, 1777

9. *Ketubbah, Ancona, 1781*

1.

Circumcision Knife

Amber; silver: engraved
Germany: 1697 (date of inscription)
Marks: none
7 x ⅞" (17.8 x 2.2 cm)
D 153

The tang of the double-edged blade of this knife is inserted in an octagonal amber handle with silver fittings. The upper fitting has a scalloped edge and is decorated with incised leaves. A solder repair remains at top, which may indicate a missing finial. The lower fitting bears the following inscription:

וימל / אברהם / את / יצחק / בנו בן / שמונת / אלעזר / ב׳
מהורר / יהודה / ש׳ בשנת / תנז לפק.

("And when his son Isaac was eight [days] old, Abraham circumcised him . . . [Gen. 21:4] Elazar b[en] the revered Rabbi Yehudah . . . , in the year [5]457"=1697.) The shapes of the handle and fittings of this knife are closest to two late 18th-century knives from Austria: one in the Feuchtwanger Collection (Shachar, *Osef Feuchtwanger*, no. 3); and another in The Jewish Museum (JM 8-61).

REFERENCES: Danzig, 1904, no. 100; Danzig, 1933, no. 11. pl. 2.

2.

Circumcision Knife

Steel and silver plate on copper
Europe: 18th-19th century
6¾ x ¹¹⁄₁₆" (17.2 x 1.7 cm)
D 152

A floral design framed in a triangular field decorates the upper half of the handle. Similar motifs set within a smaller triangle also appear at the lower end, overlapping the steel blade. Between the two triangles are engraved the words

וימל אברהם.

("And . . . Abraham circumcised . . ."; Gen. 21:4.) Portions of the handle are broken off at the point where the blade meets the handle.

REFERENCES: Danzig, 1904, no. 98; Danzig, 1933, no. 13, pl. 2.

3.

Circumcision Knife

Steel; silver filigree; agate
Europe: 18th-19th century
6⅛ x ¹¹⁄₁₆" (15.5 x 1.7 cm)
D 154

A fan-shaped filigree mount masks the juncture of the steel blade and agate handle. A second, petal-shaped filigree mount covers the lower end of the handle socket.

REFERENCES: Danzig, 1904, no. 99; Danzig, 1933, no. 14, pl. 2.

1.   3.   2.

4 a-d.

Circumcision Set

Pewter: engraved and hammered; niello
Danzig or Elbing: 1801
Maker: Johann Jacob Bietau
Mark: Hintze[3] 473
a. spice flask: 5 x 2″ (12.7 x 5.1 cm)
b. powder flask: 2⁷⁄₁₆ x 1³⁄₈″ dm (6.2 x 3.5 cm)
c. oil flask: 2³⁄₈ x 1³⁄₈″ dm (6 x 3.5 cm)
d. plate: 4³⁄₄″ dm (12 cm)
D 157-60

This set of objects used during the circumcision ceremony includes a short flask inscribed

פלווער

("powder"); another marked

עהל

("oil"); a tall flask engraved

געווירץ

("spice"); and a plate to hold the flasks engraved

מילה

("circumcision"). All of these Judeo-German and Hebrew inscriptions are filled with niello so that they stand out against the ground. An owner's initials,

C.G.D., and the date, 1809, are also engraved on the tall container. The shorter flasks are cylindrical and are furnished with screw-on covers. The larger one is more elaborate in form and decoration. It has a bulbous base rising into a cylindrical neck and a screw top terminating in a thin finial. Raised moldings and bands of hammering decorate the surface.

Bietau's mark appears only on the plate, but from the workmanship and size of all the objects they appear to have been made as a set. They are designated as such in the Danzig catalogues. Bietau became a master in Danzig in 1801, but then moved to Elbing in the same year. He died there in 1842.

REFERENCES: Danzig, 1904, no. 99; Danzig, 1933, no. 14, pl. 2.

5.

Bowl for Circumcision Ceremony

Silver: engraved
Danzig: 1837–38
Maker: Johann Jakob Raths
Marks: Czihak[2] 10, 535, 541 (control mark of Gottlieb Ephraim Wulstein)
1⅛ x 4″ dm (2.9 x 10 cm)
D 161

This plain shallow bowl rests on a low foot. Within the bowl is inscribed:

להניח בזה עפר לכסות הערלה. שייך לקהל דק״ק
מאטטענבודען. נעשה ע״י הגבאים ר׳ איצק ב״ר״מ
גאלדשטיין / ור׳ ברוך קראנהיימער / תקצח.

("For placing ashes to cover the foreskin / belongs to the Mattenbuden congregation made for the *Gabbaim* Itzig b[en] Moshe Goldstein / and Baruch Kronheimer [5]598"=1838.)

The inscription mentions Itzig Goldstein, the first president of the Mattenbuden synagogue and donor of many of its ceremonial objects (nos. 41, 69, 88, 89, 121, 126, 127, 129, 132, 185, 202, 226, 235, 278, 281). For other bowls of similar use, see Shachar, *Osef Feuchtwanger,* no. 23c; H. Frauberger, "Uber alte Kultusgegenstände in Synagoge und Haus," *Mitteilungen der Gesellschaft zur Erforschung jüdischer Kunstdenkmäler,* 3–4(1903), p. 86, no. 10, fig. 134.

6.

6.

Curtain for the Circumcision Ceremony

Beige pile; blue silk; metallic embroidery; stumpwork; sequins
Hannover or Danzig: 1760
79½ x 43½" (202 x 110.5 cm)
D 250

The background textile is an unusual beige silk pile. A large Crown of Torah executed in stumpwork and embroidered with metallic threads and sequins is the dominant motif at top. Below it are a pitcher and covered container. Various dedicatory inscriptions are arranged around these images: above the crown,

כתר תורה וכתר כהונה

("Crown of Torah and Crown of Priesthood"); to either side of the crown,

זאת נדר ונדב / ר' אליעזר ליפמן כ"ץ / מהנובר / ואשתו מרת / רבקה דארוש / ת"י

("This was vowed and donated by Eliezar Lipmann K[at]z of Hannover and his wife Rivkah Darush [?]"); below the metallic fringe,

ר' אברהם / ישראל / סגל / ע"א מ' / טויבה / תי.

("Avraham Yisrael Siegel w[ith his] w[ife] Toibe . . ."); and above the mirror,

קדש לה' / ביום ה' כ"ג אלול מ'ב'ר'כ'י'ך' ב'ר'ו'ך' לפ"ק.

(". . . holy to the Lord . . . [Ex. 31:15] on Thursday, 23 of Elul . . . 'Blessed are they who bless you . . .' "; Num. 24:9 = [5]520 = Sept. 4, 1760.)

A large blue satin mirror banded by metallic braid covers most of the remaining area of the curtain. It is embroidered with the standard text of the circumcision ceremony, beginning with the blessing over the wine and concluding with the sentence, "As he has been entered into the covenant, so may he be introduced to the study of Torah, to the *huppah,* and to good deeds." This last passage also appears on Torah binders made from circumcision swaddling cloths (cf. nos. 55, 56, 190).

Curtains such as this one and no. 138 may have been hung above the chair on which the infant was held during the circumcision ceremony. Most known examples were made in Germany or in areas under German influence. The Jewish Museum owns a third 18th-century example from Mannheim (JM 4-49).

The inscription on this curtain specifies that one of the donors, Eliezer Lipmann, came from Hannover. Thus, the curtain may have been made in Hannover and brought by Lipmann to Danzig when he moved there, or it may have been made in Danzig with the information on Lipmann's birthplace specified in the commission. Instances of both practices are known; see O. Herbenová, "Synagogenvorhänge des 17. Jahrhunderts aus Böhmen und Mähren," *Waffen- und Kostümkunde* 10(1968), pp. 107ff., esp. 110ff.; F. Landsberger, "Old Time Torah-Curtains, *Beauty in Holiness,* pp. 125ff., esp. pp. 142–56.

7.

Pidyon Ha-Ben Plate

Brass: repoussé and engraved
Eastern Europe: 18th-19th century
2¼ x 18½" dm (5.6 x 47 cm)
D 116

60

7.

This circular plate has a wide flange decorated with an abbreviated blessing executed in repoussé letters. The text is drawn from the ceremony for the redemption of the first-born, the *Pidyon ha-ben:*

.ב׳. א׳. יי׳. א׳. מ׳. ה׳. א׳. ק׳. ב׳. ו׳. על. פדיון. הבן.

("Praised are You, O Lord our God, King of the universe, who has sanctified our lives through His commandments, commanding us concerning the redemption of the first-born.") The remainder of the flange is engraved with a flowering vine and a Star of David. At the center of the cavetto is the image of a baby in swaddling cloths, executed in deep repoussé, surmounted by the priestly hands in blessing. A wavy ribbon border is engraved near the edge of the cavetto, and a later, German inscription is engraved across the center field: "Gieldzinski'sche Samlung" (sic) ("Gieldzinski Collection").

During the *Pidyon ha-ben* ceremony, the father of the first-born redeems his son from priestly service through an offering of money. After accepting the gift, the *kohen* blesses the child with the traditional threefold benediction, symbolized on the plate by the open hands above the child in swaddling cloths. A cutout leaf shape replaces the nose, in keeping with the religious proscription against complete representation of the human form (*Shulhan Arukh,* Yoreh De'ah, 141).

REFERENCES: Danzig, 1933, no. 116; Kanof, *Jewish Ceremonial Art,* p. 187, fig. 198.

8.
Bridal Belt and Pouch

Weave-patterned silk; gold metallic appliqués; buckle; silk lining
German: 18th-19th century
Belt: 4 x 26¼" (10 x 66.7 cm)
Pouch: 7½ x 9¼" (19 x 23.5 cm)
D 268

Both belt and pouch are constructed of a rose, grey and white woven silk with green and white flowers and white fronds. The border of the pouch is edged in metallic braid. Metallic appliqués are sewn on both objects. The same appliqués are fused together and attached to a frame to form the belt buckle. Each appliqué is a rosette whose circumference is formed of a series of hives with swarming bees, symbols of industriousness.

The fabric used may be earlier than the manufacture of the belt. However, it is impossible to determine from internal evidence when the cloth was adapted to its present form. A letter to L. Gieldzinski from the director of the Stadtisches Historisches Museum, Frankfurt a. M., dated May 25, 1906, discusses the German-Jewish custom of having bride and groom exchange belts decorated with gold (*Sivlonotgürtel*). We may infer that the present example was acquired by Gieldzinski prior to the date of his inquiry to the Frankfurt Museum. Most extant German marriage belts are made of metal; the Danzig example, made out of silk, is thus rare.

REFERENCES: Danzig, 1933, no. 120; pl. 4.

8.

*9.

Ketubbah

Watercolor on parchment
Ancona: 1781
34½ x 23¼" (80.7 x 59 cm)
D 305

This marriage contract was written at Ancona, Italy on Wednesday, the 14th of Tishri, 5542 (October 3, 1781) between

יעקב שלמה שבתי יצ"ו / בן ... יוסף חיים צינגולי
וספיראנצא שמחה מבת בת ... ברוך הלוי.

("Jacob Solomon Shabbetai ben Joseph Hayyim Zinguli and Speranza Simḥah daughter of Barukh Halevi.") The standard text of the *ketubbah* begins with the Hebrew word

ברביעי

("on Wednesday") written in large square letters within the inner gold frame. Below it, in cursive writing, is the text of the *tenaim,* the legally binding articles of engagement specific to this marriage. The names of the two witnesses, in Hebrew, follow. Surrounding the text is an elaborate border with framed scenes, allegorical figures, and decorative elements. The scenes are drawn from the lives of the two Biblical heroes whose names the bridegroom and his father bore. At top is Jacob's dream of the ladder, labeled

ויחלום והנה סולם מוצב ארצה וראשו מגיע השמימה והנה
מלאכי אלקים עולים ויורדים בו.

("He had a dream; a ladder was set on the ground and its top reached to the sky, and angels of God were going up and down on it"; Gen. 28:12.) This scene is supported by two large *putti.* Below it, in red lettering, is a standard passage often appearing at the top of Italian marriage contracts:

בסימנא טבא ובמזלא מעליא לחתנא ולכלתא ולכל ישראל אחינו
אמן כן יהי רצון.

("With good signs and good fortune to the bride and groom and to all Israel our brothers. Amen. May it be Your will.") Near the bottom of the *ketubbah* is a depiction of Joseph as governor of Egypt, accompanied by the passage

ויוסף הוא השליט על הארץ

("Now Joseph was the vizier of the land . . .";

Gen. 42:6.) The allegorical figures, who symbolize the virtues of marriage, flank the text. On the right side, Righteousness stands supported by a console inscribed

בצדקה תכונני

("You shall be established through righteousness"; Isaiah 54:14.) At left is Hope standing above the text

ויש תקוה לאחריתך

("And there is hope for your future"; Jeremiah 31:17.) The remainder of this large and elaborate frame is filled with scroll and foliate motifs which serve to interlock all the figurative elements. The basically rectangular shape of this *ketubbah* is modified at the top, formed as a symmetrical undulating shape culminating in a rounded tip filled with a coat of arms. A vertical line divides the device in two. The right side is filled with a pitcher and laver symbolic of the tribe of Levi to which the bride belonged. Unfortunately, the left side is indecipherable.

During the 18th century, a school of artists working in Ancona produced a series of large and elaborate *ketubbot.* Like other Italian marriage contracts, the Ancona *ketubbot* are characterized by bright colors and a wealth of ornamental motifs and decorative elements drawn from late Renaissance and Baroque art. **Characteristic of Ancona contracts are the undulating upper edge of this *ketubbah,* the arrangement of its** text and the use of contrasting scripts for the *ketubbah* proper and auxilary texts. Commissions for such large and impressive *ketubbot* probably resulted from a 16th-century innovation in the marriage ceremony, the public reading of the contract (cf. Barnett, nos. 476 and 479; *Beauty in Holiness,* pp. 391, 412.)

REFERENCES: Danzig, 1904, no. 101; Danzig, 1933, no. 62; D. Davidovitch, *The Ketuba: Jewish Marriage Contracts Through the Ages,* Tel Aviv, 1968, p. 91, no. 53.

10.

Wedding Sofa

Birch veneer over pine; lindenwood; painted and gilded; upholstery
Possibly Danzig: 1838
38¼ x 63 x 28" (97 x 160 x 71 cm)
D 280

This interesting sofa is both an excellent example of

10.

Biedermeier style furniture and possibly a unique surviving example of a Jewish marriage couch. The frame is formed of pine veneered with birch. Its basically rectangular shape is softened by the addition of circular forms: the arched top piece flanked by semi-circular finials; the round armrests that are supported by gently curved posts and legs, and finally the carved drapery festoons suspended on the front and sides. Gilt lindenwood appliqués articulate the edges of major sections: palmettes on the armrests; slender leaves at the base of the posts and legs; floral motifs on the finials and on the top piece. The center of the arched top is an oval cartouche painted a deep blue, bearing two clasped hands executed in relief. These hands are carefully differentiated to indicate that the woman sat on the right side of the sofa and the man on the left. Below the hands is a dedicatory inscription carved in relief, the letters set off by gilding against a blue ground:

ז״נ ה״ה היקר המרומם הרר שלמה פרידלענדר / עם זוגתו הצנועה מרת דאברה שתחי׳: תקצח.

("T[his was] d[onated] by the revered Rabbi Shlomoh Friedländer with his modest spouse Dobrah . . . [5]598"=1838.) The pendant festoons are also painted blue and gold to simulate fabric edged with fringe and braid. From the use of blue paint on the wooden portions of the sofa, we may suppose that the upholstered seat, back, and side panels were originally covered in a blue fabric. In its present state, the sofa shows evidence of prior restoration to both its framework and upholstery covering. However, an interesting original feature of its construction is the upholstery stuffing composed of kelp and seashells which indicate that this sofa was made near the sea, probably in Danzig itself.

Biedermeier is the name given to furniture produced in Germany and Austria between the years 1815 and 1848 in what was basically a neo-classical style with Empire and other influences. Characteristics of the Biedermeier style which are evident in the wedding sofa are the stress given to a single major viewpoint, the use of decorative elements derived from antique art and a respect for materials. Biedermeier furniture is generally not conceived as a single overall shape but as a series of juxtaposed geometric forms; the same is true of this sofa. Characteristic, too, is the use of draped fabric, both real and simulated. Biedermeier furniture was ample, functional and comfortable, and well-suited to the needs of the middle class for whom it was made.

It is the function of this sofa which makes it unique. The presence of a dedicatory inscription indicates that the sofa was given to a synagogue, and the clasped male and female hands suggest that it was used during marriage ceremonies. Also the relative placement of the man and woman on the couch replicates the positions of the bride and groom beneath the *huppah*. The 1933 Danzig catalogue explains that the sofa was used during the *Bedeckung*, the veiling of the bride by the groom before the ceremony.

REFERENCES: Danzig, 1933, no. 121.

11.

Wedding Ring

Silver: engraved
Europe: 19th century
Marks: none
1³⁄₁₆ x 1¹⁄₁₆" dm (2.1 x 2.7 cm)
D 279

Two plain raised moldings mark the edges of this wedding band. The center is engraved with the words

מזל טוב

(*"mazzal tov"*) framed in a cartouche.

According to the 1933 Danzig catalogue, this ring came to the Synagogue Museum from the Gieldzinski Collection, together with the bridal belt and pouch and the silver-covered prayer book (nos. 8 and 102), although it is not listed in the earlier catalogue. Since Gieldzinski died in 1910 and there is reason to date the belt and pouch at latest in the 19th century, we may suppose the same date for the ring. However, documentary evidence for the use of marriage rings inscribed *mazzal tov* occurs as early as the 18th century; see J. Gutmann, "Wedding Customs and Ceremonies in Art," *Beauty in Holiness,* pp. 323–24, no. 21.

REFERENCES: Danzig, 1933, no. 120, pl. 4.

12.

Cover of a Mezuzah

Silver: cast and engraved
Warsaw: 1878
Maker: Pogorzelski   o.c.
Marks: Lepszy, nos. 316–9 and 1878
5⅞ x ⅞" (15 x 2.3 cm)
D 81

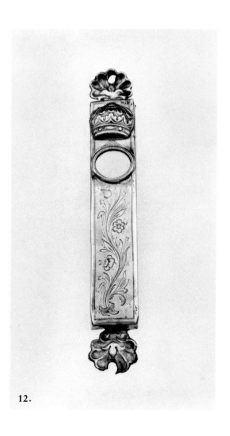

12.

A delicately engraved flowering vine decorates the top of the *mezuzah* cover. Above is an oval glass protected by a raised frame which would have permitted the viewing of the name of God inscribed on the parchment within. A cast crown is affixed to the top of the cover above the glass, and palmettes with drilled holes are affixed to either end to allow for securing the *mezuzah* to a doorpost. The name "T. S. Kohn," scratched inside the cover, is presumably the name of the owner.

The Biblical injunction to write the words of God upon the doorposts of the house (Deut. 6:9; 11:20) gave rise to various forms of containers for the required scriptural passages. These passages are written on parchment whose back is inscribed *Shaddai,* meaning Almighty, but also an acronym for the Hebrew words, "Guardian of the doors of Israel" (*Tur,* Yoreh De'ah, 288). The parchment is always rolled to allow the name *Shaddai* to be visible through an aperture such as the glass oval frame of this *mezuzah.*

REFERENCES: Danzig, 1904, no. 75; Danzig, 1933, no. 86, pl. 10.

13.

Mezuzah

Fruitwood; ink on parchment; glass
Europe: 19th century
6 x 1⁵⁄₁₆ x ⅞" (15.5 x 2.3 x 2.1 cm)
D 85

The *mezuzah* is in the form of a baluster decorated with leaves framed by plain moldings. A square aperture at center allows for viewing the name of God, *Shaddai,* inscribed on the parchment within. This rolled parchment was inserted with the prescribed passages from Deuteronomy (6:4-9; 11:13-21); its outer side has *Shaddai* written three times, and written once, the fourteen-letter name of God

כוזו במוכסז כוזו

The fourteen-letter name is formed by *temurah,* or "substitution," for each letter of the phrase

ה' אלהינו ה'

the succeeding letters of the alphabet. This name is commonly inscribed on amulets, and its presence on the parchment is witness to the popular belief in the apotropaic powers of the *mezuzah.*

REFERENCES: Danzig, 1904, no. 74; Danzig, 1933, no. 85.

14.

Miniature Torah Ark

Brass and copper: cast and chased; wood
Danzig: 19th century
23 x 16⅝ x 16⅝" (58.5 x 42.2 x 42.2 cm)
D 1

This miniature ark for home use was designed as a small temple set within a sacred precinct that is defined by a low wall of openwork. Four small pinnacles mark the corners, and two tall columns flank the entry. The building rises from a raised platform approached by steps. It is hexagonal and roofed by a ribbed dome topped by a rectangular turret with bulbous dome and projecting finial. Appliquéd Stars of David decorate each panel of the main dome, and cast scroll ornaments overlay the juncture of the ribs and the architrave, except at the front, where appear the Tablets of the Law. The sides of the building are richly

ornamented with a tapestry-like design of birds and foliage. All of these elements are mounted on a wooden base with ball feet. The textile panels set in the doors are embroidered with Stars of David and quotations from the penitential prayer *Avinu malkenu*, recited on fast days and during the Ten Days of Penitence between Rosh Hashanah and Yom Kippur. At right,

א׳ מ׳ / שמע קולנו / חוס ורחם / עלינו.

("Our Father, our King, hear our voice, have pity and compassion upon us"); at left,

א׳ מ׳ / פתח שערי / שמים / לתפלתנו

("Our Father, our King, open the gates of heaven to our prayer".)

Various types of miniature Torah arks have survived, but these are usually cabinets. This Danzig example is interesting for its development as an architectural complex. A comparison with the 17th-century tower of the Brigittenkirche in Danzig reveals that the turret of the ark is closely modeled after it and that this Torah ark must therefore have been made in Danzig. The chased decoration of the sides is similar in theme to that of the book cover, no. 106, but the forms on the ark are more elegantly designed and finer in execution. A pair of small brass candlesticks in the collection (no. 271) was once used together with this ark.

REFERENCES: Danzig, 1904, no. 1; Danzig, 1933, no. 1.

15.

Miniature Torah Scroll

Ink on parchment; silver: cast and filigree
Poland (?): 19th century
Marks: none
9½ x 4½ x 2" dm (24 x 11.5 x 5 cm)
D 276

This miniature Torah is written in a fine, clear hand on a parchment scroll fitted with silver rollers. The lower ends of the staves are shaped as handles and worn smooth from use. The upper ends are decorated with removable filigree finials.

In the two Danzig catalogues, this scroll was associated with the small mantle (no. 16), the crown (no. 18), the shield (no. 17) and the pointer (no. 95). It may have been used in a home and enclosed in an ark such as no. 14.

REFERENCES: Danzig, 1904, no. 4; Danzig, 1933, no. 136.

14.

63

16.

Miniature Torah Mantle

Velvet; silver foil; silver-wrapped silk threads; copper
threads
Poland: 19th century
6⅛ x 5⅞" (15.5 x 15 cm)
D 277

A wide scalloped ribbon of silver foil and silver-
wrapped silk threads, woven into stylized foliate
forms, is overlaid on a maroon velvet foundation to
form this miniature Torah mantle. Bands of loosely
woven copper threads are attached to the top and
bottom of the velvet.

This mantle was made for the small Torah, no. 15.
The ribbon is similar in workmanship and materials to
those of the Gieldzinski *yarmulke* and *atarah* made in
Włocławek, 1816–78 (nos. 38, 39) and suggests the
same dating and provenance for the mantle.

17.

Miniature Torah Shield

Silver: filigree, cast, parcel-gilt
Eastern Europe: 19th century

Marks: none
6½ x 4⅞" (16.5 x 12.5 cm)
D 151

The center of the shield is a hexagonal silver plaque
edged in parcel-gilt that is decorated with Tablets of
the Law flanked by two crowned rampant lions. A
third crown surmounts the Tablets. Flowering vines
executed in filigree form a rectangular frame around
the central plaque. From the botton edge hang festoons of silver chains and two filigree flowers whose
centers are Stars of David. The shield was hung from
the staves of the miniature Torah by means of a chain
attached to two filigree branches affixed at the top
corners.

REFERENCES: Danzig, 1904, no. 23; Danzig, 1933, no. 126.

18.

Miniature Torah Crown

Silver: filigree
Eastern Europe: 19th century
Marks: none
4 x 3⁷⁄₁₆" dm (10.3 x 8.7 cm)
D 54

The crown consists of two graduated bulbous sections
of filigree set on a short, cylindrical base.Each section

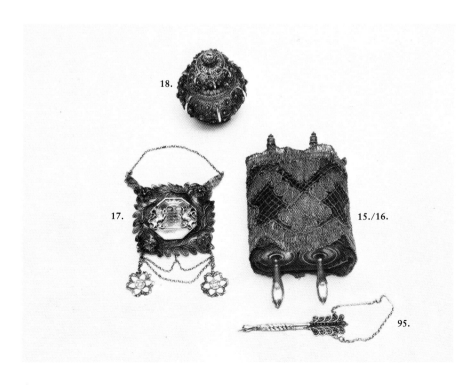

is composed of filigree rosettes bounded by plain bands of silver. The center of each leaf and the center of the rosette are decorated with three-dimensional beads shaped as flowers, and additional beading appears on the base.

This crown belongs to the miniature Torah scroll, no. 15, and forms a set with the pointer, no. 95, the mantle, no. 16 and the shield, no. 17.

REFERENCES: Danzig, 1904, no. 18; Danzig, 1933, no. 54, pl. 6.

*19 a-c.

Miniature Reader's Desk and Furnishings

(a) Reader's Desk

> Wood; brass: cast, cut-out, engraved; silver: engraved; velvet
> Danzig: 19th century
> 13¹¹⁄₁₆ x 7¾ x 5¾" (34.6 x 19.6 x 14.5 cm)
> D 274

This reader's desk for home use is a fully developed miniature version of an architectural furnishing for the synagogue. Its sloping top is supported by four knops rising from short pillars that rest on a footed wooden base. An engraved and hammered diaper pattern enclosed in a cartouche decorates each face of the pillars. The top and back panel are covered with brown velvet overlaid with metal decorations. A metal molding nailed into the top also served as a guard for the miniature candlesticks that illuminated the reading. The remaining top surface was covered with a silk brocade cover on which was placed the *siddur* (prayer book). The back panel is formed of a square lower section and a pediment, whose broken contour is banded with strapwork. Within the pediment is a symmetrical design of foliate scrolls, executed in cut-out brass, that frames a Star of David and a silver banner inscribed

דע לפני מי אתה עומד

("Know before whom you stand"; a variation on Babylonian Talmud, *Berakhot* 28b.) Similar foliate scrolls fill the upper corners of the center panel whose main decoration are two rampant lions holding a silver shield engraved

שויתי / ה' / לנגדי / תמיד

("I have set the Lord always before me"; Ps. 16:8.) This shield rests on an elaborate pedestal covered with a cloth, and itself supports an openwork crown. All of the cut-out metal forms are enriched by engraved details. An elaborate wooden frame carved with intersecting wavy lines surrounds this central back panel.

Elements of this miniature desk suggest that it may have been made as a set with the miniature ark (no. 14). Both pieces are noteworthy for their fine architectural detailing, graceful engraving, their use of metals of contrasting color and their emphasis on the Star of David. In addition, decorative details such as the cartouches filled with diaper patterns that adorn the pillars are nearly identical in execution to those on the ark.

(b) Reader's Desk Cover

> Silver and silver foil embroidered on weave-patterned silk; metallic sequins
> Germany (?): 18th century (fabric)
> 6 x 11" (15.4 x 28 cm)
> D 273

The background material is an ecru, silver, and aqua silk with a continuous vine formed of silver and white threads, silver foil, and gilded silver foil, with added flowering green shoots and blue flowers. Part of an undulating line of metallic sequins remains at bottom. A strap and buckle sewn to the back were used to attach this cover to the miniature reader's desk.

(c) Candlesticks

> Brass: cast
> Danzig (?): 19th century
> 3½ x 1⁹⁄₁₆" (8.9 x 4 cm)
> D 104a, b

Each small candlestick is supported by a baluster stem rising from a circular base that rests on a plinth.

A metal frame nailed to the sloping top of the desk is set just far enough from the back panel to accommodate the base of each candlestick and to prevent its slipping.

REFERENCES: Danzig, 1904, no. 39.

20.

Amulet for Healing

Silver: cast and engraved
Venice: ca. 1742 *(menorah)*
Mark: R 7486
2⅞ x 1¹⁵⁄₁₆″ (7.3 x 4.9 cm)
D 2

The center motif, the *menorah,* is a cast relief that has been joined to a cut-out ovoid frame on which is engraved:

שלח רפואה שלמה.

("Send complete healing"; from the penitential prayer, *Avinu malkenu.)* A gadrooned edging protects the inscription and decoration. A short chain is attached through two small holes at top.

21./20./22.

contrasts with the thinness of the two remaining frames and their polished surfaces. The base of the altar on no. 22 was evidently cut to fit its frame and it must have originally been identical to that of no. 21. Since the hallmark in use on all three pieces is only stamped on the central motifs, it is impossible to determine when these plaques were transformed into amulets. In the Danzig collection is a Torah shield (no. 196) on which similar unmarked Italian decorations are applied to a background plate probably produced in Germany.

REFERENCES: Danzig, 1904, no. 90; Danzig, 1933, no. 2, pl. 1.

21.

Amulet for Healing

Silver: cast and engraved
Venice: probably 18th century
Mark: R 7486
3¼ x 1⁷⁄₁₆″ (8.2 x 3.7 cm)
D 3

A two-storey "tempietto" is set above a fanciful base consisting of volutes, vines, and a shell. Each story of the building has four columns and a center doorway with two additional side doorways on the ground floor. The whole is surmounted by a sectioned dome terminating in a ring for suspension. Along the top stair is inscribed (as in no. 20)

שלת [כך!] רפואה שלמה

and below the stairs,

This amulet is one of three from the Danzig collection which bear identical marks and are similarly executed and constructed (cf. no. 21 and no. 22). The major decorative motifs, cast separately from the frames, were evidently used to decorate a variety of ritual objects. Thus, an identical *menorah* is applied to an Italian Torah crown of 1742 now in The Israel Museum (see *Picture History of Jewish Civilization,* ed. B. Narkiss, New York, 1973, p. 163.) All three examples from Danzig were transformed into amulets by the inscriptions, which were poorly executed by someone ignorant of Hebrew. On the piece we are considering, the *aleph* is improperly formed and the inscription reads from left to right, rather than from right to left. Also, the treatment of the major motifs, cast in high relief and roughly finished on the reverse,

שדי

(Shaddai, "Almighty"; a name of God commonly found on amulets.)

For the relationship between this piece and others from the Danzig collection, see no. 20.

REFERENCES: Danzig, 1904, no. 91; Danzig, 1933, no. 3, pl. 1; E. R. Goodenough, *Jewish Symbols in the Greco-Roman Period,* IV, New York, 1954, p. 128 and fig. 92.

22.

Amulet

Silver: cast and engraved
Venice: probably 18th century
Mark: R 7486
3³⁄₁₆ x 2⅛" (8.1 x 5.3 cm)
D 4

Above the same fanciful base occurring on the preceding example is placed a flaming altar whose structure is enriched through a variety of motifs including moldings, columns, and diamond shapes. The altar and base are joined to a triangular frame with gadrooned edging. The frame bears the Hebrew name *Shaddai* (repeated twice).

The decoration of the altar, together with the very sculptural flames and the convex and concave forms of the base, create a rich play of projecting and receding surfaces. Flaming altars are a generalized symbol which may be associated with various Biblical episodes, such as the Sacrifice of Isaac. On the structure of this amulet and its relation to others in the Danzig collection, see no. 20, and for the inscription, see no. 21.

REFERENCES: Danzig, 1904, no. 92; Danzig, 1933, no. 4, pl. 1.

23.

Two Amulets Suspended from a Belt Clip

(a) Hand-shaped amulet

Silver: cast, engraved, punched
Tunisia: 1856-1905
Mark: Beuque 2952
2⁷⁄₁₆ x 1¾" (6.2 x 4.5 cm)
D 10

23.

The hand-shaped amulet, or *hamsa*, is symmetrically shaped and adorned with cut-out foliage designs that are chased for added detail. A Tunisian silver mark appears on one side.

Hand-shaped amulets have a long history in North Africa, going back to the Carthaginians. Until recently, they were commonly used by both Moslems and Jews, who considered them particularly effective against the Evil Eye. An almost identical example is in the Feuchtwanger Collection of The Israel Museum (see Shachar, *Osef Feuchtwanger,* no. 992), but the Israeli example lacks any mark.

(b) Oval amulet box

Silver: engraved
Italy: 1810–72
Mark: R 7329
2¹⁄₁₆ x 1⁵⁄₁₆ x ⁷⁄₁₆" (5.3 x 3.3 x 1.1 cm)

The edge of the lid is highlighted by concentric arc shapes, while the center field is inscribed above, in Hebrew,

א״ג״לא

(Agla) and below "E F, 20.9.82." *Agla* is an acronym for the phrase "You, O Lord, are mighty forever," taken from the daily prayers. The initials and date were presumably added by an owner. On the back face is the Hebrew inscription *Shaddai,* commonly used on amulets (see no. 21). The ring bears a single

mark current in Italy between 1810 and 1872.

Boxes shaped like this one were widely used for many purposes in the 19th century. Two others that were also made into amulets are part of The Jewish Museum's collection (no. 145a, b and F 2516); another was published by Shachar, *Osef Feuchtwanger,* no. 801.

(c) Belt Clip

> Silver: cast
> Italy: ca. 1860–72
> Mark: R 7328
> 3⁹⁄₁₆ x 1¹³⁄₁₆″ [width of clip] (9.1 x 4.6 cm)

A nearly symmetrical curvilinear design of scrolls and flowers forms the front of the belt clip. Suspended from it is a ring terminating in an elephant's head from which hang five chains of varying lengths.

There are three marks stamped on the back plate of the clip: a cluster of grapes, a rosette, and a bird. The first is the only one which can be identified with certainty (R 7328). It was used in northern Italy between 1810 and 1872 to mark small pieces of silver. Although the bird is nearly obliterated, traces of the outline resemble northern Italian marks dated 1863 and later (e.g., C. G. Bulgari, *Argentieri Gemmari e Orafi d'Italia,* IV, 1966, nos. 2417, 2675).

In essence, this clip has no Jewish content apart from the amulets which are suspended from it.

24.
Hanging Sabbath Lamp

> Brass
> Germany: late 18th century
> 14¼ x 7½″ (36.2 x 19 cm)
> D 94

A knopped shaft suspended from a horseshoe-shaped hook (ring missing) supports six open oil containers in the shape of a star. The drip bowl hanging below is different in color from the rest of the lamp and may not have originally belonged to it.

This is a typical German *Judenstern,* or star-shaped lamp, used for the benediction over the Sabbath lights. Its use by Jews for the Sabbath can be traced back to the 14th century, for representations of it first appear in Hebrew manuscript illuminations at that time; but these lamps may even have been used earlier. The

Jewish Museum also possesses a larger version of the same lamp, F 2969.

REFERENCES: Danzig, 1904, no. 77; Danzig, 1933, no. 109.

25.
Kiddush Goblet

> Silver: repoussé, engraved, chased, acid-etched
> Erfurt: early 19th century; Danzig, before 1848
> Maker: Carl Moritz Stumpf
> Marks: E, 12; Danzig city mark and Czihak[2] 545
> 11½ x 5¹⁄₁₆″ dm (29 x 12.8 cm)
> D 65

The upper portion of this large presentation goblet consists of a flaring cylindrical cup attached to a bulbous lower section decorated with repoussé flowers enclosed in cartouches. Each of the four cartouches bears a different design of flowers. The same variety of design can be seen in the four chased and engraved sections of the baluster stem and in the floral and fruit band engraved on the circular foot. The most

25.

elaborate decoration appears on the cup. Two engraved and chased cartouches formed of pairs of putti holding hunting paraphernalia enclose a dedicatory inscription which reads:

"Dem hochverehrten Stifter und Vorsteher des Vereins für den Unterricht armer Kinder Herrn Itzig Goldstein. am Jubeltag fünf und zwanzig jähriger treuer Wirksamkeit für den Verein./ geweiht von sämtlichen Mitgliedern am 11ᵗ. Februar 1848 überreicht von S. Friedländer und H. Hirschsohn."

("To the most honored founder and a president of the Society for the Education of Poor Children, Mr. Itzig Goldstein, on this jubilee day of twenty-five years of loyal work for the Society. Dedicated by all the members, on the 11th of February, 1848. Presented by S. Friedländer and H. Hirschsohn.") The two sets of marks on the foot indicate that the cup was made in Erfurt and then redecorated by Stumpf in Danzig.

For Itzig Goldstein, see no. 5. Salomon Friedländer was the donor of the marriage couch, no. 10, and of dedicatory plaques, no. 210.

26.

Covered Kiddush Goblet

Silver: repoussé and engraved
Danzig(?): 1855, date of earliest inscription
Maker: G. H.
Marks: GH and 12
15¾ x 5" dm (37.5 x 12.7 cm)
D 64

This is the second large *Kiddush* goblet extant that was presented to Itzig Goldstein in recognition of his charitable works. A Hebrew inscription engraved below the lip reads:

מנחת זכרון ותודה מאת העדה הקדשה מאטטענבודען ביום
מלאת חמש ועשרים שנה גבאי צדקה דקהילתינו / ה"ה התורני
הנגיד והקצין כ"ה איצק ב"ר משה גאלשטיין [כך!] נ"י בשנת
י"ב'ר'ך' א'ד'נ'י' ח'י'ל'י'ך' ו'פ'ע'ל'י' י'ד'י'ם' לפ"ק.

("A gift, in remembrance and in gratitude, from the holy congregation of Mattenbuden on the anniversary of twenty-five years as *Gabbai* of the charities of our congregation [to] t[he] scholar r[abbi], the leader and the officer, the revered Itzig b[en] . . . Moses Goldstein . . . in the year 'Bless, O Lord, your substance, And favor your undertakings' "; a variation on Deut. 33:11 = [5]615 = 1855.) A second Hebrew inscription begins in a cartouche on the cylindrical portion of the cup:

26.

שותה נא ידידנו מכוס הישע / עשית צדק מאסת רשע — עוד
ימים רבים תהיה בקרבנו / ראש החברות ראש לכל שמחותנו.
/ שם טוב כאחד הגדולים לך קנה / על אדני צדק ואמת ביתך
בנה.

("Please drink, our friend, from the cup of salvation. You have done justice, and despised evil./ For many more days may you be in our midst,/ Head of our societies and in charge of our celebrations./ Acquire for yourself a good name, as one of the great ones./ On the Lord of justice and truth, build your house.")

Opposite the cartouche is a later inscription flanking an engraving of the interior of the Mattenbuden Synagogue, which was erected in 1838 largely through the efforts of Itzig Goldstein. It reads: "Geschenk an die Mattenbuden Gemeinde von den Itzig Goldsteinschen Erben 1871." ("A gift to the Mattenbuden Community from the heirs of Itzig Goldstein 1871.") The engraving is captioned: "Das Innere der neuen Synagoge auf Mattenbuden in Danzig." ("The interior of the new synagogue at Mattenbuden in Danzig.") Below this inscription, the cylindrical portion of the cup flares outward into a bulbous lower section decorated with repoussé flowers enclosed in cartouches. Similar floral designs decorate the baluster stem, the cusped base and the cover. A bud-shaped finial set on a circular base forms the handle of the cover.

See no. 25 for a similar cup presented to Itzig Goldstein. It is ironic that the only word misspelled in the florid Hebrew inscription is Goldstein's name.

REFERENCES: Danzig, 1904, no. 45; Danzig, 1933, no. 64.

27.

Covered Kiddush Goblet

Silver: cast, repoussé, acid-etched, chased, engraved
Erfurt: first half of the 19th century
Marks: E, 13
10⅝ x 3¹³⁄₁₆" dm (27 x 9.7 cm)
D 70

The paneled upper portion of the cup rises from a bulbous lower section consisting of a series of bosses. Each panel is decorated with foliate scrolls set off against striated ground. Engraved flowers and scrolls decorate the stem, while the foot is ornamented by a band of etched ivy vines and cupids in various attitudes. Two bands of repoussé beads frame the etched band, and a third band of beads appears on the lid. Below the beads on the lid is another band of etched work with various flora and fauna including wheat, pineapples, dolphins, a bull, a bird and two lizards represented in a naturalistic style. The handle of three

cast flowers is executed in a similarly naturalistic fashion. A German inscription was later engraved below the lip: "Der Danziger Synagoge geweiht von Frau Rosette Paradies geb. Deutschland an ihrem 70. Geburtstage." ("Dedicated to the Danzig Synagogue by Mrs. Rosette Paradies, née Deutschland, on her 70th birthday.") On a cartouche affixed to the panel below the word "Geburtstage": "den 15 Schwat 5637" (January 29, 1877).

28.

Covered Kiddush Goblet

Silver: parcel-gilt, cast, repoussé, acid-etched, chased, engraved
Erfurt: first half of the 19th century
Marks: E, an indeterminate second mark, and R 7555
12¼ x 4⁷⁄₁₆" dm (31.1 x 11.2 cm)
F 4276

The forms of the stem and base of this cup are identical to those of no. 27 and its lid is also very similar. Only the upper portion of the cup is substantially different: it is cylindrical rather than paneled, and the texture of the etched areas is mottled rather than striated. Its decoration is organized around two central motifs: a lyre enclosed in a wreath guarded by two griffins standing on flowering vines, and a large cartouche formed of scrolls, foliage and flowers. Within is a dedicatory inscription in Hebrew and Judeo-German:

מנחת תודה / להרב המאה״ג חריף ובקי מהור״ר / אלחנן
בהר״ב מה״ר זנוויל ראזענשטיין זצ״ל / מאלופי קהל דק״ק
מאטענבודען בדאנציג. / איבעררייכט דורך דיא פארשטעהער
/ ר׳ איצק בר״מ גאלדשטיין / ר׳ אלחנן מאנקעוויטש / תר״ד
לפ״ק.

("A gift in gratitude to Rabbi . . . Elhanan b[en] . . . Zanvil Rosenstein . . . from the directors of the h[oly] c[ongregation of] Mattenbuden in Danzig. Presented by the directors Itzig b[en] . . . M. Goldstein and Elḥanan Mankiewitz [5]604" = 1844.)

This goblet came to The Jewish Museum as a gift from Dr. Harry G. Friedman, who purchased it from an Amsterdam dealer. From the Dutch mark on the lid, it must have been in Holland by 1909, perhaps taken there by the Rosenstein family. It appears to be a work of the same master who created no. 27, and it was likewise dedicated in Danzig. Rabbi Elhanan must have been the son of Samuel Zanvil Rosenstein, rabbi of Mattenbuden until his death in 1824. For Itzig Goldstein, see no. 5.

28.   27.

29.

Kiddush Goblet

Silver: repoussé and engraved
Eastern Europe(?): 1927 (date of inscription)
Marks: OX, ▨, I/C
7¾ x 3⅝" dm (19.5 x 9.2 cm)
D 66

A simple, flaring silhouette unifies the stem and foot of this goblet into one unit, decorated only by a single band of repoussé rosettes and rectangles. The relatively short cup is decorated with ovoid Art-Deco motifs, also executed in repoussé. The following German inscription appears on the cup: "Zur Einweihung 25.9. 1927 Hilfsverein für jüdische Emigranten in Danzig 'Emigdirect.' " ("For the opening, Sept. 25, 1927, of the Aid Association for Jewish Emigrants in Danzig 'Emigdirect.' ")

Emigdirect was an affiliated branch of the Joint Distribution Committee later responsible for making possible the emigration of Danzig Jews in 1939 (see the introductory essay by Gerson Bacon). The same organization and date are engraved on no. 88, an early 19th-century Torah pointer that was originally given by I. Goldstein and a second *Gabbai,* probably to the Mattenbuden Synagogue. This *Kiddush* goblet may, therefore, have been given to the same congregation.

30.

Spice Box and Candleholder

Silver: cut-out and engraved
Germany(?): probably 18th century
Marks: none
8¹⁄₁₆ x 2¾" (20.4 x 7 cm)
D 197

This combined spice box and candleholder houses two of the three elements required for the *havdalah* ceremony held to mark the end of the Sabbath and the beginning of the new week. The circular base ornamented with engraved flowers supports a short stem and a small perforated box containing a drawer to hold spices. From the box rise four rods topped by pennants that are fitted with a movable platform serving as a candle holder.

Stylistic parallels for this piece suggest an 18th-century date and a possible German provenance (cf.

Synagoga, no. 120; F. Landsberger, "The Origin of the Ritual Implements for the Sabbath," *Beauty in Holiness,* p. 192).

REFERENCES: Danzig, 1904, no. 52; Danzig, 1933, no. 20, pl. 1.

31.

Spice Box

Silver: cast and filigree
Austrian Empire: late 18th century
Marks: none
10 x 1⅞ x 1¹⁵⁄₁₆" (25 x 4.7 x 4.8 cm)
D 191

This spice box for *havdalah* is in the form of a three-storey tower resting on a quadrilobed base supported by ball and claw feet. All of the surfaces are composed of filigree with added cast elements serving as borders and applied ornament. The first stage of the tower is closed. Gadrooned edging topped by small orbs mark the corners, and an applied rose decorates one face. The second stage is conceived as a belfry. It is surmounted by an onion-shaped cupola and a similar, but smaller third stage. A tall spire with orb and pennant surmounts the whole.

The closest parallels to this spice box are two taller examples of the same design that are part of The Jewish Museum's collection (F 2601 and F 2178). A more elaborate version in the Museum für Kunst und Gewerbe, Hamburg, bears late 18th-century marks (cf. *Synagoga,* no. 122).

REFERENCES: Danzig, 1904, no. 49; Danzig, 1933, no. 17, pl. 1.

32.

Spice Box

Silver: cast, openwork, engraved
Danzig: 1760
Maker: undetermined
Marks: Czihak² 5, 445 (control mark of Johann Carl Dietrich) and a third mark that is either u or n.
10¼ x 2" (26 x 5 cm)
D 190

The two-storey tower of this spice box rests on a short curved stem set on a square base inscribed:

נדבה לבה"כ מקו"פ: ח"ק: ע"י הגבאים ר' יאקב בר"י: / ור'
גרשון: במנ.

("A donation to the synagogue from the Treasury of
the Burial Society through the *Gabbaim* Yaakov Bari
and Gershon b[en] Mn.") The first storey has two
rows of windows on three sides and a small door on
the fourth. Bands of zigzags set against a striated
ground border these openings as well as those of the
second storey. The bottom and top of the first storey
are scalloped and four slender spiral turrets mark its
corners. A small bell is suspended inside the second
storey. From its top rises a tapering turret surmounted
by a ball finial and a pennant inscribed:

שנת תקפא

("the year [5]581"=1821.)

REFERENCES: Danzig, 1904, no. 50; Danzig, 1933, no. 18,
pl. 1.

33.
Spice Box

Silver: cast, openwork, engraved, parcel-gilt; brass
Danzig: 1778–84
Maker: Johann Gottlieb Stegmann
Marks: Czihak² 3, 501, 507
12¼ x 3⅝" (31 x 9.1 cm)
D 193

The cubic form of this tower is engraved with foliate
scrolls, and plant forms overlay the stem and circular
base. The sides of the box and the dome rising from it
are pierced with holes and various shapes to permit
smelling of the spices. (A small door cut in one side
allows for their insertion.) A brass pennant with engraved decoration tops the tall spire and gilt ball finial
which rise from the dome, and four smaller brass pen-

30.   35.   33.   34.   32.   31.

36.

nants mark the corners of the spice box. Finally, a series of small brass bells suspended from the lower edge of the box complete the decoration.

Johann Gottlieb Stegmann also made the Torah shield, no. 68.

REFERENCES: Danzig, 1904, no. 48; Danzig, 1933, no. 16, pl. 1.

34.

Composite Spice Box

> Silver: cast, chased, engraved
> Danzig and Russian Poland: 18th-19th century
> Mark: Verzeichnis 12
> 13 x 3¹⁵⁄₁₆″ (33 x 10 cm)
> D 192

This spice box is in the form of a tower set on a baluster stem and fluted base. The architecture consists of a cube decorated with chased floral designs and cast foliate scrolls, topped by a steep roof with dormer windows that is surmounted by a turret with an onion-shaped dome and a pennant flag. One side of the tower is a hinged door for placement of the spices; pierced openings in all the walls would allow the aroma to escape. Palmette leaves with pendant bells are suspended from the lower edge of the tower.

The box is a composite of works made in two different places. The baluster stem and fluted base bear a Russian weight mark in use during the 18th and 19th centuries and were, therefore, not made in Danzig. These parts are heavier and of a different quality silver and workmanship than the rest of the box. The upper section, however, must have been fashioned in Danzig, since its architectural features and their relative proportions and arrangements are closely modeled on the Stockturm, a Danzig landmark completed in 1509.

REFERENCES: Danzig, 1904, no. 47; Danzig, 1933, no. 15, pl. 1.

35.

Spice Box

> Silver: cast, engraved, cut-out
> Eastern Europe: 18th-19th century
> Marks: none
> 9¾ x 2¾″ dm (25 x 7 cm)
> D 195

A hexagonal tower with hexagonal steeple forms the body of this spice box. Each of the faces is decorated with engraved designs, foliate forms alternating with a plaited motif, and the lower edge is adorned with a band of cut-out leaves. The last motif is repeated at the point where the stem meets the base, and the foliate scrolls of the tower are also engraved on the lowest zone of the base. Six small bells hang from the corners of the tower. Half of the sides of the tower are cut out to allow the aroma of the spices to emerge. Interestingly, no aperture was provided for inserting the spices, which can only be done by unscrewing all of the parts.

REFERENCES: Danzig, 1904, no. 51; Danzig, 1933, no. 19, pl. 1.

36.

Shofar

> Horn with engraved decoration
> Europe: 18th century
> 19¼ x 2½″ (49 x 6.3 cm)
> D 117

The entire length of the *shofar* is decorated with a border of incised triangles outlined in dots. Three bands of cross-hatching are engraved at either end and at the bend of the horn. Portions of a broken loop remain at the wide end. An inscription begins at this end and runs to the mouthpiece, continuing on the second side:

תקעו בחודש שופר בכסה ליום חגינו כי / חוק לישראל הוא
משפט לאלקי יעקב.

("Blow the horn at the New Moon, at the full moon for our feast day. For it is a statute for Israel, an ordinance of the God of Jacob"; Ps. 81:4–5.)

Two *shofarot* with identical decoration are in the collection of The Jewish Museum (F 502 and F 1746). Another similar example in the London Jewish Museum bears an inscription date of 1745 (see Barnett, no. 195.)

REFERENCES: Danzig, 1904, no. 57; Danzig, 1933, no. 117.

37.

Plaque for Rosh Hashanah: Order of Sounding of the Shofar

Brass: repoussé and cast; silver: cast; wood
Europe: 19th century
16⅞ x 18¼" (43 x 46.9 cm)
D 107

The rectangular lower portion of this brass plaque is topped by a curvilinear pediment bearing two symbolic representations, a repoussé *shofar* and an appliqué silver crown. The lower section holds a text indicating the order of the sounding of the *shofar* on Rosh Hashanah executed in repoussé letters:

תקיעה: שברים: תרועה [כך!]: תקיעה ג"פ /
תקיעה:שברים:תקיעה: ג"פ / תקיעה:תרועה:תקיעה ג"פ /
גדולה.

("*Tekiah: Shevarim: Teruah: Tekiah:* 3 t[imes]/ *Tekiah: Shevarim: Tekiah:* 3 t[imes]/ *Tekiah: Teruah: Tekiah:* 3 t[imes]/a long one.") Two flanking poles with hooks that attach to slots on the back of the plaque hold it in position. These poles are supported by collet bases nailed to a wooden platform. A small plaque attached to the wood is engraved "Gieldzinski'sche Sammlung" ("Gieldzinski Collection").

Unlike the other stands in the Danzig collection,

which were designed to hold prayers recited repeatedly throughout the year (nos. 107, 108, 256), this stand could only be used on Rosh Hashanah to signal the order of sounds blown on the *shofar*. A *tekiah* is an unbroken sound; *shevarim* is a grouping of three sounds; and a *teruah* consists of nine short sounds emitted in rapid succession.

REFERENCES: Danzig, 1933, no. 119, pl. 3.

38.

Yom Kippur Yarmulke

Silk taffeta; linen; silk; silver foil; silver-wrapped silk threads
Włocławek (Poland): ca. 1816–78
7 x 7½" dm (17.7 x 19 cm)
D 269

The silk taffeta foundation of this *yarmulke* is formed of two pieces of fabric that are lined with linen. A wide scalloped ribbon of silk, silver foil, and silver-wrapped silk threads, woven in a brocade design of rosettes and mountain motifs, is applied to the top and bottom of the *yarmulke*. This ribbon is banded by a woven looped edging.

A paper label written by Lesser Gieldzinski came stitched to the *yarmulke*: "Das Jom Kipur Käppchen meines seligen Vaters Michael Gieldzinski Włocławek." ("The Yom Kippur *yarmulke* of my late father Michael Gieldzinski, Włocławek.") White is traditionally worn on Yom Kippur as a symbol of purity. This symbolism is made explicit in the inscription on a similar *yarmulke* now in The Israel Museum (no. 164/4), which reads in part: ". . . you shall be clean before the Lord" (Levit. 16:30); see Shachar, *The Jewish Year*, pl. XIIIC.

REFERENCES: Danzig, 1933, pl. 10.

39.

Decorative Panel for Prayer Shawl

Silk taffeta; silk; silver foil; silver-wrapped silk threads
Włocławek (Poland): ca. 1816–78
2½ x 20½" (6.4 x 52 cm)
D 270

37.

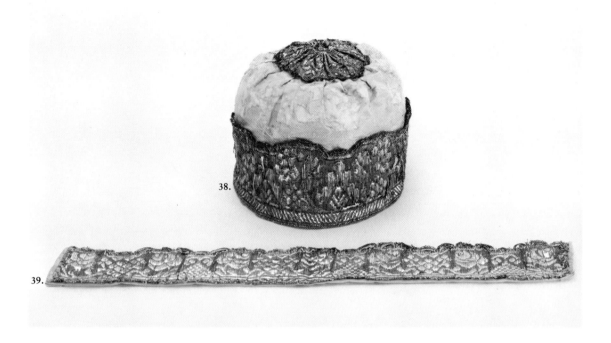

38.

39.

This ribbon is similar in construction to that decorating the Gieldzinski *yarmulke* (no. 38). Silk, silver foil, and silver-wrapped threads are woven into a brocade design of two alternating motifs. In one, two roses, which are mirror images of one another, flank a rosette with leaves. The second consists of a stepped triangle surmounted by a volute. A woven looped edging, identical to that on the *yarmulke,* is woven to the scalloped edge of the panel; the opposite side is straight. Bands of silk taffeta bind the short sides.

R 3787, and a man's profile facing left. The 750 mark on this Danzig piece was established in 1858. The earliest *etrog* container in The Jewish Museum in the form of a citron is an Augsburg piece dated 1670–80 (F 4390; see J. Gutmann, *Jewish Ceremonial Art,* New York, 1964, pl. 45). A melon handle also occurs on JM 55-72, a silver box from Königsberg made in 1851 that may have been used to hold an *etrog.*

REFERENCES: Danzig, 1904, no. 56; Danzig, 1933, no. 33; *Jüdisches Lexikon,*II, pl. LXVI, no. 1.

40.

Etrog Box

Silver: repoussé and chased
Germany: late 19th century
Marks: B(R?) & R, 750
6¼ x 4¾ x 3″ (15.5 x 12.2 x 7.5 cm)
D 74

This richly textured box is shaped like a citron (*etrog*) resting on a leaf and twig base. A small melon on a bed of leaves affixed to the top serves as a handle.

In the collection of The Jewish Museum are three other *etrog* boxes that are identical to the Danzig example except that they lack handles (F 6a, F 87, and F 6172). One of these, F 6172, bears a system of marks established in Germany in 1886: R 2, 800, R 321 or

40.

41.

Footed Box

Silver: cast and engraved
Königsberg: 1818
Maker: probably David Benjamin Kahl
Marks: Czihak[1] 9, 18, DBK
3⅝ x 5½ x 4¹⁄₁₆″ (9.2 x 14.5 x 10.3 cm)
D 290

Small claw and ball feet support this octagonal box decorated with appliqués. On the lid, two putti holding containers of fruit and mounted on griffins flank a

42.

41.

large bowl of fruit and foliage set on a tall pedestal and bowl. On the front, winged female creatures support a vase of flowers, below which is a keyhole. The figures are surmounted by a later Judeo-German inscription:

אייגענטוהם דקהל דק״ק / מאטטענבודען / דורך בעמיהונג של
הגבאי ר' איצק ב״ר משה / גאלדשטיין אנגעשאפט בשנת תר״ב
לפ״ק.

("Belongs to the congregation of the h[oly] c[ongregation of] Mattenbuden. Acquired through the efforts of the *Gabbai* Itzig b[en] Moshe Goldstein in the year [5]602"=1842.)

Boxes such as this one were generally made to store sugar (see Scheffler, figs. 123, 124, 127). This one was probably converted into an *etrog* container.

42.

Hanukkah Lamp and Case

Silver: cast, repoussé, engraved; wood
Europe: 19th century
Marks: none
4¼ x 8⅝ x 2″ (10.8 x 21.9 x 5.1 cm)
D 201

The case is a wooden rectangular box whose front is carved in a lattice design. Two thin silver cartouches affixed to the top bear a somewhat enigmatic Hebrew inscription: on the right plaque,

ל״ה מרדכי / ג׳ש׳ט׳.

("To . . . Mordekhai G.S.T."; perhaps an abbreviation for Goldstein or Goldschmidt), and on the left plaque,

ה / לח״ק.

(Translation uncertain.) A silver *menorah* came with the case. It consists of eight small urns for oil which sit on a plain base. Two flat wing and claw feet with paired tabs form clamps that affix the *menorah* to the front of the open case.

This unique *menorah* in a case was probably designed for a traveler, though it could also have served for home use. Since only eight containers for oil are provided, a candle must have been used as the *shammash* ("servitor").

REFERENCES: Danzig, 1904, no. 84; Danzig, 1933, no. 26, pl. 10.

43.

Hanukkah Menorah

Silver: cast, chased, parcel-gilt
Eastern Europe: 19th century
Marks: 12 and a stag running left in an oval cartouche

11½ x 12 x 2¾" (29.2 x 30.5 x 7 cm)
D 206

The relatively plain gilt back panel of this *menorah* serves as a foil for richly worked silver appliqués that suggest a magical garden guarded by protective beings. A rampant lion and griffin stand to either side, overlapping the edges of the *menorah*. Their paws embrace trees in which nest a pair of birds. Near the center, a rampant stag and unicorn, cast in the round, stand on stumps facing inward toward a bird with outstretched wings fastened to a spring in order to

43.

appear in flight. Three birds enclosed in a wreath are affixed to a shield on the back panel behind the bird in flight. Near the top of the panel is the servitor or *shammash* light attached to a movable arm from which is suspended a bird on a ring. Surmounting the whole is an openwork crown flanked by two griffins which overlap the cusped top. The remaining edges of the back panel are overlaid with luxuriant grapevines that tend to obscure its exact shape. The garden theme of the upper portion is continued in the base (which holds the requisite eight containers for oil) in the form of a flowering vine decorating the front and the feet. Pairs of empty holes on either end once held recumbent lions, so that the protective being theme is extended to the base.

The Jewish Museum possesses an almost identical *menorah* (JM 34–66), bearing the mark 84 in a rectangular shield, a hallmark in use in areas ruled by Russia during the 18th and 19th centuries. Other examples from the Museum (e.g. F 494) and other collections were obviously made in the same workshops and are adorned with some, but not all, of the same motifs as the Danzig *menorah* (cf. H. Gutmann, *Hebraica, Documents d'art juif,* Paris, 1930, pl. XVII). JM 34–66 and no. 43 are noteworthy for the richness of their decoration and iconography.

REFERENCES: Danzig, 1904, no. 83; Danzig, 1933, no. 25.

44.

Hanukkah Menorah

Brass: cut-out and engraved
Eastern Europe: ca. 1800
9¼ x 9⅛ x 3¼" (23.5 x 23.2 x 8.3 cm)
D 202

The decoration of the back panel includes different types of ornament—abstract, architectural and zoomorphic, among others. A horizontal band, largely comprised of a wavy ribbon executed in openwork, forms the base of the back panel. From it rise two sets of corbels framing a broken pediment that supports two lions and a crown. Below the pediment is an urn filled with flowers flanked by two large birds to which are affixed two candlesticks that could be used for Sabbath lights. A trough divided into eight holders is suspended between the side and back panels, its front obscured by a bowed panel of zigzag openwork.

Though no exact parallel for this *menorah* is known, it may be related to a series of similar examples decorated with broken pediments, scrolls, and urns with flowers (e.g., Jewish Museum, nos. F 142, F 904, F 2853, and JM 79–69; see also Narkiss, *Menorat ha-Hanukkah,* pl. XXVII, no. 76).

REFERENCES: Danzig, 1904, no. 86; Danzig, 1933, no. 28, pl. 3.

44.

45.

Hanukkah Menorah

Brass: cast
Probably Poland: 18th or early 19th century
10¾ x 9¼ x 5½" (27.3 x 23.5 x 14 cm)
D 207

Two rows of openwork zigzags serve as a base for the major ornamentation of the back panel: two scrolls supporting a seven-branched *menorah* with interwoven branches on which is perched a double-headed eagle holding an orb and sceptre. Two vine scrolls bearing lions and birds flank the central *menorah,* and two spiral columns topped by bowls filled with leaves decorate the remaining area of the panel. Openwork diamonds are the main motif of the side panels; these are topped by finials. A single Sabbath candleholder of the original pair remains affixed to the right side panel. The missing one has been replaced by a cast bird so that in its present form, the *menorah* can only be used for the Hanukkah lights. The divided oil receptacle may likewise be a later addition to the lamp. Its fabric differs from that of the original portion.

The basic elements of this *menorah* are identical to three others in the collection of The Jewish Museum (F 98, F 145, and M 76) and to various published examples. M. Narkiss suggested stylistic comparisons with Polish paper-cuts and gravestones (*Menorat ha-Hanukkah,* pp. 40–41, figs. 19–20, pl. XXX, no. 85).

REFERENCES: Danzig, 1904, no. 85; Danzig, 1933, no. 27, pl. 3.

46.

Hanukkah Menorah for the Synagogue

Brass: cast
Danzig (?): ca. 1810
19⅝ x 31¼" (55.5 x 79.4 cm)
D 211

This *menorah* rises from a round stepped base bearing a German inscription: "Den Kindern der Danziger Synagogen Gemeinde. Simon Anker Chanukah 5696." ("To the children of the Danzig Synagogue

46.

Congregation. Simon Anker Hanukkah 5696"=1935.) The lower part of the center shaft is formed of a series of knops; the upper part, of three spaced rings with sockets for the hooks of the arms; an openwork finial is affixed to the top. The arms flare outward into shallow curved tree branches which metamorphose into dolphins' heads and then again into branches, finally terminating at a flat horizontal bar which bears eight prickets. The arm for the servitor (*shammash*) is broken near the center shaft.

The Jewish Museum possesses two identical *menorot* (F 6171, JM 68–79) the second of which bears an inscription dated [5]570(=1810). Another, similar in form with branches and dolphins' heads, is inscribed [5]577(=1817). These comparisons suggest a dating between 1810 and 1820 for the Danzig *menorah.* The same form of dolphins' head can be traced back to the 18th century on two of the Torah pointers, nos. 91 and 93.

Simon Anker headed one of the most important grain firms in Danzig. He was a member of the Board of Trustees of the Danzig Synagogue from 1907 to 1928.

47.

Hanukkah Menorah for the Synagogue

Brass: cast
Probably Poland: 18th century
38 x 35⅞" (96.5 x 91.1 cm)
D 213

The tall baluster stem of this *menorah* rises from a circular base. Its lower portion is composed of rounded elements, while the top consists of squared and angular forms. Brackets attached to the squares hold the ends of the curved arms. There are four of these in graduated sizes on either side of the stem. Each is cast as a vine with projecting tendrils that terminate in a candleholder with drip trays. The *shammash* or servitor is held by a bracket affixed to the front. Like the arms, it too is removable.

The large size of this *menorah* indicates that it was used in a synagogue where it was kindled for the benefit of wayfarers not able to hear the blessings recited at home. A record book of the Mattenbuden Synagogue demonstrates that the maintenance of such Hanukkah *menorot* was the responsibility of the Eternal Light Society. A number of similar *menorot* have been preserved (cf. Barnett, no. 233 and Narkiss, *Menorat ha-Hanukkah,* no. 180).

48.

Scroll of Esther

Parchment: engraved and manuscript
Italy: before 1641
Engraver: Salom d'Italia
7¹⁵⁄₁₆ x 98⅝" (20 x 250.5 cm)
D 76

The beginning of the scroll is cut out to form a tip for ease of handling. Its scalloped edge is bordered by a variety of birds, rendered in a naturalistic manner. Partially set within the tip is a baroque cartouche which is blank. There follows an urn filled with a very large bouquet of variegated flowers flanked by a small monkey, a squirrel and two small birds. The lip of the urn is inscribed:

ע"י שלום איטאליאה.

("By Salom d'Italia"). A piece of silk brocade cloth is sewn to the back of this portion of the scroll to protect the parchment.

The text is contained in a series of twenty elaborately decorated portals adorned with fanciful motifs that were printed from a single plate, repeated five times. All of the architectural details are naturalistically drawn and clearly articulated. Each of the four pediments of a single plate contains a different genre

48.

scene; but all are surmounted by two lions framing an urn with flowers. More elaborate urns fill the space between the pediments. Below each is a mask with a dangling bunch of fruit suspended from its mouth. A series of four figures taken from the story of Esther are placed between the arched portals: Ahasueros, Esther, Mordekhai and Haman. They stand on socles decorated with individual scenes from the narrative, nineteen in all. These small scenes were printed from separate plates superimposed on the main engraving. The text is handwritten.

Salom D'Italia was a Jewish engraver, born in Mantua in 1619, who descended from a well-known family of printers. Some of his works are engraved with elements of the Italia coat of arms (e.g., the squirrel on this scroll). He must have left Mantua by 1630, when all Jews were expelled from the city after the Austrian conquest. In 1641, Salom d'Italia settled in Amsterdam, where he died around 1655. His earliest engravings, those produced in Italy, are signed in Hebrew. Seven of his eighteen known works are Scrolls of Esther and he is credited with popularizing the so-called portal-type, in which the text is framed by portals as in this example. The Danzig scroll is the only known copy of a type distinguished by the use of lions atop the portals.

REFERENCES: Danzig, 1904, no. 62; Danzig, 1933, no. 76; Kayser-Schoenberger, no. 149; M. Narkiss, "The Oeuvre of the Jewish Engraver Salom ben . . . Mordecai Italia," *Tarbiz* 25 (1956), p. 446, ill. 2.

49.
Seder Plate

Pewter: engraved
Germany (perhaps Saxony): 1751
Maker: IS(?)
Marks: A woman turned to the right holding an anchor and a bird with I,S, 7 in a heraldic shield; ⊠
16¾" dm (42.5 cm)
D 112

The original engraved inscription on the flange begins at top right with the blessing over the wine. Only the first word is written out in full, the remainder appears as an acronym. There follows a name partially enclosed in a wreath,

ר' נ' ליב ר'

("Rabbi N. Leib R.") presumably that of the owner, and then the order of the Seder ritual beginning with

49.

the small circle at left. The date is engraved in Hebrew at the top of the cavetto

תקי"א לפ"ק

("[5]511") and at bottom, in Arabic numerals, 1751. A second name engraved near the bottom of the cavetto appears to be a later addition:

חיים / ז[?] עעפעלד

("Hayyim [S?]eefeld") and may be the name of a subsequent owner. A representation of the two Israelite spies bearing bunches of grapes from Canaan (Num. 13:23) fills the center of the plate. This image is superimposed on a fanciful tree that grows from a pomegranate-like form at bottom. A single bird perches at right.

The bird-like nose of the figure at right may represent the influence of 13th- and 14th-century Hebrew manuscripts (cf. J. Gutmann, *Hebrew Manuscript Painting*, New York, 1978, pl. 26). Unfortunately, the maker's marks cannot be identified. However, they closely resemble Hintze 789 and 790, Saxony marks of the period indicated by the inscription.

REFERENCES: Danzig, 1904, no. 79; Danzig, 1933, no. 112.

50.
Seder Plate

Pewter: engraved
Germany: 1751

50.

Maker: IL
Mark: A rose enclosed in a wreath surmounted by the
letters I, L and a crown
13¼" dm (33.7 cm)
D 113

A series of mountain shapes engraved on the flange
divide it into compartments, each containing the name
of one of the fourteen prescribed rituals for the Seder,
the date

תקבט ל

("[5]511" = 1751), and the letters

שלמ

("SLM"), which may be the initials of the owner. The
cavetto is decorated with a series of representational
motifs, some decorative and others having a basis in
Scripture. At the center, two men sit at a table holding
goblets; the paschal lamb on a platter rests between
them. This is the only framed motif; the remainder are
arranged in series around the perimeter of the cavetto.
They include three pairs of animals facing urns, deer,
lions and birds, and two men in a rowboat—the latter
an illustration of Abraham crossing the river (Joshua
24:2-4 and part of the *Haggadah*).

In the collection of The Jewish Museum is a second
Seder plate (F 4872), nearly the same size, with almost
identical decoration, bearing the same inscription

date, the same owner's initials and a similar hallmark.
These similarities suggest that both pewter plates were
decorated for the same individual for use as a set,
perhaps even by the same engraver. The subject of
Abraham crossing the river is not generally found on
pewter Seder plates. Its representation here appears to
derive from that in the Prague *Haggadah* of 1526; see
*Die Pesach Haggadah des Gerschom Kohen gedruckt
zu Prag 5287–1527,* Berlin, 1925, pl. 7b.

REFERENCES: Danzig, 1933, no. 113.

*51.

Tiered Seder Plate

Brass: cast, cut-out, engraved; wood: painted and
stained; ink on paper; silk, embroidered with silk
threads
Poland: 18th century
13¾ x 14" dm (35 x 35.5 cm)
D 115

The bottom section of this Seder plate is formed of
three wooden tiers for holding *matzot,* the unleavened
bread eaten during Passover. A grille of brass openwork encloses the wooden trays, which are further
hidden by strips of embroidered silk that covered the
matzot prior to its use in the Seder. Three pairs of rampant lions cast in brass rest on the top of the openwork
grille. They support crowned oval frames containing
papers inscribed with the blessings over ceremonial
foods, placed in wooden containers that rest on top of
the tiers. The blessings read:

ברוך אתה / ה' אלקינו / מ'ה'א'ק'ב'ו' / על אכילת / מצה

("Praised are You, O Lord our God, King of the
universe, who has sanctified our lives through His
commandments, commanding us to eat unleavened
bread.")

ברוך אתה / ה' אלקינו / מ'ה'א'ק'ב'ו' / על אכילת / מרור.

("Praised are You, O Lord our God, King of the
universe, who has sanctified our lives through his
commandments, commanding us to eat bitter herbs.")

כן עשה / הלל / בזמן שבית / המקדש / קים

("Thus did Hillel, at the time the Holy Temple was in
existence.") All three quotations are from the *Haggadah,* the service book read during the Seder. The
symbolic foods to which these blessings refer are bitter
herbs, horseradish and *haroset* (a mixture of apples,
nuts, and other ingredients), all eaten in remembrance

of the bondage in Egypt. The two additional chalice-shaped containers held an egg, recalling, according to tradition, the festival sacrifice, and a roasted bone, symbolic of the paschal lamb sacrificed in the Jerusalem Temple. The tall container in the center, which is circled by a band of brass decorated with cut-outs, may have held the Cup of Elijah, a goblet of wine reserved for the prophet who is eagerly awaited on the Seder night, the night of redemption.

The openwork grille surrounding the trays recalls in both design and technique various brass Hanukkah lamps from Poland dated to the 18th century. The large heart-shaped forms and intersecting arcs closely resemble the decoration on a lamp in the collection of The Jewish Museum (F 482).

REFERENCES: Danzig, 1904, no. 81; Danzig, 1933, no. 115; Kayser-Schoenberger, no. 109; C. Roth, *Jewish Art,* 2nd ed., New York, 1971, pl. 25.

52.
Seder Plate

Faïence
Central Europe: 1850–1900
18″ dm (45.7 cm)
D 114a

The center of the plate bears the standard text for the Passover *Kiddush,* plus the order of the Seder service. Leafy vine scrolls frame the title. On the flange, raised brown floral designs surround eight cartouches framed by raised yellow moldings. Four single figures labeled in Hebrew occupy each of the small cartouches: Solomon, Moses, Aaron and David. To the right and left of the text are two large cartouches bearing similar floral designs. Above it is a representation of Joseph revealing himself to his brothers, inscribed

אני יוסף אחיכם

("... I am you brother Joseph ..."; Gen. 45:4); while below is the scene of the first Passover meal inscribed

ואכלתם אותו זמן

("And you shall eat it [Ex. 12:11] time").

This plate is one of a series of fifteen faïence plates in various collections that are similarly decorated. Although the central text varies slightly, and alternative scenes from the Bible appear, the style and com-

position are constant. This composition, comprising raised floral designs and frames, scenes and central text, is remarkably similar to silver Seder plates of the second half of the 19th century. Most plates in the series are signed on the reverse with the maker's name, an Italian place of manufacture and the date. Yet these plates are quite dissimilar to other faïence plates manufactured in Italy during the 17th and 18th centuries. In this case, the reverse is inscribed,

יצחק כהן פזרו שנת השעד

("Isaac Cohen, Pesaro, 5379" = 1614.) Other factors contradicting such an early dating include the late style of the flower painting and the lack of wear on the edges. Most significant, however, is the dependence of the iconography of the plates on that of *Haggadot* published in the second half of the 19th century. Moreover, since this plate was part of Gieldzinski's 1904 donation to the Danzig community, and because another of the series was included in the London exhibition of 1887, a date in the second half of the 19th century seems appropriate.

REFERENCES: Danzig, 1904, no. 80; Danzig, 1933, no. 114, pl. 12; Kayser-Schoenberger, no. 104; *Jüdisches Lexikon,* IV/2, pl. CLVI, no. 2; C. Roth, "Majolica Passover Plates of the XVIth-XVIIIth Centuries," *Eretz-Israel* 7(1963), pp. 106ff.; Shachar, *The Jewish Year,* pl. XL/d.

53.
Tablets of the Law

Wood: painted and gilded
Danzig: 1818
40 x 27″ (101.5 x 68.5 cm)
D 283

The first words of the Ten Commandments are carved and gilt in raised lettering set against a deep blue background. The edges of the Tablets are also gilt, as are portions of the crown surmounting the tablets. The remainder of the crown is painted red.

Carved plaques of the Ten Commandments were generally set above the Torah ark of the Danzig synagogues, as can be seen from photographs of the Great Synagogue and from the engraving of the interior of the Mattenbuden Synagogue on no. 26. According to Dr. Erwin Lichtenstein (oral communication), this set came from the Schottland Synagogue, which was built in 1818. The practice of placing the

Tablets of the Law above the ark in European synagogues can be traced back only to the 17th century; see J. Gutmann, "How Traditional Are Our Traditions?" in *Beauty in Holiness*, p. 418.

* 54.

Torah Ark Curtain

Red velvet; weave-patterned silk with silk embroidery; cut velvet with metallic lace; stumpwork; couched embroidery; metallic foil and fringe; glass stone
Danzig: 1795
102 x 64″ (259 x 163 cm)
D 248

Two twisted columns decorated with grapevines and flowers frame the central portion of this large and elaborate Torah curtain that once hung in the Great Synagogue of Danzig. Each column is set off against a pilaster of brown cut velvet with metallic lace, surmounted by a vase filled with flowers and two spheres. The same cut velvet is used as a secondary mirror at bottom center, where it is bordered by couched silver bands, metallic braid and fringe, and gold metallic embroidery. These border elements also surround the larger, central mirror, a panel of cream-colored brocade adorned with flowers. Above, in high relief, are two rampant lions supporting the Tablets of the Law and a jeweled crown decorated with couched embroidery, metal foil and multi-colored glass stones. The inscriptions are all in the center zone: at top,

כתר תורה

("Crown of Torah"); on the tablets, an abbreviated version of the Ten Commandments; to either side,

ליב / רחל

("Leib/Rachel"; the names of the donors); and below the tablets,

שנת תקנה לפק

("the year [5]555"=1795).

The remaining two inscriptions are problematical. On the large mirror,

ד״נ [כך!] היורשים מן הבח / חיים ליזר ז״ל לחק

which may possibly be read: "T[his was] d[onated] by the heirs of t[he] y[outh] Ḥayyim Leiser z.l. to the B[urial] S[ociety]"; and below the small mirror,

מי אני כי אעצר כוחו להת״נדב / כז״ה ראה וק״ורש [כך!]
מידך הוא ו״לך הפל.

("Who am I that I should be able to gather my strength and willingly offer? [variation of I Chr. 29:14] What did he see and sanctify? '. . . it is from Your hand, and all is Yours' "; I Chr. 29:16=[5]546=1786.) Both of these inscriptions include misspelled words and improperly formed letters, e.g. the inverted *mem* on the large mirror and the two letters *kuf*. These mistakes, analogous to those which appear on the very similar curtain, no. 179, suggest that one or more of the embroiderers who worked on these curtains was ignorant of Hebrew, or perhaps not Jewish. The carelessness evident in the rendering of the inscriptions is in sharp constrast to the quality of the workmanship and the beauty of the design. Another problem is the meaning of the marked letters in the lowest inscription, based on I Chronicles 29:14. On the seventh word, a deliberate departure from the text, the mark falls between two letters, suggesting that more than one is to be included in the resulting word or chronogram. If the letters form a chronogram, there are three possible dates, the latest of which is sixteen years before the dedication date embroidered at the top. One would have to suppose that the earlier date represents the first fabrication of this curtain, perhaps connected to the name of the donor on the large mirror, and that Leib and Rachel were the patrons who restored the curtain in 1795. Another possibility is that the letters form a name or are an acrostic, in which case Leib and Rachel would be "The heirs of t[he] y[outh] Ḥayyim Leiser."

The earliest examples of this portal type of curtain with its frame of twisted columns.and its central mirror date from the 17th century and are preserved in the Prague State Jewish Museum. Elkone of Naumburg and Jakob Koppel Gans, famous makers of Torah ark curtains, popularized this composition in 18th-century Germany. Its origins have been traced to the title pages of Bavarian *maḥzorim,* which feature the same combination of twisted columns resting on fanciful bases and vases of flowers.

REFERENCES: Danzig, 1933, no. 102, pl. 9 and p. 3 for another illustration.

55.

55.

Torah Binder

Undyed linen, embroidered with silks
Western Europe: 1737
6 x 102¼" (15 x 260 cm)
D 262

The decoration of this *Wimpel* consists of an elaborately embroidered inscription with accompanying illustrations, banded above and below by a border of repeated trefoils. The inscription reads:

ברוך (המכונה בענדיט) בכם יצחק (המכונה איצק) שנולד במט
יו ד ב טבת תצחל ה' יתן לגדל לתורה לחופה ולמט אמ . . .

("Barukh (called Bendit) the son of Yitzḥak (called Itzig) who was born u[nder a] g[ood] c[onstellation] on W[ednesday], the second of Tevet [5]498 [=December 25, 1737]. May God raise [him] to Torah, to *huppah* and to g[ood] d[eeds]. Ame[n])." Each letter contains floral and animal forms solidly filled in with stitchery. The small letters used in the inscription are similarly treated. Inserted in the date is a cartouche framed by wreaths enclosing the zodiac symbol Capricorn and a flowering branch. This cartouche is surmounted by a crown which interrupts the trefoil border. Two other images illustrate the blessing which concludes the inscription: an open Torah scroll, and a marriage scene showing a rabbi and a bridal couple standing beneath a canopy held by four male figures. It is interesting to note that the work was never completed; three of the letters and portions of the border remain unfinished. A section of the left edge is missing as well.

Late medieval documents provide the first evidence for the transformation of the swaddling cloths used at circumcision ceremonies into binders for Torah scrolls such as this one. The earliest known Ashkenazi examples date from the 16th century and were used in the synagogue at Worms until its destruction by the Nazis. Following the ceremony, the cloth was cut into strips and reassembled to form a binder on which was embroidered or painted an inscription based on the text used at circumcision.

REFERENCES: Danzig, 1904, no. 5; Danzig, 1933, no. 155; Kayser-Schoenberger, no. 14, pl. IX.

56.

Torah Binder

Undyed linen, embroidered with silk
Western Europe: 1788
5½ x 137" (14 x 345.4 cm)
D 267

An embroidered inscription fills the length of the binder. Its letters are decorated with various floral and zoomorphic motifs. The single independent representational image, an open Torah scroll surmounted by a crown, is embroidered after the word Torah:

אריה (המכונה ליב) בן כ''ה יעקב (המכונה יאקב) שליט נולד
במ''ט ביום א' ה' אלול תקמ''ח לפק ה' יגדלהו לתורה (תורת
משה אמת) ולחופה ולמעשים ט' א' ס'

("Aryeh (called Leib), the son of . . . Jacob (called Yaakov) . . . born under a good constellation on Sunday the 5th of Elul 5548 [=September 8, 1788]. May God raise him to Torah (the Torah of Moses is Truth), to *huppah* and to good deeds, Amen, Selah.")

For a discussion of *Wimpeln,* see no. 55. This work came to The Jewish Museum wrapped around the pole on which was hung no. 113.

REFERENCES: Danzig, 1904, no. 10; Danzig, 1933, no. 160.

*57.

Torah Mantle

Green satin embroidered with colored silks and metallic thread; lower edge: metallic braid and green velvet

Prussia: 1713–50
26 x 15″ (66 x 38 cm)
D 254

Along the edges of both the front and back of this mantle are embroidered fanciful pavilions with delicate floral decorations executed in shades of yellow and pink. Two different pavilion motifs alternate along the sides; a more elaborate third type decorates the corners. A dark green velvet field, bordered by gold metallic thread, fills the center of the front side. In its upper section is a jeweled crown executed in stumpwork; a Prussian heraldic device fills the center, and the letters

כ[תר] ת[ורה]

("C[rown of] T[orah]") occupy the lower portion. The lower border of the mantle consists of silver metallic braid on a band of dark green velvet.

The heraldic appliqué provides the most secure evidence for dating the mantle. The device, an eagle holding a sword and orb, with the letters FW superimposed on the body, was used by Friedrich Wilhelm I, who ruled Prussia from 1713 to 1740. In addition, the floral designs are similar to those incorporated into the very popular silk sashes woven in Poland by Persian weavers during the 18th century. Tulips, carnations, asters and other Polish flowers and grasses were especially favored motifs on these textiles. One such sash was incorporated into a Torah curtain now in The Jewish Museum (M 611), demonstrating a direct link between this Polish art form and Judaica. The embroidery on the Danzig mantle represents the influence of these motifs in another medium.

58.
Torah Mantle

Silk cannelé; weave-patterned silk; silk brocade; silver gilt and gold threads; stumpwork and couched work with sequins and glass stones
Germany or Poland: 18th-19th century
29 x 16¾″ (73.6 x 42.5 cm)
D 256

In its present state, this mantle appears to be a restoration which includes portions of an earlier mantle. The top piece, a beige silk cannelé patterned with branches bearing maroon flowers, is probably 18th century. The later, larger material has a woven design of

58.

parallel zigzags of fronds that rise vertically, alternating with zones of large and small flowers, set against a latticed ground. Curiously, the pattern is inverted on the front of the mantle. Two rampant lions, supporting a crown above which the letters

כ[תר] ת[ורה]

("C[rown of] T[orah]"), are appliquéd to the upper half of the mantle. This embroidery is elaborately executed in stumpwork and couched work. Glass stones and sequins (some now missing) decorate the crown.

A comparison of the forms of the lions and the shape of the letters with other German and Polish mantles and curtains suggests that the embroidery dates to the 18th century and that it belonged to an earlier mantle, as did the top piece. These were then reused together with the 19th-century fabric which makes up the front and back.

59.
Torah Shield

Silver: cast, repoussé, chased, engraved
Nuremberg: 1800-3
Maker: Wolfgang Schubert
Marks: R 3767, 3782, 4305
10⁵⁄₁₆ x 8½″ (26.2 x 20.8 cm)
D 136

A plain molding outlines the shape of this shield, a rectangle with arcuated top. Within are two fluted pilasters set off from the background on tall pedestals, which support rampant lions turned towards the center field. Along the axis of the shield, the following elements are arranged contiguous to one another (from bottom to top): the Tablets of the Law (inscribed with the Roman numerals I-X); oval holy day plaques surrounded by a beaded frame and a wreath which extends downward to embrace the Tablets; a *menorah* with flowering branches; and a crown which projects from the surface to enclose a bell. A bossed semi-circular band connects the center of the crown to the top of the arcade. The following German inscription is engraved on the lower border: "Gestiftet v. Herrn Erich Berghold." ("Donated by Erich Berghold".) The Berghold family were prominent mortgage bankers in Danzig.

The Jewish Museum possesses an earlier, somewhat smaller version of the same design, F 4885, dated 1794-97, as well as a variant version from the same period (F 1982). A Torah shield by Schubert is in the Germanisches Nationalmuseum Nürnberg (inv. no. JA 22; see *Synagoga,* no. 232 and *Monumenta,* no. E373); and another is in the collection of The Israel Museum (no. 148/153, inv. no. 241-2-50; see Y. Cohen, "Torah Breastplates from Augsburg in The Israel Museum," *The Israel Museum News* 14 (1978), p. 84, fig. 20).

REFERENCES: Y. Cohen, p. 85. no. 21.

60.

Torah Shield

Silver: cast, repoussé, engraved, parcel-gilt
Berlin: 1854–60
Maker: M
Marks: Scheffler 15, 21 and M
15⅝ x 12¹⁄₁₆″ (39.7 x 30.6 cm)
D 122

The basic shape of this shield is an oblong to which has been added a cusped extension. Large repoussé leaves and scrolls decorate the borders and the upper sections. Background areas are covered with an engraved lattice pattern in varying sizes. Overlaid on this background are two fluted columns with leafy capitals resting on S-shaped corbels; all are cast in high relief. A three-dimensional crowned eagle with extended wings perches on each capital. Between the columns is the container for the holy day plaques, the Tablets of the Law, and two lions supporting a crown. The three pendant plaques are inscribed: right,

שנת כתר לפ״ק

("The year 'crown'" = [5]620 = 1860); center,

שייך / לר׳ ישראל משה / ב״ר מרדכי ז״ל / גרטה.

("This belongs to . . . Israel Moses b[en] . . . Mordekhai, of blessed memory, Gerth [?]")

60.

59.

62.

ע״ז / מ׳ אסתר בת״ר יעקב / זצל.

("with his spouse . . . Esther daughter of Jacob of blessed memory".)

In contrast to contemporaneous Torah shields from Berlin (e.g., no. 63), the lions on this example were fashioned in relatively low relief and set parallel to the background. The Tablets, however, are angular and jut out from the surface, echoing the strong spatial projection of the columns and eagles at the sides. Another similar shield in the Danzig collection is no. 68, which closely resembles F 244 in the collection of The Jewish Museum. Both of these shields may be dated after 1858.

REFERENCES: Danzig, 1904, no. 19; Danzig, 1933, no. 122, pl. 7.

61.

Torah Shield

Silver: repoussé, parcel-gilt, engraved, cast; glass stones
Berlin: after 1858
Mark: Scheffler 29
13⅝ x 11⅜" (34.5 x 29 cm)
D 134

This oblong shield is framed by winding repoussé foliate scrolls. The remaining surface is covered by a lattice pattern ornamented with punched circles. Two fluted columns with foliate capitals, resting on S-shaped corbels, project in high relief. They each bear an eagle with outspread wings. The base and capitals are set with inlaid glass stones, a form of decoration which also appears on the crown and Torah ark overlaid on the center field. Adjacent to the column capitals are two rampant lions cast in low relief, and below the ark is a container for the holy day plaques. The ark is in the form of a small aedicula framed by columns and topped by a foliate arch. Its two doors, shaped like Tablets of the Law and bearing an abbreviated version of the Biblical text, enclose a small Torah scroll inscribed:

קדש / ל״א.

("Holy to the L[ord]"; Ex. 28:36). The back of the central pendant plaque is inscribed with a "W," indicating that this Torah shield was once the property of the Weinberg Synagogue; see no. 60 for a discussion of a similar shield.

62.

Torah Shield

Silver: parcel-gilt, repoussé, cast, engraved; glass stones
Berlin: ca. 1750–80
Maker: Joachim Hübner
Marks: Scheffler 494 (110); Berlin mark of indeterminate year
15½ x 10¾" (39.4 x 27.3 cm)
D 150

A pair of plain columns, set on square bases decorated with engraved flowers and blue glass stones and surmounted by identical capitals terminating in foliate finials frame the lower part of this shield. Rocaille scroll and shell motifs fill the center and frame a holder bearing plaques with names of the holy days, on which portions of the Torah are read. Similar motifs encircle the Tablets of the Law on the upper portion of the shield. Above the tablets is a large, oval blue glass stone and, on either side, a rampant lion executed in high relief. The two lions support a jeweled crown which projects from the surface. Two small plaques with dedicatory inscriptions are suspended from the lower edge: at left,

עי הג״ב / נעשה / בריצוי החכ״ק / יצ״ו.

("Made for the G[abbaim] according to the specifications of the B[urial] S[ociety]. . ."); at right,

ור / שמואל / פח.

("and Shmuel . . ."). The content of the missing third plaque is known from the 1933 catalogue. The plaque bore the name of the second Gabbai responsible for the commission, Shimon. In all probability, the left plaque was originally in a different position so that the inscription could be read in proper sequence from right to left.

Another shield by Hübner in the Danzig collection (no. 63) is very similar to this one, and a third was once in the Breslau Jüdisches Museum (Hintze, Katalog, no. 214). The same master was also responsible for a pointer, no. 87, and a Torah crown, no. 74. The donors of this shield also donated the Hübner crown.

REFERENCES: Danzig, 1933, no. 147a.

63.

Torah Shield

Silver: parcel-gilt, repoussé, cast, engraved
Berlin: 1776
Maker: Joachim Hübner
Marks: Scheffler 8b, 494 (110)
15 x 9⅞" (38 x 25.1 cm)
D 146

The lower portion of this shield is framed by two columns entwined with vine scrolls, which are set on cubic bases engraved with floral and scroll motifs. Identical forms surmount the columns and terminate in bud-shaped finials. From these spring two rampant lions, executed in high relief. A projecting crown rests on their heads. The lower portion of the center field is decorated with repoussé scroll forms, which asymmetrically frame the plaques bearing the names of the holy days on which the Torah is read. From this frame arise scroll forms that support and enclose a flaming glory on which is superimposed the Tablets of the Law.

Most of the ornamental and iconographical elements of this shield can also be found on a Torah shield by the same master, no. 62 (q.v. for other works by Hübner). The grapevines entwined around the columns are also found on the two large Torah curtains from the Danzig Synagogue (nos. 54, 179).

Comparison with the illustration of this shield in the 1933 Danzig catalogue shows that the plaques once suspended from the lower edge are today missing. According to the catalogue, the shield was a donation of the Burial Society in 1806.

REFERENCES: Danzig, 1933, no. 138b, pl. 10.

64.

Torah Shield

Silver: parcel-gilt, repoussé, cast
Berlin: 1804-8
Maker: August Ferdinand Gentzmer
Marks: Scheffler 30b, 1296 (219), and Berlin bear with H
15¾ x 11¹¹⁄₁₆" (40 x 29.7 cm)
D 139

Two parcel-gilt tapering columns with cubic bases and "capitals" surmounted by egg-shaped finials frame the

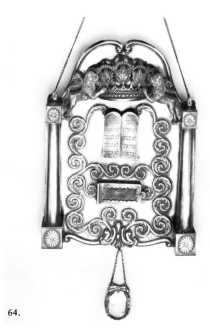

64.

shield. Floral appliqués decorate both bases and capitals. The most prominent decorations of the center field are the container for the holy day plaques and the Tablets of the Law. These project from the surface in high relief and are parcel-gilt to contrast with the silver background decorated with a symmetrical design of repoussé scrolls. Two lions, cast in high relief, spring out at a three-dimensional angle from the background to embrace a crown affixed to the top of the shield. The lions, the crown and the upper and lower edges are emphasized through gilding. The suspended cartouche reads

זאת נדבת

("This was donated by . . .").

The majority of Gentzmer's known works are Torah shields once in the collections of synagogues in Dessau, Lissa, and Königsberg (Scheffler, p. 263; R, p. 262). An early Gentzmer shield now in The Jewish Museum (F 2562), dating from the 1770s, contains some of the elements found on another of his works, no. 198 (e.g., the Tablets, the wreath and the crown). However, the 1770s piece lacks the coloristic effects obtained by contrasting parcel-gilt and plain silver that is such a dominant stylistic feature of the three later Gentzmer pieces from Danzig (nos. 64, 80, and 198).

65.

Torah Shield

Silver: repoussé, engraved, stamped, cast, parcel-gilt
Berlin: 1821–41
Maker: Johann August Gebhardt
Marks: Scheffler 1714 (336) and two unintelligible marks
12⁵⁄₁₆ x 9¾" (31.3 x 24.7 cm)
D 148

This shield is oblong in shape with the sides and base composed of scroll and leaf motifs. Two fluted columns adorned by composite Corinthian and Doric capitals form an inner frame for the center field. Atop the columns are two urns filled with flowers; these flank a cupola consisting of overlapping leaves surmounted by a ball-shaped finial, on which are written two Hebrew letters

א ג

of uncertain meaning. A diaper pattern stamped with flower buds fills the background of the center field. Superimposed on this ground and set off from it through gilding are the major symbolic components of the design: a crown, two lions and the Tablets of the Law. These three elements overlap one another in a dynamic manner. Below them is the container for the holy day name plaques. The single remaining pendant plaque is inscribed

החברה קדישא

("the Burial Society.")

In the collection of The Jewish Museum is another smaller shield by Gebhardt, very similar in design (F 254). It bears a clear set of hallmarks dating it 1821–41, which suggests the same date for the Danzig example. See also Barnett, no. 144, for a similar shield.

REFERENCES: Danzig, 1933, possibly no. 144a.

66.
Torah Shield

Silver: repoussé, cast, engraved, stamped, parcel-gilt
Berlin: 1821–50
Maker: Johann Christian Samuel Kessner
Marks: Scheffler 1455 (264) and an indeterminate Berlin city mark
12½ x 10¼" (31.8 x 26 cm)
D 142

The sides and base of this oblong shield are decorated with foliate scrolls. Two fluted columns set on tall

bases and crowned with Corinthian capitals surmounted by urns with flowers frame the center field. Along the central axis are the following parcel-gilt elements: a container for holy day plaques, the Tablets of the Law, and two confronted lions supporting a crown. Above the crown are two leafy swags and a canopy of leaves. The background is decorated with a lattice design.

This shield is by the same master who executed no. 200, which it resembles. Another, very similar shield was once part of the Feinberg Collection (see Parke-Bernet, *Feinberg Collection,* no. 402).

REFERENCES: Danzig, 1933, possibly no. 144a.

67.
Torah Shield

Silver: cast, engraved, repoussé, parcel-gilt
Danzig: probably 1821–34
Maker: ANL, perhaps August Nathanael Lehnhard
Marks: Danzig city mark, ANL (August Nathanael Lehnhard?) and S (possibly Czihak² 525, control mark of Carl Benjamin Schultz)
13⅞ x 10¾" (35.3 x 27.3 cm)
D 133

The side borders of this oblong shield are decorated with foliate scrolls. Along the bottom, the same motifs, with added leaves and rosettes, are arranged as

67.

overlapping festoons which form a series of curves running counter to the outlines of the leafy cupola and flowered urns at top. Three-dimensional columns with finely articulated bases and capitals are attached inside the side borders. Two cast eagles perch atop the capitals. Above and behind them are small crowns, soldered to the main plate of the shield. The major decorations are arranged along the central axis: below, the holy day plaques; at center, the Tablets of the Law; above, a crown guarded by two crowned lions. The background behind them is a simple diaper pattern of incised diamonds without stamped motifs. Two oval plaques suspended from the bottom are inscribed:

שייך לחברה / תלמוד תורה / דק״ק / מאטטענבודען.

("This belongs to the Talmud Torah Society of the h[oly] c[ongregation] of Mattenbuden") and

תקצד לפ״ק

("[5]594" = 1834).

The style of this work differs from that of other Torah shields of similar composition (cf. nos. 65, 66, 200). The repoussé is more shallow, while linear elements, such as the outlines or the veins of leaves, are given greater visual emphasis. The lions closely resemble those of nos. 66 and 200, related Torah shields made by J. C. S. Kessner, a Berlin silversmith. Two iconographic details also distinguish this shield from the rest of the series: the engraved priestly hands on the Tablets (instead of the usual crowns) and the eagles and crowns above the columns.

The control mark S, which is stamped on this shield, also appears on no. 81, a pair of *rimmonim,* and on no. 280, an alms dish with an inscribed date of 1822. J. G. Ulrich, who fashioned the *rimmonim,* was active in Danzig between 1804 and 1839. Carl Benjamin Schultz was the only Danzig assay master with the initial S to hold office during this period and whose mark is not published. He was control master in 1821 and 1822, the probable date of this Torah shield. Only one Danzig master had the initials ANL: August Nathanael Lehnhard, active 1799–1841, the period indicated by the control mark and the inscription. The base of the columns and the back shield are lightly engraved with the number 14, which is perhaps an assembly mark.

According to the 1933 Danzig catalogue, the (now missing) pendant plaque recorded the name of the donor, Josef Mendel Bramson.

REFERENCES: Danzig, 1933, no. 146a, pl. 6 (where it is erroneously numbered 122).

68.
Torah Shield

Silver: repoussé and parcel-gilt
Danzig: 1778–84
Maker: Johann Gottlieb Stegmann
Marks: Czihak² 10, 501, 507
11⅝ x 9¾″ [without pendants] (29.5 x 24.7 cm)
D 143

This shield is in the form of a rectangle with rounded top that is outlined by a beaded border. Two vine-covered spiral columns with fanciful bases and capitals frame the center field. Within is a flowering vine that supports two rampant lions holding a crown superimposed on a radiating glory. The crown and the container for the plaques naming the holy days on which the Torah is read are fashioned from separate pieces of metal and attached to the shield. (Two plaques are missing.) Between them, at center, are the Tablets of the Law set within forms which recall a Torah ark. Two of the originally three oval pendant decorations still remain. In addition to the standard inscriptions (names of the holy days and the Tablets of the Law), two names of donors are engraved within the bow at bottom center:

ארון / רבקה

("Aron, Rivkah").

A comparison with the illustration of this piece in the 1933 catalogue indicates that the missing pendant and holy day plaques were lost after 1933.

REFERENCES: Danzig, 1933, no. 143a, pl. 6.

69.
Torah Shield

Silver: repoussé, engraved, punched
Probably Danzig: ca. 1805
Marks: none
11 x 8 1/16″ (27.9 x 20.5 cm)
D 126

In its present state, this shield consists of the original plaque with its curved pedimental headpiece, and a later section appended to the base. Two columns with bulbous finials fill the sides of the main plaque and frame the central stepped section. Its lowest level is decorated with a diaper pattern. The second level

69.

serves as a base for tablets that are inscribed with the first words of the Ten Commandments; the Commandments are not in the correct order. The dedicatory inscription is spread over all three levels:

נר תמיד / נעשה / מצדקה / נ״ת ע״י / הגבאי / מה יוסף /
במ יואל / כהנא / מדאנ / ציג / יום א׳ / ד״ / ד״חי״ה״ס״ /
של / סוכות / לפרט / ו׳ער׳י׳כת נ׳ר׳ לׄבן׳ י׳שׄ׳ / לפ״ק

("Eternal Light. Made through the charity of the E[ternal] L[ight Society] by order of the *Gabbai* . . . Yosef b[en] . . . Yo'el Kahana from Danzig. Sunday, the fourth day o[f] H[ol] ha-M[o'ed]of *Sukkot,* in the year 'and the setting up of a light for the son of Jesse' "; Babylonian Talmud, *Berakhot* 29a = [5]566 = October 13, 1805.) The lower edge of the main plaque was apparently trimmed when the pendant section was added. It is, therefore, impossible to determine now whether or not the beaded design which borders the sides and top once continued along the base as on no. 68. The undulating outline of the lower section is decorated with an engraved vine. A second dedicatory inscription is engraved within reading

זאת נעשה ע״י הגבאי ר׳ איצק ב״ר משה גאלדשטיין תקפפ.

("This was made for the *Gabbai* Itzig b[en] Moshe Goldstein [5]589" = 1829.)

This shield was the second known donation by Yosef ben Yo'el Kahana, *Gabbai* of the Eternal Light Society, in 1805. The first was a Torah pointer (no. 90) bearing a similar inscription specifying that the donor came from Danzig. The phrasing of both inscriptions together with the secondary dedication of the shield by Itzig Goldstein, prominent member of the Danzig Mattenbuden community, indicate that both the shield and the pointer were originally made for a synagogue in the area near that city and later came to Danzig. The wars of 1807 and 1812 caused

much destruction in surrounding communities and led many Jews to seek a haven in Danzig. From the evidence of the inscription plus the fact that the pointer bears Danzig hallmarks, we may suppose that the shield was also made there.

70.
Torah Shield

Silver: repoussé, parcel-gilt, engraved, cast; colored glass
Eastern Europe: before 1809
Maker: MONIK
Marks: Scheffler 30c; MONIK ;
12⅝ x 10¾″ (32 x 27.4 cm)
D 137

A parcel-gilt beaded border emphasizes the simple rectangular shape of this shield. Two spiral columns set on tall pedestals and surmounted by crowns run the entire length of the shield and frame the central section on which appear a repoussé cartouche, the box for holy day plaques and a large crown set with glass stones. The cartouche is inscribed:

ח״ק / ד׳ ק׳ ק׳ שאטטלאנד.

("B[urial] S[ociety] o[f the] h[oly] c[ongregation of] Schottland.")

Three ornately decorated dedicatory plaques are suspended from the lower edge. All have wide borders decorated with the faces and wings of cherubim and vines executed in repoussé. Addorsed birds also appear on the smaller, side plaques. The inscriptions read: right plaque,

זנה / יאקב עים [כף!] בנו ה׳ שמעי / עא ה / אברם.

("T[his was] d[onated by] Yaakov with his son Shim'[i] w[ith his] b[rother] Avram"); center plaque,

ז״נ / הרר ליב עי [כף!] / אשתו מרת / פריידל עבא / הבחור
שמו׳ / ע׳ א׳ / מרדכי.

("T[his was] d[onated by] R[abbi] Leib wit[h] his wife Freidel w[ith] h[is] n[ephew] the youth Shmu[el] w[ith his] b[rother] Mordekhai"); left plaque,

ז׳נ׳א׳ / יענטה / עב שואל / עב ליזר.

("T[his was] d[onated by the] w[oman] Yenta w[ith] her] s[on] Shoal w[ith her] s[on] Leiser.")

The style of the decoration and engraving of the dedicatory plaques is strikingly different from those

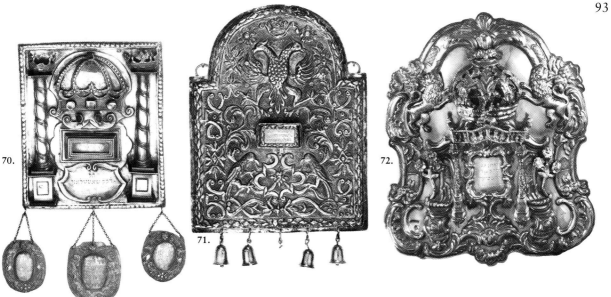

70.

71.

72.

features of the shield, which would seem to indicate that they were not made for one another. Yet all four pieces bear the same assembly mark, the number 17, lightly engraved on the back. Similar assembly numbers are engraved on no. 67, a Danzig Torah shield. Thus, the cartouches may have been added to this shield in Danzig. Both the style of the border decoration of the small pendant plaques and the beaded border of the shield are characteristic of Polish Torah shields of the 18th and early 19th centuries.

REFERENCES: Danzig, 1933, no. 137a, pl. 11.

71.

Torah Shield

Silver: repoussé and chased
Poland: early 19th century
Marks: none
7¾ x 6⅛" (19.1 x 15 cm)
D 131

This small, rectangular Torah shield with an arcuated top is decorated with a symmetrical pattern of strap-work, foliage, flowers and birds. A crowned Polish double-headed eagle dominates the arcuated section. Beneath it is affixed a small box inscribed:

נעשה עי הגבאי / ר' איצק ב"ר משה / גאלדשטיין

("This was made for the *Gabbai* Itzig b[en] Moses Goldstein.") A wreath border decorates the outline of the shield. Four (of the originally five) brass bells are suspended from the lower edge.

Shields with arcuated tops such as this one were made in Poland during the 18th century. This Danzig example shows that the form continued to be used into the early 19th century. For Itzig Goldstein, mentioned in the inscription, see no. 5. He gave his first donation in 1813–14 (no. 278) and his last in 1841–42 (no. 41). This shield must have been given during the same period. Another similar Polish shield with an early 19th century date is F 5290 in The Jewish Museum, inscribed 1816. Stylistically and iconographically, the Danzig example closely resembles a copper Torah shield in the Mintz collection (Jewish Museum, M 286), which is missing its inscription plaque.

REFERENCES: Danzig, 1904, no. 28; Danzig, 1933, no. 131, pl. 7.

72.

Torah Shield

Silver: cast, repoussé, engraved, parcel-gilt
Warsaw: ca. 1875
Maker: A. Riedel
Marks: A. RIEDEL, Ⓐ , and a crowned double-headed eagle in a circular field
11⅞ x 10¼" (30.2 x 26 cm)
D 149

An elaborate border design of scrolls, foliage, flowers, and lattice patterns frames this cartouche-shaped shield. Rising from the lower edge is a fanciful architectural ensemble consisting of curving bases, pilasters and arches. Two vine-covered columns on elaborate bases cast in high relief are set within the larger architectural form. These columns bear an openwork arch surmounted by two lions and a deer. Within the arch is a cartouche bearing the following inscription:

לזכרון אכינו [כך!] / יצחק בן דוד / הלוי שפייער ז"ל / תרכ"ו — כ"ח סיון תר"פו.

("In memory of our father, Yitzhak b[en] David Halevi Speier, z.l. [5]626[=1866] 25 Sivan [5]686"=June 7, 1926.) In the upper section, two addorsed rampant lions support an openwork crown containing the same flowers that appear next to the architectural ensemble.

This shield is one of a series produced by A. Riedel during the second half of the 19th century that are nearly identical in overall design, but vary in individual details (e.g., F 2520 and F 2575 in the collection of The Jewish Museum; Berger, *Judaica*, no. 109). The basic composition appears to have been based on Warsaw shields of the second half of the 18th century (cf. Jewish Museum, M 6; and *Synagoga*, no. 234, fig. 92). A. Riedel also fashioned a pair of *rimmonim* in the Danzig collection (no. 86).

73.
Torah Crown

Copper: openwork, repoussé, chased, engraved
Bolzano, Italy: 1699
6⅛ x 7⅛" dm (15.5 x 18 cm)
D 58

This cylindrical crown consists of two sections—a

73.

short, solid band which serves as a base and a tall band of openwork. The upper section was originally formed of a single unit of decoration, repeated six times, with each unit comprised of two addorsed S-shaped foliate scrolls enclosing further scrolls and ornamental motifs symmetrically arranged along a central axis. Flowering vines filled the spaces between the units, so that the upper contour would have been scalloped. Only one of these decorative units has survived in its entirety. Two convex moldings engraved with diagonal lines frame the lower band. Its center is engraved with a repeated cartouche design engraved with the following inscription:

נדבת / יורשי / כמר / זלמן / ב"ש / ז"ל / בבל [?] / יריד / בולזאן / שנת תנט / לפ"ק.

("Donated by the heirs of . . . Zalman b[en] S. . . . [?] the fair[?] of Bolzan in the year [5]459"=1699.)

The form of this crown, a solid lower band supporting a zone of openwork, is typical of Italian Torah crowns from the 17th to the 19th century. Most extant examples are made of silver. The use of copper in this one is, therefore, unusual. Another brass crown dated 1797 is in the collection of the Skirball Museum, Los Angeles (inv. no. 58.5). The Danzig crown came to the Seminary mounted on a brown velvet stand with a label offering the following information: "Diese bei einem Pogrom in Russland geraubte und wieder erstandene." ("This was plundered during a pogrom in Russia and acquired again.")

REFERENCES: Danzig, 1933, no. 58.

*74.
Torah Crown

Silver: parcel-gilt; semi-precious stones; glass
Berlin: 1779
Maker: Joachim Hübner
Marks: Scheffler 10c, 494 (110)
16 x 8¾" dm (40.6 x 22.2 cm)
D 61

The base is formed of a broad circlet set with six colored stones and embossed with garlands and wreaths containing the following inscription:

כתר תורה / שייך לאלופי חברה קדישא / וג"ח י"צו / ד"ק"ק שאטלנד שנת תקסג לפ"ק.

("The Torah Crown belongs to the leaders of the Burial Society and B[enevolent] S[ociety] . . . of the h[oly] c[ongregation of] Schottland, the year [5]563" = 1803.) The top of the circlet is shaped into acanthus leaves; the lower edge is bordered by a wreath below which is a second inscription:

נעשה ע״י הגבאים ר׳ שמעון ור׳ שמואל . . .

("This was made for the *Gabbaim* Shimon and Shmuel.") Above this base are six arches set with colored stones that terminate in a round base surmounted by a multi-level finial including a brass ball and disk, a star inset with glass, and a jasper surmounted by an agate. Seven bells are suspended from the arches and the finial.

In Ashkenazi communities, two types of ornaments are traditionally used to adorn the staves of Torah scrolls: finials (*rimmonim*) and crowns. The crown form symbolizes the royal position and exalted spiritual value accorded to the Torah in the life of every Jew (cf. *Midrash Rabbah,* Kohelet, 7). This example is one of four works by Hübner in the Danzig collection (cf. nos. 87, 63, 62), three of which may be dated to the period 1770–80, the last decade of his life. Shimon and Shmuel, the *Gabbaim* named in the inscription, also donated the Torah shield, no. 62.

REFERENCES: Danzig, 1933, no. 138c.

75.

Torah Crown

Silver: cast, engraved, openwork; glass stones
Probably Berlin: ca. 1870
Marks: none
9⅞ x 10¼″ dm (25 x 26 cm)
D 62

The bulbous form of this crown is decorated with engraved and repoussé leaf and scroll motifs and openwork shapes. A convex molding divides the crown horizontally and separates the two largest zones of decoration. The most prominent feature of the upper zone is a series of heart-shaped cut-outs enframing repoussé palmettes; wider versions of the same cut-out motifs appear in the bottom zone, equipped with pendant bells. Large glass stones of various colors are attached between the cut-outs of the lower section. The base of the crown is a wide convex molding engraved with a running diamond pattern marked by punched circles. The top is decorated with rampant lions which support the Tablets of the Law. These three-dimensional motifs are set on a textured rocky promontory, cast separately and attached to the

75.

top. The two sockets that once fit into the slotted base, and that were used to affix the crown to the staves of the Torah scroll, are today missing. A "W" engraved on the underside indicates that this crown belonged to the community of Weinberg.

The loss of the sockets is particularly unfortunate because of the absence of marks elsewhere on the crown. A stylistic comparison with a crown bearing a Russian hallmark once in the Hessisches Landesmuseum, Kassel, and now in a private collection, would seem to suggest a similar dating and provenance for the Danzig crown. The overall shape of both crowns is identical, as are the cut-outs and bells of the lower zone; see Parke-Bernet, *Feinberg Collection,* no. 467, p. 133. However, a third crown in the Altonaer Museum, Hamburg, equally similar, is said to possibly bear a Berlin hallmark; see *Monumenta Judaica,* no. E343, fig. 92. Three other crowns of the same type were once in the Hamburg Synagogue at Bornplatz (photostats in The Jewish Museum). The predominant number of such crowns known to have been in German collections suggest that the type originated there.

76.

Upper Portion of a Torah Crown

Silver: cast, repoussé, chased, parcel-gilt; glass stones
Danzig: ca. 1800
Mark: Danzig city mark
8½ x 5⅛″ dm (21.5 x 13 cm)
D 53

76.

The base of this portion of the crown is a circular band ornamented with parcel-gilt bosses, glass stones, and six swans holding bells. Behind the swans rise six staves in the form of flowers from which spring six deer who support a small dome decorated with scrolls and pendant bells. The dome is surmounted by a series of three finials decorated with flowers and leaves.

Six slots are cut in the base, indicating that this crown once served as the upper section of a larger Torah crown. Similar slots pierce the upper section of another Jewish Museum crown that is still attached to its lower portion (JM 17-64). The use of cast animal figures to support part of a Torah crown can also be seen on no. 77.

It is impossible to date the crown on the basis of the city mark as these marks were often reemployed after the period of original use. From a comparison with no. 77 and similar crowns of the late 18th and early 19th centuries, a dating of ca. 1800 seems appropriate.

REFERENCES: Danzig, 1904, no. 15; Danzig, 1933, no. 53, pl. 5; S. Kayser, "A Polish Torah Crown," *Hebrew Union College Annual* 23 (1950–51), p. 495; The New York Historical Society, *City of Promise*, exhibition catalogue, New York, 1971, no. 149, illustrated p. 18.

77.
Torah Crown

Silver: cast, engraved, parcel-gilt
Poland: ca. 1809–10
Maker: B.M.
Marks: ℬℳ
9⁷⁄₁₆ x 4¹⁵⁄₁₆" dm (24 x 12.5 cm)
D 52

The lower portion of this circular crown is decorated with two bands of silver foliate scrolls alternating with parcel-gilt channel moldings. From this base rise seven doves alternating with seven rampant lion staves which support a canopy with leaf pendants and suspended bells. A small crown rests on the canopy. It is inscribed:

כתר תורה כתר כהונה כתר מלכות כתר שם טוב לפרט ת' ק'
ע'

("Crown of Torah / Crown of Priesthood / Crown of Royalty / Crown of a Good Name [5]570" = 1810; a variation on *Ethics of the Fathers* 4:17). A parcel-gilt sphere surmounted by an acorn finial rises from the center of this small crown.

This Torah crown is one of a series that are nearly identical in basic composition but which vary in ornamental detail. All bear engraved inscriptions dating between 1809 and 1819 (see Kayser-Schoenberger, no. 39; Parke-Bernet Galleries, New York, *Jewish Ritual Silver Belonging to Mrs. Mira Salomon*, December 6, 1949, no. 115; idem, *Feinberg Collection*, no. 460.

REFERENCES: Danzig, 1904, no. 14; Danzig, 1933, no. 52; Kanof, *Ceremonial Art*, no. 115.

77.

78.

Torah Crown

> Brass: cast, cut-out, engraved; silver; colored glass stones
> Central Europe: early 19th century
> 8¾ x 6″ dm (22.2 x 15.2 cm)
> D 59

The base is a circlet ornamented with glass stones and topped by various foliate forms (fleur-de-lis, etc.). From it rise five curved staves decorated with floral buttons supporting a composite pedestal whose base and top are covered with leaves. A cast silver swan with outstretched wings surmounts the whole.

A similar crown from Brno, dated 1813, is now in the Prague State Jewish Museum (inv. no. 10.377) and suggests a similar dating and provenance for this crown (see The State Jewish Museum, Prague, *The Silver Objects from Czech Synagogue* [*sic*], n.d. unpaginated, s.v. "Crowns").

REFERENCES: Danzig, 1933, no. 59, pl. 5.

*79.

Pair of Rimmonim

> Silver: cast, cut-out, chased, engraved, hammered, parcel-gilt
> Berlin: 1788–1802
> Maker: AG, probably August Ferdinand Gentzmer
> Marks: Scheffler 11, 30c; AG
> 18½ x 4¼″ (70 x 40.7 cm)
> D 184 a,b

The two-storey-tower forms of these *rimmonim* rise from plain shafts each of which terminates in an echinus whose bottom is covered with leaves and whose upper section is pierced by cut-out forms. Both stages of the graduated towers are cubic with beveled edges. Each face is decorated with swags of leaves and cut-outs which surround an open arch in which hangs a pendant, parcel-gilt bell. A spool-shaped intermediate zone decorated with similar motifs connects the two stages. Parcel-gilt openwork crowns surmounted by double finials top the towers. Each shaft is engraved

ח״ק דק״ק שאטלאנד

("B[urial] S[ociety] o[f the] h[oly] c[ongregation of] Schottland.")

Though the mark AG is not recorded by Scheffler or Rosenberg, stylistic similarities between these *rimmonim* and other works by Gentzmer in the Danzig collection suggest that he was the master. The cubic stages decorated with cut-outs, pendants-bells and swags of leaves can also be seen on no. 80, a pair of *rimmonim* bearing Gentzmer's usual hallmark. Characteristic of all the silver by this master in the Danzig collection is the use of contrasting colored metal as an effective part of the design. (See no. 64 for a discussion of other known Jewish ceremonial objects by Gentzmer.)

REFERENCES: Danzig, 1933, no. 143b, pl. 11.

80.

Pair of Rimmonim

> Silver: parcel-gilt, cast, cut-out, repoussé, engraved
> Berlin: 1788–1802
> Maker: August Ferdinand Gentzmer
> Marks: Scheffler 11, 30b, 1296 (219)
> 21¹¹⁄₁₆ x 4⅝″ (53.5 x 11.7 cm)
> D 173 a,b

80.

The tower forms of these *rimmonim* rise from gradually tapering shafts that terminate in an echinus decorated with repoussé leaves. The towers themselves consist of three storeys of diminishing size decorated with garlands, cut-outs and arches in which hang gilt bells. Above each storey is a molding ornamented with repoussé leaves. In contrast to the lower storeys, which are cubic, the last stages are cylindrical. They serve as a base for the gilt, openwork crowns with ball and acorn finials which top the whole.

The forms of these *rimmonim* are harmoniously proportioned and shaped into a graceful whole. The subtlety of Gentzmer's design can best be appreciated by comparing these *rimmonim* to a copy made in Danzig (no. 81). Although the shapes and motifs of both pairs are identical, their execution and relative proportions differ considerably. For further discussion of Gentzmer's work, see no. 64.

81.

Pair of Rimmonim

Silver: parcel-gilt, cast, cut-out, engraved
Danzig: probably 1821–28
Maker: Johann Gottlieb Ulrich
Marks: Danzig city mark; Czihak² 526, S (possibly Czihak² 525, control mark of Carl Benjamin Schultz)
21¹⁄₁₆ x 3¾″ (53.5 x 9.5 cm)
D 174 a,b

These *rimmonim* are identical to no. 80, the work of A. F. Gentzmer (1759–1808), with the exception that all the foliate ornamental motifs are engraved, rather than executed in repoussé.

Gentzmer's *rimmonim* can be securely dated 1788–1802 from their hallmarks. They also bear a Prussian control stamp established in February, 1809. Ulrich became a master goldsmith in 1804; he is last mentioned in archival sources in 1839. The only Danzig assay master of this period whose initial is S, and whose control mark is not published, is Carl Benjamin Schultz, who held office in 1821 and 1828. Taking into account the priority of Gentzmer's career to Ulrich's, and Ulrich's comparatively weaker, less harmonious version of the common design, we may conclude that the Danzig master copied the Berlin silversmith's work.

Ulrich also executed two similar alms vessels, no. 120 and 278, dated 1809–19. The S control stamp also appears on the alms dish, no. 280.

82.

Pair of Rimmonim

Silver: cast, parcel-gilt, cut-out, engraved, filigree
Danzig: probably 1821–34
Maker: ANL, perhaps August Nathanael Lehnhard
Marks: Danzig city mark, ANL (August Nathanael Lehnhard?) and S (possibly Czihak² 525, control mark of Carl Benjamin Schultz)
19 x 3¾″ (48.3 x 9.5 cm)
D 181

These *rimmonim* rise in three tiers of different form that are harmonized visually through the use of repeated shapes. The first stage is cylindrical with oval cut-outs linked by a plain horizontal band. Additional cut-outs that curve inward form the lower portion of the second tier; these are surmounted by cupolas composed of ovoid sections of filigree. A short stem rises from each cupola to support an open crown composed of more ovoid sections of filigree. A distinctive feature of these *rimmonim* are the arched brackets with hand-shaped terminals which held bells on the first and second stages. Many of the bells are now missing.

For a discussion of the marks, see no. 67, a Torah shield bearing the same hallmarks. Three other pairs of *rimmonim* of similar design are in the Danzig collection: nos. 83, 224, and 225.

REFERENCES: Danzig, 1933, no. 146b.

83.

Pair of Rimmonim

Silver: cast, parcel-gilt, cut-out, engraved, filigree
Danzig: 1770–1835
Maker: GFS (?)
Marks: Danzig city mark, GFS (?)
11½ x 2½″ dm (29 x 6.3 cm)
D 176

Repeated oval shapes link the three tiers of these *rimmonim*. The first storey is cylindrical with oval cut-outs joined by a plain horizontal band. The second stage is formed of wider ovals that curve inward to support a cupola composed of filigree ovoid leaves. From a short stem set atop the cupola rises a crown of similar filigree leaves alternating with small cast heraldic forms. A ball finial terminates the whole. Curved arms holding pendant bells are attached to the first two stages.

This pair of *rimmonim* is the smallest of a group of

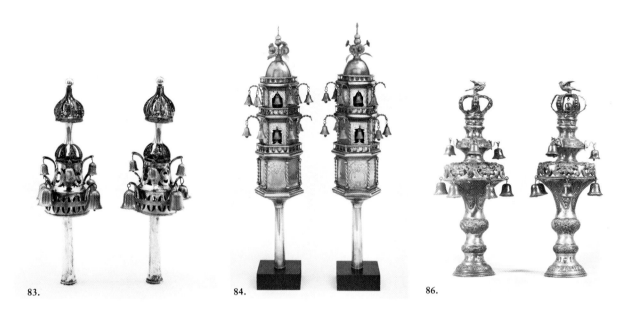

83.   84.   86.

four of similar design (cf. nos. 82, 224, and 225). The three other pairs may be dated between 1770 and 1835 on the basis of their hallmarks, which suggests that the present set was made during the same period.

REFERENCES: Danzig, 1904, no. 13; Danzig, 1933, no. 105.

84.

Pair of Rimmonim

Silver and brass: cast, cut-out, engraved
Danzig(?): 18th-19th century
Marks: none
23 x 4⅝″ (58.4 x 11.7 cm)
D 183

These *rimmonim* were designed as architectural forms to which fanciful details were added. Each is a three-storey hexagonal tower topped by a dome with a conventional spire. The first storey is a blind one. Spiral brass shafts mark the corners, and foliate and scroll designs are engraved on the silver faces. The second and third stages are more elaborate. Every other face is cut-out and holds a bell, and balconies surround the base of each tier, as well as the base of the dome. On these upper stages, the brass corner shafts are playfully elongated into arched supports for pendant bells. The most fanciful detail is the addition of cast flowers and leaves to the base of the spire.

Visually, these *rimmonim* are impressive because of their size, their fine detailing and the effective use of the contrasting colors of silver and brass. Though no

exact model for the tower can be identified among the extant buildings of Danzig, the hexagonal shape, blind lower storey, balconies, and spire are paralleled in the Danzig Rathaus, a major city landmark.

REFERENCES: Danzig, 1933, no. 108, pl. 11.

85.

Pair of Rimmonim

Silver: parcel-gilt, cast, cut-out, repoussé, engraved
Breslau: 1840–49
Maker: Carl Friedrich Korok
Marks: R 1386, 1455 and a Breslau city mark, the head of John the Baptist with a 4–[?].
11 x 3″ (28 x 7.5 cm)
D 177 a,b

Atop the short tapering staff of each *rimmon* is set a fluted echinus that supports a cylindrical band ornamented with repoussé palmettes. A zone of cut-out flowers and moldings rises from this band and tapers inward to form the base of a small melon-shaped cupola that is surmounted by a crown with acorn finial. This finial as well as the bells attached to the palmette band and the cupola are parcel-gilt. Four of the bells are missing and three of the extant ones are replacements. One of the shafts bears the following German inscription, which must have been added later: "Lesser Gieldzinski gewidmet der Israel [itischen] Gemeinde zu Danzig." ("Donated by Lesser Gieldzinski to the Israelite Congregation in Danzig.")

100

Similar *rimmonim* are in the Friedman collection, Budapest (unpublished). Korok also fashioned an alms box in the Mintz collection of The Jewish Museum (M 29), dated 1847; and several objects once in the collection of the Jewish Museum in Breslau (see Hintze, *Katalog,* nos. 201, 228, 229, 250).

86.
Pair of Rimmonim

Silver: cast, repoussé, hammered, parcel-gilt
Warsaw: ca. 1875
Maker: A. Riedel
Marks: A. RIEDEL, 🛆 , AR, and a crowned double-headed eagle in a circular field
15¾ x 5¼" dm (40 x 13.3 cm)
D 186

The baluster stem of each *rimmon* consists of alternating zones of concave bands and of repoussé floral and scroll motifs. Each stem terminates in a row of tall acanthus leaves which supports a wide, openwork zone of flowers framed by cartouches from which hang pendant bells. Above the openwork, a second stem of alternating zones supports an openwork crown surmounted by a bird finial. Other cast birds attached to the upper stem hold wires with pendant bells.

Another work by A. Riedel in the Danzig collection, a Torah shield (no. 72), displays many of the same elements as the *rimmonim.* Compare, for example, the forms of the flowers and scrolls and the incorporation of animal motifs.

87.
Torah Pointer

Silver: cast and engraved
Berlin: 1749–50
Maker: Joachim Hübner
Mark: Scheffler 494 (110), R 1201
9¹⁄₁₆ x 1¹⁄₁₆" dm (23.3 x 2.7 cm)
D 23

This pointer consists of three segments: a rectangular handle with beveled edges, a spiral shaft, and a hand with extended forefinger. Each joint is articulated in a different manner. A Hebrew inscription is engraved on three sides of the handle:

שייך להה״ כה שלמה ברה זל / ואשתו מ׳ פריידה בת כה״
זלמן זל / בשנת י׳ונ׳ת׳י׳ תמ׳תי לפ״ק.

("This belongs to . . . Shlomoh b[en] H., z.l., and his wife Freida daughter of Zalman, z.l. in the year 'my dove, my perfect one' "; [5]510 = 1750.)

The leafy forms separating the shaft and handle are unusual, as is the decoration of the ball finial, a continuous scalloped line and stippling. Although the hallmark is very worn as a result of use, the letters and forms remaining are identical to one of the marks occurring on the Torah crown, no. 74.

88.
Torah Pointer

Silver plate: engraved
Danzig: 1814–15 or earlier
Marks: none
10½ x 1⅛" dm (26.7 x 2.8 cm)
D 24

The form of this pointer closely resembles that of no. 89, except for the dedicatory inscription engraved on the sides of the handle:

שייך לאלופי חברה גמילת חסדים / ונעשה מן נדבת אנשי
אלופי חברה ג״ח / ע״י הגבאים ר׳ איצק בר״מ גאלדשטיין /
ור׳ הירש בר״ע ערב ר״ה שנת תקעה לפ״ק

("[This] belongs to the leaders of the Benevolent Society and was made through the donation of the leaders of the B[enevolent] Society f[or] *Gabbaim* Itzig b[en] M. Goldstein and Hirsch b[en] E. on the eve of R[osh] Ha[-Shanah] year [5]575" = 1814.) A later inscription, "Emigdirect Danzig 25.9.27," appears on the topmost finial. For Emigdirect, see no. 29 and the introductory essay by Gershon Bacon.

This pointer probably served as a model for no. 89 which was also donated by Itzig Goldstein.

89.
Torah Pointer

Silver: cast and engraved
Danzig: 1831
Maker: Master L
Marks: Czihak² 10, 535 (control mark of Johann Jakob Raths)
8½ x 1" dm (21.6 x 2.5 cm)
D 19

The gradually tapering form of this pointer begins in the rectangular handle, continues along the spirally fluted shaft, and terminates in a hand with extended index finger. The scalloped cuff above the hand is echoed in the scalloped bands decorating the ball finials that divide the shaft from the handle, and the handles from the ring above it. A dedicatory inscription is engraved on the handle:

זאת נדר ר' איצק גאלדשטיין לחברה ת" ... ד'ק'ק מאטענבודען / עבור נשמת אביו ר' משה ב'ר' מרדכי / ונשמות אשתו הצנועה מרת חנ ... / בת ר' חיים צוטרויען ז"ל / תקצא לפי"ק.

("This was vowed by Itzig Goldstein to the T[almud Torah] Society of t[he] h[oly] c[ongregation of] Mattenbuden on behalf of the soul of his father Moses b[en] Mordekhai and the soul of his modest wife Han[nah] daughter of Ḥayyim Zutreuen, z.l. [5]591" = 1831.)

The inscription is partially obliterated by a soldering repair at the bottom of the handle. The Mattenbuden Talmud Torah Society is also mentioned in the inscription of no. 67.

Another pointer in the Danzig collection (no. 88) is identical in design to this one, and may have served as its model since it bears an inscription dated 1814–15 and was also donated by Goldstein. For Goldstein, see no. 5. The hallmark of the unknown master is nearly obliterated on this pointer but appears to be the same as that on a pair of rimmonim, also made for Mattenbuden (no. 225). Raths was control officer of the Danzig goldsmiths guild from 1829 to 1833.

REFERENCES: Danzig, 1933, no. 143c.

90.

Torah Pointer

Silver: cast and engraved
Danzig: 1801–5
Maker: Johann Christoph Wonecker II
Marks: Czihak² 3, 495 and 511 (control mark of Johann Carl Hecker)
9¼ x 1¹⁄₁₆″ dm (23.5 x 2.7 cm)
D 25

The tapering rectangular shaft of this pointer terminates in a small hand with extended forefinger. A knop with raised molding divides the shaft in two, and a second, larger knop serves as the upper finial to which the chain is still attached. The shaft is engraved with the following inscription:

נעשה מצדקה נ"ת / עי הגבאי מה יוסף במה / יואל כהנא מדאנציג / נר תמיד יום ד עיכ' ת'ק'ס'ו לפק.

("Made through the charity of the E[ternal] L[ight Society] by the order of the Gabbai ... Yosef b[en] ... Yo'el Kahana from Danzig/Eternal Light/Wednesday e[ve] of Y[om] K[ippur] [5]566" = October 2, 1805.) The only other decoration is a series of wavy lines stippled along the beveled edges of the shaft and along the circumference of each knop.

The inscription contains two interesting pieces of information. The first is that it was purchased with the funds of an Eternal Light Society and donated by its Gabbai. It would appear, then, that the activities of such groups went beyond those indicated in the Mattenbuden Society Book (no. 131): maintenance of the Eternal Light in the synagogue and the kindling of the Hanukkah menorah. Second, the inscription specifies that the Gabbai, Yosef ben Yo'el Kahana came "from Danzig"; a meaningless phrase if he were still living there in 1805. Inscriptions that mention the donor's previous place of residence are not uncommon. (See no. 6 for another example and pertinent references.) Yosef ben Yo'el Kahana's name is also mentioned in a similar inscription on a Torah shield (no. 69) that was later rededicated by Itzig Goldstein, a leader of the Mattenbuden community in Danzig. It is probable that both the pointer and shield were brought to Danzig from one of the surrounding Prussian communities, perhaps after the war of 1807 or that of 1812, when nearby suburbs and towns suffered great destruction.

* 91.

Torah Pointer

Silver: cast and engraved
Danzig: 1766–1812
Maker: possibly Johann Christian Franck
Marks: Czihak² 6 (?), 501, part of a third mark
11 x 1³⁄₁₆″ dm (28 x 3 cm)
D 31

The handle of this pointer is a rectangular shaft whose edges are decorated with engraved zigzags and whose faces bear the following inscription:

זאת נדב ר' צבי ב'ה'ה' ר' מרדכי / אלעכסאנדר ז"ל / ניפטר י"ד אייר תרכ"ח / ע"א" מ' קאשה ט"ו בת הח"ר יעקב / לחברה קדישא וב"ח דק"ק שאטלאנד.

("This was donated by Tzvi b[en] the revered Rabbi

Mordekhai Alexander, z.l. who died on 14 Iyyar [5]628 [May 6, 1868] w[ith his] w[ife] Ka'sha . . . daughter of . . . Yaakov to the Burial Society and V[isiting the] S[ick Society] o[f the] h[oly] c[ongregation of] Schottland.") Knops decorated with raised moldings are attached to both ends of the shaft. The head of a dolphin(?) emerges from the lower knop. From its open mouth projects a human arm and hand grasping a second arm and hand whose index finger is extended to point to the text.

The use of a dolphin's head motif on this and related Torah pointers is extremely rare. Dolphins occur in 3rd- to 4th-century Jewish catacombs in Rome, but to suppose any connection between these early Jewish works and Polish examples of the 18th century would be farfetched. Dolphins have always symbolized the sea, and the fact that Danzig was the most prominent seaport of its day may explain the popularity of the motif there. See also nos. 92, 93, 94, 95, and 46 for other pointers and a Hanukkah *menorah* incorporating dolphins' heads.

Two complete hallmarks and portions of a third are stamped on the shaft. Thus, Franck's mark may signify that he was the silversmith or the control master. If his is indeed an assay mark, then the date of the pointer may be more precisely fixed to the years between 1778 and 1784. (Franck was control master in 1778, 1782, and 1784.) In any case, the dedicatory inscription was engraved many years after the manufacture of the pointer, indicating that the current practice of dedicating synagogue furnishings already in use is an old one.

For similar Torah pointers, see nos. 92, 93, and 94.

REFERENCES: Danzig, 1933, possibly no. 147c.

92.

Torah Pointer

Silver: cast and engraved
Danzig: 1727–30
Maker: Wilhelm Raths
Mark: Czihak[2] 448
11⅞ x 1³⁄₁₆″ dm (30.2 x 3 cm)
D 37

A rectangular shaft whose edges are engraved with zigzags serves as the handle of this pointer. A knop with raised molding is attached to each end. The upper bears a ring and chain; the lower leads to the head of a dolphin(?) from which emerges a human hand and

arm grasping a second arm and hand with extended forefinger.

This pointer may be precisely dated to the years between 1727 and 1730 because of the absence of the assay master's mark, a requirement established in 1730. Thus, this pointer is earlier than no. 91 which is almost identical in form and could have served as its model.

For a discussion of the dolphin motif, see no. 91.

REFERENCES: Danzig, 1933, possibly no. 147c.

93.

Torah Pointer

Silver: cast and engraved; red glass stone
Danzig: 1739 (date of inscription)
Marks: none
10⅛ x 1³⁄₁₆″ dm (25.7 x 3 cm)
D 33

The handle of this pointer consists of a tapering rectangular shaft whose edges are adorned with braided wire. A dedicatory inscription is engraved on all four sides:

ז״נ האלוף הרר שכנא . . . במ [?] זל / עבור בנו מאיר שי׳
נולד במזט / ביום ו׳ עש״ק ח״י תמוז תצ״ט לפי״ק ה״ש יגדל
לתורה ולחופה ולמעט אמן.

("This was donated by Shakhne b[en] M[eir] z.l. in honor of his son Meir . . . born with good fortune on Friday the eve of the holy Sabbath, 18 Tammuz [5]499 [July 24, 1739] May G[od] raise [him] to Torah, *huppah* and g[ood] d[eeds]. Amen.") At the top of the shaft is a ball finial with star-shaped cut-outs to which is attached a ring and chain. At the lower end is a smaller knop with an inset red glass stone aligned with the beginning of the inscription. Presently, this knop is affixed to the shaft by a soldering repair. A dolphin's(?) head emerges from the knop, and from its open jaw projects a human arm and hand with its forefinger extended. This hand is adorned with a pinkie ring whose stone is lost.

The inscription follows the text of the circumcision ceremony. The same formula was also used on Torah curtains and binders (cf. nos. 6, 55, 56, 138, and 190). The form of this pointer is a variant of nos. 91, 92, and 94.

REFERENCES: Danzig, 1933, no. 137c, pl. 11.

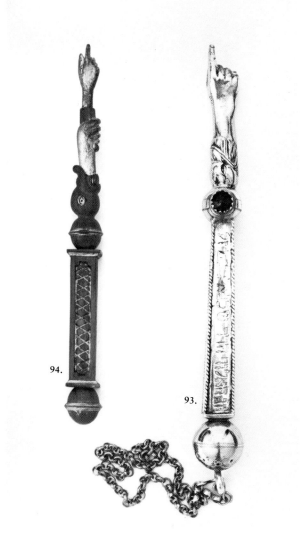

94.

93.

95.
Miniature Torah Pointer

Silver: cast and filigree; pyrope garnets; amethyst
Danzig(?): 18th-19th century
Marks: none
5¼ x 1¹⁄₁₆" (13.3 x 2.7 cm)
D 50

The handle of this pointer consists of a short cylinder attached to a longer, spiral shaft that terminates in a dolphin's(?) head. A hand with extended forefinger emerges from the head. Attached to the upper end of the shaft is an elaborate foliate branch whose leaves are composed of filigree, and whose spine is adorned with eight small garnets and a larger amethyst.

The combination of the spiral shaft with an animal head and a pointing hand recalls the four other Danzig Torah pointers which incorporate the same elements (nos. 91, 92, 93, 94). However, the treatment on the miniature pointer differs from that of the other pieces. For example, this dolphin's head is not complete, but a doubled mirror image of the upper half, whose dorsal fin is indicated by a leaf form.

In the 1933 Danzig catalogue, this pointer was designated as a set with a miniature Torah, no. 15, its mantle, no. 16 and the filigree crown, no. 18 and Torah shield, no. 17. However, the style of the filigree used on the pointer and the higher quality of its workmanship make it unlikely that all three filigree accoutrements were made by the same master.

REFERENCES: Danzig, 1933, no. 50.

94.
Torah Pointer

Walnut with gilding
Danzig: 18th century
8½ x ⅞" dm (21.5 x 2.2 cm)
D 43

The rectangular shaft of this pointer is decorated with an incised diamond pattern that has been painted gold. Similar painting highlights the square moldings and the ball knops at either end. The head of a dolphin(?) emerges from the lower knop. From its open mouth there projects a human arm and hand grasping a second arm and hand with extended forefinger.

This pointer may be dated and placed in 18th-century Danzig on the basis of its close similarity to two silver pointers (nos. 91 and 92) bearing definitive hallmarks. On the dolphin symbolism, see no. 91.

REFERENCES: Danzig, 1904, no. 30; Danzig, 1933, no. 43; *Jüdisches Lexikon,* IV/2, pl. CLXXIII.

96.
Torah Pointer

Silver: parcel-gilt
Warsaw: 18th-19th century
Marks: none
8³⁄₁₆ x 1" dm (20.7 x 2.5 cm)
D 17

Three knops segment the shaft of this pointer into two sections decorated with flowering vines and grape clusters. The top end terminates in an ornate finial formed of foliage and scrolls to which a ring and chain are attached. The lower end is inserted into a separate unit consisting of a hand with extended forefinger and a flaring sleeve.

A similar pointer in the Stieglitz Collection, Tel Aviv, bears hallmarks dating it to the second half of the 18th century (see *Synagoga*, no. 245, fig. 100). However a later date should probably be given to the Danzig pointer for a number of reasons. It bears no marks and the workmanship appears to be less fine than that of the Stieglitz example. In addition, the decorative motifs used on the Danzig pointer also appear on 19th-century works based on 18th-century models (e.g., no. 72, the columns of the Torah shield).

REFERENCES: Danzig, 1933, no. 47.

97.

Torah Pointer

> Mediterranean coral; silver: parcel-gilt
> Moscow: 18th-19th century
> Marks: none
> 6⅝ x ¹¹⁄₁₆″ dm (16.9 x 1.7 cm)
> D 44

This pointer is composed of a series of silver and coral beads threaded on a shaft. The top bead is in the form of a crown; below it is a cylindrical silver bead, two coral beads, and a silver gilt filigree bead. A coral hand with clenched fist terminates the whole. Small silver caps in the shape of radiating petals frame each bead. A double ring is affixed to the top of the shaft.

Three double-headed crowned eagles are affixed to the center bead. On each eagle's chest is a heraldic shield with a representation of St. George slaying the dragon. Double-headed eagles appear on Russian silver, and the St. George scene was the hallmark of Moscow from 1741 until the early 20th century. Thus, these devices suggest a Moscow provenance. A similar pointer is in the collection of the London Jewish Museum where it is given an Italian provenance; see Barnett, no. 149.

REFERENCES: Danzig, 1904, no. 31; Danzig, 1933, no. 44; *Jüdisches Lexikon*, IV/2, pl. CLXXII.

98.

Eternal Light in Cupboard

> Brass: cast and openwork
> Poland: 1856
> 30 x 17⅝ x 7½″ (76 x 44.8 x 19 cm)
> D 90

98.

This cupboard is in the form of a small building resting on a corbel. Two columns set on high bases support the curvilinear pediment adorned with two finials. Within the pediment is a dedicatory inscription:

להעלת / נר תמיד / אש תמיד תוקד לא תכבה / ז"נ החי"ר
נחמן הירשפעלד ע"א מ' הדס שתי' / שנת תרט"ז לפ"ק.

("To cause a lamp to burn continually [Ex. 27:20]. A perpetual fire shall be kept burning . . . , not to go out [Lev. 6:6]. This was donated by . . . Nachmann Hirschfeld w[ith] h[is] wife . . . Hadas . . . in the year [5]616" = 1856.) A large glass door ornamented with a fantail and two rosettes gives access to the cupboard. Inside hangs a perforated lamp suspended by three chains.

A similar lamp from which light was taken for the Hanukkah *menorah,* is illustrated in the Book of the Eternal Light Society, no. 131.

REFERENCES: Danzig, 1904, no. 42; Danzig, 1933, no. 90; *Jüdisches Lexikon*, IV/1, col. 454.

* 99.

Prayer Book for Morning Services (Seder Shomrim Laboker)

Ink; watercolor, gouache and gold paint on parchment
Ashkenazi Europe: 1725
10¼ x 7″ (26 x 17.7 cm); 120 fols.
D 168

The title page of this manuscript bears two inscriptions setting forth its purpose, extolling its script and appearance, and praising the Lord. The major inscription is framed between the columns of an aedicula; the second is contained in a cartouche inserted between the column bases. Of the remaining folios in the manuscript, thirty-six are illuminated with floral decoration executed in watercolor, gouache and gold paint.

The earliest extant example of this devotional text, *Seder shomrim laboker,* dates from the 16th century. The composition of this title page may have been modeled on printed books such as that of the Sulzbach Haggadah of 1711 (see Y. H. Yerushalmi, *Haggadah and History,* Philadelphia, 1975, pl. 65).

The name "Yehudah" appears in the lower inscription, where it is accented—a device sometimes used to indicate the name of the scribe.

REFERENCES: Danzig, 1904, no. 65; Danzig, 1933, no. 34.

100.

Reader's Prayer Book

Ink on paper; leather with gold tooling; brass
Prussia: 1861–88
11⅜ x 13¾″ (28.9 x 35 cm); 841 fols.
D 289

The first title page of this manuscript bears the following inscription:

סדר / תפלות ישראל / מכל השנה

("The Order of the Prayers of Israel for the Entire Year.") Indeed, this large volume contains prayers for daily worship, the Sabbath, festivals, plus benedictions for various occasions, all handwritten on paper.

Its decoration is confined to the letters comprising the first words of selected prayers. These letters are greatly enlarged and filled with a variety of abstract ornamental motifs set off against a cross-hatched ground. The manuscript is bound in brown leather ornamented with gold tooled scrolls and borders, and the edges of all the papers are gilded. The word "Gebetbuch" ("Prayer Book") is printed on the spine. Only portions of the original brass clasps remain.

From its very large size, we may suppose that this prayer book was written for use by the cantor of a synagogue. That it was written in Prussia between 1861 and 1888 is indicated by the prayer on behalf of Wilhelm I inscribed on pp. 547–49.

* 101.

Prayer Book for the Evening Service

Printed on paper; leather with gold tooling; silver: cut-out
Dyhernfurth: 1777 (book); after 1888 (cover)
Printer: Mikhal May
Marks: R 4, ES
3¼ x 2⅜″ (8.4 x 5.5 cm); 43 fols.
D 163

This small book contains only the evening service (*Ma'ariv*) and the order of the Counting of the *Omer,* the days between Passover and Shavuot. It is bound in leather tooled with gold-leaf decoration, and the front cover is further adorned with cut-out silver corners in a foliate design.

The title page bears the information that it was printed by Mikhal May of Breslau in Dyhernfurth in the year [5]537 (= 1777). Dyhernfurth is a town near Breslau (Wrocław) that was a center for the printing of Hebrew books from 1688 until 1834.

REFERENCES: Danzig, 1904, no. 67; Danzig, 1933, no. 36, pl. 10.

102.

Prayer Book with Silver Cover

102.

103.

Silver: openwork; ink on paper
Breslau: 1837
Scribe: Hirsch Jaretzki
Marks: none
4⅜ x 2⅞″ (11 x 7.3 cm); 66 fols.
D 169

This ornate silver cover of openwork leaf and scroll designs encases a handwritten book of prayers for special occasions. The title page bears a pen drawing of two columns joined by a crown, enclosing the following Hebrew inscription:

שמחו בני יעקב! צבאותיו הריעו! / ביין הטוב בטן התמלאו /
תענוגי הנפש בל רחקו — / יען השמחה וגיל / תדבקו— !

("Rejoice children of Yaakov. His hosts shout out! Fill your stomach with good wine. Do not distance yourself from pleasures of the spirit—because of the joy and gladness—stay near!") Below is a Judeo-German inscription containing information on the date, the donor, and scribe:

דיזער אייבנבאנד של כסף איזט פאן מיינען שעעצבאארען פריינד
וועלכעס דער / פרט אנצייגט מיר צום אנגעדענקנען פערעהרט
וארדען / לפרט ש'מ'ו'א'ל' ב'ן' מ'ה' ו'ו'א'ל'ף' נאא לפק. /
געשריבען פאן הירש יארעטצקיע קאנטאר אין ברעסלויא.

("This is the silver cover from my esteemed friend that indicates the year [in which it was] given to me as a tribute in my honor by Samuel ben Wolf Noa, [5]597 [=1837] written by Hirsch Jaretzki, Cantor in Breslau.")

REFERENCES: Danzig, 1904, no. 66; Danzig, 1933, no. 35, pl. 4.

103.

Prayer Book (Iyyun Tefillah)

Printed on paper; leather with gold tooled decoration
Prague: 1858
Publisher: M. I. Landau
4⁵⁄₁₆ x 3″ (10.8 x 7.6 cm); 256 fols.
D 164

This book contains daily prayers, as well as those for Sabbaths, holy days and special occasions in the original Hebrew and also in German translation. The first page bears the title

עיון תפלה

("*Iyyun Tefillah,*" "Devotion in Prayer.") and the information that the book contains prayers for travelers on the railroad and over the sea. Opposite is the engraved frontispiece, a scene of the dedication of the Temple in Jerusalem by Solomon. It is framed by an arch on which is inscribed a passage from the Biblical account of the dedication:

ושמעת אל תחנת עבדך ועמך ישראל.

("And when You hear the supplications which Your

servant and Your people Israel . . ." [I Kings 8:30].) On the same page, Lesser Gieldzinski wrote the following information: "Gebetbuch meines seeligen Vaters zu Włocławek er starb am 21ten Ijar, 24 Mai 1878, L. Gieldzinski, meine seelige Mutter starb in Włocławek am 28 Siwan 1882 Juni Lesser Gieldzinski." ("The prayer book of my late father from Włocławek; he died on the 21st of Iyar, May 24, 1878. L. Gieldzinski. My late mother died in Włocławek on 28 Siwan 1882, June. Lesser Gieldzinski.") Michael Gieldzinski's name also appears on the fly leaf.

104.

Prayer Book (Siddur Moreh Derekh)

Printed on paper; leather with gold tooling
Europe: before 1904
2⅝ x 1⅞" (6.5 x 4.7 cm); 255 fols.
D 165

Unfortunately, the title page of this small prayer book is missing. Thus, there is no information about its place and date of publication. The covers are decorated with embossed quatrefoils enclosed in rectangular frames whose corners are filled with flowers. The title

סידור מורה דרך

("Prayer Book Guide") is stamped inside the front quatrefoil. Additional embossed designs appear on the spine.

REFERENCES: Danzig, 1904, no. 39.

105.

Book Cover

Velvet: embroidered with silk, silver and gold-wrapped threads, gold and silver foil and sequins, couched embroidery, stumpwork, metallic fringe and braid
Prague: 1827
18¾ x 11½" (40.8 x 20.9 cm)
D 281

A vine-like design executed in couched embroidery and stumpwork frames both the front and back halves of this book cover. Long flowers project from the corners into the center field. On the front is an alle-

gorical scene with two kneeling, faceless female figures with feathered headdresses. The figure at left holds a shield in her left hand and a spear in her right; the right figure holds aloft a ship model. Both figures gaze across a river to a city with many medieval towers. Above them is a banner embroidered

חיים אלחנן עא אסתר

("Ḥayyim Elḥanan w[ith his] w[ife] Esther") and below is the date written in Hebrew

תקפז

(= 1827). The back cover is decorated with an elaborate coat of arms: a shield, divided diagonally, shows at upper left a crowned two-tailed lion holding aloft a dagger and, at bottom right, two silver stripes. This shield is surmounted by a helmeted head and surrounded by a foliate frame. Above the head is a second crowned, two-tailed lion holding aloft a dagger. The background material of both front and back is a maroon velvet which shows extensive signs of repair. The spine is covered in gold velvet decorated with silver braid.

Inside the binding were found fragments of a Hebrew-Latin lexicon and an inscription "Reparit (1907.) Gieldzinski." ("Repaired 1907. Gieldzinski.") The 1912 auction catalogue of the Gieldzinski collection lists a 1570 Hebrew-Latin lexicon in a leather binding and describes it as defective (Rudolph Lepke's Kunst-Auctions-Haus, Berlin, *Sammlung Gieldzinski Danzig,* December 3-9, 1912, no. 2288). This cover may have once been associated with that lexicon.

A Prague provenance is indicated by the coat of arms. Crowned lions with two tails appear on

105.

numerous Judaica objects from that city (e.g., H. Volavková, *Schicksal des Jüdischen Museums in Prag,* Prague, 1965, fig. 121.) Similar faceless allegorical figures appear on a valance for a Torah ark dated 1732 now in the Prague State Jewish Museum (ibid., fig. 106.) The city was often depicted as having many medieval towers.

REFERENCES: Danzig, 1933, no. 40.

106.

Book Cover

Silver: engraved, repoussé, cast
Russia or Poland: 19th century
Marks: none
5⅜ x 3⅛ x 2¼" (13.7 x 8 x 5.7 cm)
D 282

A heart-shaped medallion bearing the words

עיון תפלה

("Contemplation of Prayer") suggests that this richly decorated cover once adorned a prayer book, perhaps one furnished with commentaries intended to inspire the worshipper. Two pairs of birds flanking a central flower fill the space above and below the medallion. Their bodies are richly patterned, as are the remaining background areas. In contrast, the forms of the animals and birds engraved on the back cover and the spine are relatively free of detail and stand out against the cross-hatching and zigzags decorating the ground. A bear, lion, deer, and unicorn appear on the spine, each in its own compartment framed by repoussé

ridges. The back cover is ornamented with a crowned double-headed eagle set amidst vines and scrolls.

The crowned double-headed eagle suggests that this cover was produced in an area under Russian domination. (On the symbolism of the unicorn and associated animals, see Rüdiger Beer, *The Unicorn: Myth and Reality,* New York, 1977.)

REFERENCES: Danzig, 1904, no. 69; Danzig, 1933, no. 39, pl. 10.

107.

Stand for Prayer Text

Silver plate on copper: repoussé and engraved; ink on parchment; wood
Europe: 19th century
Marks: none
17½ x 6½" (44.2 x 16.4 cm)
D 109

The upper portion of the stand, which frames the *Kiddush* is a relief designed as a *tholos,* a small round

106.

107.

building with colonnade and dome. The text appears in the large intercolumniation at front. This framing portion is set on a bowl-shaped base whose contours and decoration echo those of the dome. A baluster stem and flaring foot with leaf and scroll ornament support the upper section. Since the front of the stand is executed in relief and is not three-dimensional, the necessary support is provided by a metal rod and wooden balance attached to the back.

This text stand is an unusual piece, both in its form and function. Extant synagogue prayer stands are few in number. This one was used at the conclusion of Friday evening services in the synagogue. *Kiddush* was said for the benefit of all those who could not hear its recitation at home. The parchment was written in an Ashkenazi hand during the 19th century, but the stand may be even earlier.

REFERENCES: Danzig, 1904, no. 46; Danzig, 1933, no. 65.

108.

Stand for Prayer Text

Brass: repoussé and cast; ink on paper
Europe: 19th century (?)
20 x 10½ x 5⁹⁄₁₆″ dm (50.8 x 26.7 x 14.1 cm)
D 108

A rectangular metal plate with a reinforcing horizontal bar frames the blessings recited before and after a reading from the Torah. The blessings preceding the reading appear above the bar:

ברכו את ה' המברך / ברוך ה' המברך לעולם ועד / ברוך אתה
ה' אלקינו מלך העולם אשר / בחר בנו מכל העמים ונתן לנו
את תורתו / ברוך אתה ה' נותן התורה. /

("Praised be the Lord, the blessed One. Praised is the Lord, Who is blessed for all eternity. Praised are You, O Lord our God, King of the universe, who chose us from all peoples by giving us His Torah. Praised are You, O Lord, Giver of the Torah.") Those which follow the lection appear below the bar:

ברוך / אתה ה' אלקינו מלך העולם אשר / נתן לנו תורת אמת
וחיי עולם נטע בתוכנו / ברוך אתה ה' נותן התורה.

("Praised are You, O Lord our God, King of the universe, who has given us a Torah of truth, and has planted everlasting life in our midst. Praised are You, O Lord, Giver of the Torah.") Both the brass baluster stem and circular base are ornamented with repoussé leaves. The small plaque attached to the top, two

rampant lions supporting the crowned Tablets of the Law, appears to be a later addition.

REFERENCE: Danzig, 1933, no. 134.

* 109.

Sheviti Tablet

Brass: repoussé and gilded; parchment
Poland: 1804 (date of inscription)
29¼ x 30⅛″ (74.5 x 76.5 cm)
D 89

This elaborately decorated *Sheviti* tablet last stood in front of the pulpit in the Great Synagogue of Danzig. An inscription running along the bottom indicates that it was originally made for another synagogue in 1804:

זאת נדב הרר מנחם מניס בר"ח משוועצזענץ ואשתו מרת פויגל
ת' שנת תקס"ד לפ"ק.

("This was donated by Rabbi Menaḥem Manus b[en] H. of Schwersenz and his wife Feigel . . . the year [5]564" = 1804.) The rectangular lower section bears repoussé representations of major elements of the Tabernacle/Temple: (from right to left) an altar for burnt offerings, the table of showbread, cherubim(?), the Tablets of the Law, the seven-branched *menorah* and the bronze laver. Above is an arched extension decorated with a heavenly cloud whose rays fall on an oval frame containing parchment inscribed with various passages from the Bible and Talmud. The most prominent of these is

שויתי ה' לנגדי תמיד

("I have set the Lord always before me"; Ps. 16:8.) Two cartouches and acanthus leaves fill the remainder of the upper extension which is flanked by two urns. A pair of candleholders project from the bottom corners.

Representations of objects from the Temple in Jerusalem are known as early as the time of Herod the Great (37-4 B.C.E.). In the medieval period, these objects were often portrayed in Hebrew illuminated manuscripts as frontispieces or as illustrations of the text. By the 18th century, they were embroidered on the valance of Torah curtains, and it is this source which may have served as a model for the maker of the *Sheviti*. His treatment of the objects does not accurately reflect their description in the Bible, and he has obviously been influenced by baroque forms in their depiction.

Menaḥem Manus, the donor, is also mentioned in the inscription of a Torah binder donated by his son Leib in 1796 that is part of the Danzig collection (no. 190). It would appear, then, that the family was in Danzig at the time of the donation of the *Sheviti* tablet, and, therefore, the mention of Schwersenz in the inscription does not indicate that the tablet came from there. See no. 6 for a similar inscription.

REFERENCES: Danzig, 1933, no. 89, pl. 8; F. Landsberger, *A History of Jewish Art,* New York, 1973, pp. 33–34, fig. 13.

110.

Sheviti Tablet

Brass: repoussé and hammered
Eastern Europe: late 18th century
43¾ x 24½" (111 x 62.2 cm)
D 88

110.

This tablet is rectangular with an arched top whose stepped edge is bordered by strapwork. A ball finial and eagle surmount the whole. The lower edge is the base of a tall platform decorated with both abstract and foliate forms. Two columns with fanciful capitals serve as framing elements along the sides. The main motifs of the center field are a jeweled crown with fleur-de-lis finial flanked by two flying birds; and a banner inscribed

דע לפני מי אתה עומד / לפני מלך מ׳ה הק׳ב׳ה.

("Know before whom you stand, before the King of Kings, the Holy One praised be He"; a variation of Mishnah *Avot* 3:1 and Babylonian Talmud *Berakhot* 28b.) Below, two rampant lions support a shield embossed with the passage

שויתי ה׳ לנגדי תמיד

("I have set the Lord always before me"; Ps. 16:8).

The iconography, composition, and even individual forms of this plaque recall Torah curtains such as no. 54 and shields like no. 68. For example, the treatment of the brass crown is reminiscent of the stumpwork embroidery of the curtain, while the columns and lions resemble those of the shield. A very rich visual effect is created by the contrast between plain and textured grounds.

REFERENCES: Danzig, 1933, no. 88, pl. 3; Kayser-Schoenberger, no. 185.

111.

Sheviti Tablet

Brass; velvet; glass; parchment; wood
Eastern Europe: 19th century
31 x 19¾" (78.7 x 50.4 cm)
D 87

A jeweled crown is affixed to the top of an elaborate arcuated frame that surrounds the central parchment of this plaque. Repoussé foliate, shell and scroll motifs, some containing velvet insets, decorate the frame. The inscriptions themselves are arranged in additional patterns: arcs, circles, scrolls and a seven-branched *menorah*. They include passages from the Bible and Mishnah, with the major emphasis given to the Tetragrammaton, inscribed in large letters and framed by a circle of flowers. Similar flowers, other foliage, and imbrication surround the *menorah* and fill the interstices between its arms. These same motifs are found on the frame.

REFERENCES: Danzig, 1904, no. 76; Danzig, 1933, no. 87.

112a.

112 a,b
Covered Urn and Basin

Copper and brass with engraved inscription
Danzig: 1845
Urn: 24 x 13½" (61 x 34.3 cm)
Basin: 19⅞ x 14½ x 12" (50.3 x 37 x 30.4 cm)
D 300 and 302

The body of the urn is divided into two sections, a fluted lower portion and a plain upper section, to which are attached lions' heads with rings and an inscribed plaque reading:

ז״נ ר' מאיר ב״ר שמואל זנוויל דאווידזאהן / בשנת ו׳ר׳ח׳צ׳ו׳
י׳ד׳י׳ה׳ס׳ ו׳ט׳ה׳ר׳ו׳ / לפ״ק ע״א מ׳ בונה ב״ר שואל הלוי

("T[his was] d[onated by] Meir b[en] Shmuel Zanvil Davidsohn, in the year 'they shall wash their hands . . .' [Ex. 30:21 = [5]605 = 1845] and be purified w[ith] h[is wife] Bunah b[at] Shoal Halevi".) Two rods project through the bottom and the urn is only watertight when these are suspended. A copper lid with brass finial handle serves as a cover. The matching

oval basin rests on a flared base whose interior is fitted with a stationary rod for fixing this vessel to a table. A pair of brass lions' heads with rings for handling are set at the ends. There is an old repair in the base.

These two vessels were depicted in a work by Wilhelm Stryjowski of 1869, "Danzig Jews in the Synagogue." From the evidence of this drawing, the urn and basin were used to store and catch the water needed for the ritual washing of the hands before prayer. The covered urn was attached to the wall by means of two large brackets, while the basin was fixed to a table set directly below. A worshipper who depressed the bolts suspended from the bottom of the urn released a small amount of water on his hands; the excess dropped into the basin. Release of the bolts rendered the urn water tight. A second set of an urn and matching basin is included in the Danzig collection (no. 263 a,b). Two similar brass basins (but without the stationary rod) came to The Jewish Museum as part of the Mintz collection (M 360 and M 493b).

REFERENCES: Danzig, 1933, no. 154.

113.
Banner for the Synagogue

Beige striped silk; beige velvet with metallic embroidery; stumpwork; glass stones; gold metallic foil; sequins; metallic braid
Danzig: last third of the 18th century
28 x 33½" (71 x 85 cm)
D 271

The background of the banner is a beige striped silk embroidered with delicate sprays of flowers and bordered on three sides by a knotted silk fringe with floral motifs. A metallic fringe is attached to the lower edge. The largest appliqué is a fragment of a Torah mantle or miniature Torah curtain. It is decorated with two rampant crowned lions which support a jeweled crown, all executed in stumpwork. Above the crown is the abbreviation,

כ[תר] ת[ורה]

("C[rown] of T[orah]"). The main inscription begins in the field between the lions and continues until the bottom of the banner:

ז״נ ה / יהודא / ליב ב״ה חנוך הענך / יצו ו׳ז מ׳ רבקה ב״ה /
ליב ז״ל שנת תק׳דו׳ לפק.

("T[his was] d[onated] by Yehudah Leib b[en]. . .

113.

Hanokh Henkh . . . and h[is spouse] Rivkah daughter of Leib, z.l. . . . in the year [5]526" = 1766.)

To either side of the velvet panel are two large heraldic badges. One, an eagle enclosed in a wreath on which is written the Latin motto, *suum cuique* ("to each his own"), is the badge of Friedrich I, in use from 1701 to 1715. The second device, three bound sheaves of wheat on a blue ground, may have been an insignia of the Danzig grain industry. Four smaller Prussian emblems are sewn to the top of the banner, all of them datable to the 18th century. A metallic ribbon in a zigzag pattern runs along the top and one side of the banner and is also used to frame the center section.

Identical badges of Friedrich I appear on two Torah curtains in the collection of The Jewish Museum, one from Danzig (no. 187) dated 1840 and an earlier 18th-century example of indeterminate Prussian origin (F 751). This banner is listed as a Torah curtain in the two Danzig catalogues; however, when it arrived at The Jewish Theological Seminary in 1939, it was attached to a pole wrapped with the Torah binder, no. 56.

REFERENCES: Danzig, 1904, no. 2; Danzig, 1933, no. 93; The Jewish Museum, *Fabric of Jewish Life,* exhibition catalogue, New York, 1977, no. 33.

114.
Pair of Sconces

Brass: repoussé
Germany: 18th–19th century
31½ x 15″ (80 x 38 cm)
D 97 a,b

These oblong sconces were formed of two sections each bearing a convex oval cartouche framed by beading and gadrooning. Symmetrical designs of repoussé flowers fill the remainder of the surface. A single candleholder is attached near the lower edges.

These sconces are similar to 18th-century examples from a synagogue in Eichsfeld (Göttingen, Städtisches Museum, inv. no. J44a n.b.; *Monumenta Judaica,* no. E 408). See also no. 116, a painting of the interior of a synagogue in which a related sconce was hung.

REFERENCES: Danzig, 1904, nos. 126 and 127.

115.
Pair of Candlesticks

Pewter: cast
Danzig: ca. 1825
Maker: Carl Wilhelm Juchanowitz
Mark: Hintze 371
31¼ x 8″ (79.4 x 20.3 cm)
D 100

Each candlestick consists of a short column on a square base supporting a knopped and ringed tapering standard. At top is a basin with pricket. The base of one candlestick bears a later inscription dated 1861 that is lightly scratched into the surface.

Candlesticks such as these served to illuminate the raised platform before the Torah ark. The Danzig collection also includes a tankard by the same master, no. 132.

REFERENCES: Danzig, 1904, nos. 118–123; Danzig, 1933, no. 68.

116.
The Worshipper: Morning Prayers

Oil on leather
Artist: unknown
Vienna (?): late 19th century
9¹³⁄₁₆ x 8″ (24.9 x 20.3 cm)
D 288

The dominant figure of this synagogue scene is the man leading the congregation in morning prayers. He stands in the foreground, caught in the middle of his chant. His face is raised upward in inner concentration, while his hands finger the prayer book on the lectern before him. In contrast to this well-lit and defined figure, the other congregants are shadowy forms. Secondary emphasis is given to a man seated beside the leader. He alone wears no *tefillin,* which may indicate his status as that of an *onen,* a mourner before the burial.

Other interesting details are the text and the sconce hung on the column, and the date prominently painted on the reader's desk cover, "in the year [5]526" (= 1766). The sconce is similar to a pair in the Danzig collection that likewise has a center panel surrounded by a pearled border and a frame of repoussé curvilinear forms (no. 114).

An inscription on the back panel of the frame records that the painting was a gift to the collection in the Danzig Synagogue from Eduard Gieldzinski of Vienna. Eduard was Lesser Gieldzinski's son.

REFERENCES: Danzig, 1904, no. 116; Danzig, 1933, no. 92.

117.
Alms Box

Silver: engraved and chased
Danzig: 1764
Maker: Johann Adam Lange
Marks: R 1499, Czihak² 486*, CT (control mark of Christoph Turck)
5 x 4⅝″ dm (12.6 x 11.7 cm)
D 217

The relatively simple tankard shape of this alms box is enlivened by the elaborate forms of the slot, hasp, and handle and by the rococo decoration. A rich pattern of chased and engraved shells, leaves, and scrolls ornaments the base, the lid, and the area to either side of the hasp. Below the hasp is a cartouche enclosing a chronogram indicating the year of dedication:

בשנת / גמ״י׳לות׳ / חס״ד״ים / לפ״ק.

("May [5]524 [= 1724] be a year of benevolence.") The remainder of the inscription appears to either side of the cartouche:

זה הקלפי נדבה / חברה הבחורים.

("This urn was donated by the Society of Young Men.") There are various signs of wear and old repairs.

117.

*The maker's mark is identical to Czihak² 527, listed as belonging to Johann Gottlieb Lange, the son of Johann Adam Lange (for whom no mark is known). The last year for which Christoph Turck was control master (1764) is also the date of the inscription, and is two years before the birth of Johann Gottlieb Lange. It therefore seems reasonable to conclude that Johann Gottlieb Lange took over the use of his father's mark. Turck's mark on this piece and on nos. 118 and 279 is identical in all respects to Czihak² 450, except that on our examples the base of the field is straight. Despite this difference, an identification of CT with Turck is certain, since there was no other Danzig control master with the same initials between 1700 and 1880.

REFERENCES: Danzig, 1904, no. 107; Danzig, 1933, no. 163.

118.
Alms Box

Silver: engraved
Danzig: 1764
Maker: Friedrich Wilhelm Sponholtz
Marks: R 1500, Czihak² 494, CT (control mark Christoph Turck)
5 x 3″ dm (12.7 x 7.5 cm)
D 221

The squat proportions of this alms box are emphasized by its decoration, raised moldings, and bands of zigzags set against a striated ground. The engraved bands are also used vertically to define the fields containing the inscriptions:

שייך לנשים / דק״ק״ דאנציג.

("Belongs to the women of the h[oly] c[ongregation of] Danzig");

לפרט / צ׳׳ד׳׳ק ל׳׳פ׳׳נ׳׳י׳׳ו׳ י׳׳ה׳׳ל׳׳ך״ / ו׳׳י׳׳שם׳ ל׳׳דרך פעמ׳׳י׳׳ו׳ / ל׳׳פ׳׳ק׳.

("Righteousness shall go before Him, and shall make His footsteps a way"; Ps. 85:14 = [5]577 = 1817.)

For a discussion of the control mark, see no. 117.

119.
Alms Box

Silver: engraved
Danzig: 1792
Maker: Ephraim Wischke
Marks: Czihak² 5, R 1598, Czihak² 505 (control mark of Johann Gottlieb Fischer)
4⅞ x 4½" dm (12.4 x 11.4 cm)
D 220

This alms box is in the shape of a tankard with sloping sides, to which has been joined a slot and a hasp. A raised channeled molding outlines the center and defines a pictorial field engraved with two couchant lions that flank a wreathed cartouche containing the following inscription:

בשנת הנ׳ה / אנ׳כ׳י׳ ש׳ול׳ח ל׳כ׳מ׳ / את א׳ליהו / הנב׳יא / לפ״ק.

("The year 'Lo, I will send the prophet Elijah to you' "; Mal. 3:23 = [5]553 = 1793.) A further inscription is engraved on two banners that float in the field above the lions.

בתורת ה׳ חפצו / ובתורתו יהגה יומם ולילה.

("... his delight is in the law of the Lord; And in His law does he meditate day and night"; Ps. 1:2.) In addition, there are trial engravings of various Hebrew letters on the slot, whose meaning cannot be determined.

120.
Alms Box

Silver: engraved
Danzig: 1814
Maker: Johann Gottlieb Ulrich

Marks: Czihak² 5, 526, 532 (control mark of Carl Stumpf)
5⅞ x 3½" dm (15 x 8.9 cm)
D 219

A high domed lid caps the simple tankard form of this box. The bottom of the lid and the top and bottom of the vessel itself are articulated by bands of engraved festoons. Likewise the slot is decorated by a band of chevrons set against a stippled ground. The inscription is divided between two cartouches engraved on either side of the handle:

זה / שייך לח״ק / דגמילות חסדים / דקק / דאנציג.

("This belongs to the h[oly] Benevolent S[ociety] of the h[oly] c[ongregation of] Danzig.")

כי / בגלל דבר הזה / יברכך ד׳ / לפק.

("... on account of this deed, God will bless you"; variation on Deut. 15:10 = [5]574 = 1814.)

The base of this box is damaged and the hasp shows evidence of an old repair. The same basic design may be seen in no. 278, also a work of Ulrich. This master also executed a pair of *rimmonim*, no. 81.

121.
Alms Box

Silver: engraved
Danzig: ca. 1830
Maker: U
Marks: Czihak² 10, U, 535 (control mark of J. J. Raths)
3¹/₁₆ x 2¾" dm (7.8 x 7 cm)
D 222

This box is in the form of a small tankard furnished with a slot and a hasp for securing the contents. Engraved foliate designs set against a textured background articulate the cover and the top and bottom of the vessel. The following inscription appears on the body of the container:

שייך / לחברה תלמוד תורה / דק״ק / מאטענבודען / נעשה ע׳׳י הגבאי / ר׳ איצק ב׳׳ר משה גאלדשטיין / שנת תקצא לפ״ק.

("Belongs to the Society for the Study of Torah of the h[oly] c[ongregation of] Mattenbuden. Made for the *Gabbai* Itzig b[en] Moshe Goldstein the year [5]591" = 1831.) For Goldstein and his donations, see no. 5.

122.

278.

119.

121.

122.
Alms Box

Silver: repoussé and engraved
Danzig: before 1883
Marks: none
3½ x 2¹¹⁄₁₆″ dm (8.8 x 6.9 cm)
D 218

The body of this alms box is formed of concave ovoid panels separated by raised moldings. Three of the panels bear symmetrical floral designs executed in repoussé. The concave forms contrast with the bulbous shape decorating the shoulder of the vessel. Alternating convex and concave moldings also characterize the stepped lid. The handle is also elaborately formed as a leafy vine scroll terminating in a swan which pecks at the handle. A German inscription is engraved on the lid to either side of the slot: "AltSchottlander Israelitscher Frauen Verein" ("Altschottland Jewish Women's Society").

The weight of the silver used for this box is very light and the box bears no marks. Nevertheless, a date

before 1883 may be established from the inscription, since the Altschottland community was dissolved in that year.

123.
Alms Dish

Silver: repoussé and engraved; inlaid silver coins
Stettin: ca. 1735–50
Maker: J. F. Timm
Marks: R 4578, 4589
1⅞ x 6¼″ dm (4.8 x 16 cm)
D 238

Seven silver coins struck in the 17th and 18th centuries for Braunschweig and Lüneburg are inlaid in the body of this footed dish. The largest is embedded in the base; six others are inlaid in the curving sides, each separated from the others by undulating forms that suggest petals. Petal shapes likewise form the upper edge. The dedication is inscribed on the underside of the base:

ז״נ אלופי ח״ק וג׳ח בק״ק שאטלנד בשנת תקס לפ״ק.

("T[his] was d[onated by] the heads of the B[urial] S[ociety] and B[enevolent] S[ociety] in the h[oly] c[ongregation] Schottland in the year [5]560" = 1800.) A second inscription is engraved on the exterior of the rim:

אמר רבי עקיבא אשריכם ישראל לפני מי אתם מטהרין ומי מטהר אתכם אביכם שבשמים שנאמר וזרקתי עליכם מים טהורים וטהרתם מכל טמאותיכם ומכל גלוליכם אטהר אתכם.

("Rabbi Akiva said: Blessed are you, O Israel. Before whom are you made clean and who makes you clean? Your Father in heaven, as it is written. 'I will sprinkle clean water upon you, and you shall be clean: I will cleanse you from all your uncleanness and from all your fetishes' " [Ez. 36:25; Mishnah *Yoma* 8:9].)

Silver dishes, tankards and cups inlaid with coins were popular in Germany during the 17th and 18th centuries. The chronological gap between the manufacture of this dish and its dedication to the Schottland Burial and Benevolent Society suggests it was not necessarily made as an alms dish or for use in the ritual purification of the dead.

REFERENCES: Danzig, 1904, no. 104; Danzig, 1933, no. 161, pl. 6 (where it is incorrectly labeled 166).

124.

Alms Dish

Silver: repoussé, filigree, engraved
Königsberg: ca. 1800–21
Maker: Daniel Ludwig Loyal
Marks: 1 + 2, 🔲 Ⓓ⸴, Czihak[1] 292a, 12 (R 2889)
1⅛ x 5⅞ x 3¹¹⁄₁₆" (2.9 x 14.9 x 9.3 cm)
D 237

This small oval dish is elaborately decorated. The bottom is ornamented with a repoussé wreath of leaves and flowers framed by a scalloped line, and the sloped sides are animated by festoons suspended from circular bosses. Similar bosses decorate the edge of the dish. Two filigree handles are attached at the ends. One of them bears the inscription "HGH / 24 Ju[ni ?] 1821," which provides a *terminus ante quem* for the manufacture of the dish. (Loyal died in 1824). A later Hebrew inscription is engraved along the outside of the dish

בשנת תקצו / לפ״ק / נעשה עי טרחת של ר׳ הירש ב׳ר׳ם׳ גדחק עם ר׳ משה מאיר ב׳ר׳ב׳א׳ מ׳ ח׳׳נ לחברה קדישא דק׳׳ק דאנציג.

("In the year [5]596 [=1836]. Made through the efforts of Hirsch b[en] M. *G[abbai]* of [the] B[urial] S[ociety] with Moshe Meir b[en] B.A.M. h[onored] f[riend] for the Burial Society of the h[oly] c[ongregation of] Danzig.")

From the inscriptions, we may conclude that this dish was made for a private owner and later dedicated to the Burial Society for a number of possible uses (see no. 126). The Hebrew inscription is interesting for its emphasis on the *efforts* of the donors.

The four hallmarks include the Königsberg city mark (similar to Czihak[1] 9), a year mark (unidentified in published sources), the master's mark, and the number 12 which indicates the weight of the silver.

125.

Alms Dish

Silver: repoussé and engraved
Danzig: 1752–64
Maker: CW
Marks: Czihak[2] 5 or 6, CW and CT (control mark of Christoph Turck)
¹⁵⁄₁₆ x 7¼ x 4¹⁵⁄₁₆" (2.4 x 18.4 x 12.6 cm)
D 162

This shallow oval dish was designed as a series of petals surrounding a central cartouche framed by shells, scrolls, and leaves, executed in repoussé; another leaf forms the handle. The inscription begins above the cartouche and continues within it:

וידר יעקב / בשנת / זה יאמר לה׳ אני / וזה יקרא ב׳ש׳ם׳ י׳ע׳ק׳ב׳ / לפק.

("Jacob then made a vow . . . [Gen. 28:20] in the year 'One shall say, I am the Lord's'; another shall use the name 'Jacob . . .' "; Is. 44:5 = [5]524 = 1834.)

The dish is cracked and bent in several places, and a small hole has been drilled above the inscription. For a discussion of Christoph Turck's control mark, see no. 117.

REFERENCES: Danzig, 1904, no. 98, where it is erroneously listed as part of a circumcision set, as also in Danzig, 1933, no. 13.

126.

Alms Dish(?)

Silver: engraved
Danzig: 1763–67
Maker: probably Ephraim Wischke
Marks: Czihak² 8, WISC, 473 (control mark of
Christian v. Hausen)
1⅝ x 7¾" dm (4.1 x 19.7 cm)
D 229

This elegant, fluted dish was made some sixty years
before it was inscribed and dedicated to the Mattenbuden Synagogue by the *Gabbaim* of the Burial
Society.

שייך לחברה קדישא דק״ק מאטענבודען נעשה ע״י הגבאים ר׳
אברהם ברוך ור׳ איצק גאלדשטיין שנת תקפה לפ״ק.

("Belongs to the Burial Society of the h[oly] c[ongrega-
tion of] Mattenbuden. Made for the *Gabbaim*
Avraham Barukh and Itzig Goldstein the year
[5]585" = 1825.)

Dishes such as this one, bearing dedications to the
Burial Society, may have been used to collect charity;
they may also have been used in the ritual purification
of the dead.

127.

Alms Dish

Silver: cast and engraved
Danzig: before 1818
Maker: MLITZ (?)
Marks: Czihak² 10, MLITZ, control mark U
(Ulrich?)
¹⁵⁄₁₆ x 5" dm (2.4 x 12.6 cm)
D 224

The body of the dish is shallow with steep sides. A
curved tongue-shaped handle with ring is affixed to
the top. Along its edge are lightly engraved zigzag
motifs on which are superimposed a broader, deeper
zigzag. Similar decoration appears on the lip and
center field of the bowl. A dedicatory inscription is
engraved in the center: in a frame,

שייך לבה״כ / דמאטינבודין / שנת תקעח / לפ״ק.

("Belongs to the s[ynagogue] of Mattenbuden the year
[5]578" = 1818); arched at top,

נעשה ע״י הגבאי ר׳ איצק גאלדשטיין.

("Made for the *Gabbai* Itzig Goldstein.")

It was generally Danzig practice for the control
master to use only one initial as his mark; therefore,
MLITZ was probably the maker and U the control
official. The identification of U with Johann Gottlieb
Ulrich, *Altermann* in 1816, is chronologically feasible
(cf. no. 121 and no. 279).

There are six similar dishes in the Danzig collection
with dedicatory inscriptions dating to the first half of
the 19th century (cf. nos. 128, 129, 279, 280, and
281.)

128.

Alms Dish

Silver: engraved
Danzig: 1842
Maker: Gottlieb Ephraim Wulstein
Marks: Czihak² 8 (?), 541, 544 (control mark of Carl

August Winkelmann)
1¹⁄₁₆ x 4⁷⁄₈" dm (2.2 x 12.4 cm)
D 228

Of all the alms dishes of this type made for the Matten-buden Synagogue during the first half of the 19th century, this one bears the finest engraved decoration. A thin undulating ribbon highlights the borders of the center field, the lip and the handle. In addition, a stylized flower appears on the handle, and the Judeo-German inscription in the center is composed around the form of a book, an appropriate symbol for the sponsoring society. Surrounding the book:

פעראיין צור אונטערהאלטונג דער ספרים לקהל דק״ק
מאטטענבודען בדאנציג.

("Society for the maintenance of books of the h[oly] c[ongregation of] Mattenbuden in Danzig.") In the open book,

נעשה / ע״י הגבאי / ר׳ משה / בן ר״ צבי / יאקאבזאן /
שנת / ת״רב״ לפ״ק.

("Made for the *Gabbai* Moshe b[en] Tzvi Jakobson the year [5]602" = 1842.)

129.
Alms Dish(?)

Silver: cast and engraved
Danzig: early 19th century
Marks: ℱ, 12
¹³⁄₁₆ x 4⁷⁄₈" dm (2.1 x 12.4 cm)
D 236

The main body of the dish is a shallow, flat-bottomed bowl whose center is engraved with a dedicatory inscription: in the square frame,

שייך לחברה קדישה / וב״ח״ דמ״ב / שנת תקפט לפק.

("Belongs to the Society for Burial and V[isiting the] S[ick] of M[atten] b[uden] the year [5]589" = 1829); and surrounding the square,

נעשה ע״י״ הגבאים ר״ אברהם ברוך בלוהם ור״ איצק
גאלדשטיין.

("Made for the *Gabbaim* Avraham Barukh Bluhm and Itzig Goldstein.")

A tongue-shaped handle with attached ring is affixed to the top. Both the edge of the handle and the tip of the dish are decorated with repeated zigzags. On the function of this dish, see no. 126. The 12 mark and the absence of the city mark indicate that the weight of the silver was below the required minimum.

130.
Lid of an Alms Box

Brass: engraved
Europe: before 1904
⁵⁄₈ x 4³⁄₈" dm (1.6 x 11.1 cm)
D 234

The lid is in the form of a shallow circular dish with an aperture for donations. Attached to the rim are a hinge and a serrated cover engraved with leaves and moldings that hide the opening. The intent of the structure is made explicit by the inscription on the base of the lid,

מתן / בסתר

("A gift in secret . . ."; Prov. 21:14.) According to Maimonides (Mishneh Torah, *Mattanot Aniyyim* 10:8-14), the highest form of charity is that which is given in secret.

REFERENCES: Danzig, 1904, no. 108; Danzig, 1933, no. 164.

131.
Book of the Eternal Light Society

Ink on paper
Danzig: 1833
8³⁄₈ x 7" (21.5 x 17.5 cm); 10 fols.
D 166

The title page of this manuscript bears the legend:

שייך להחברא נר תמיד דמאטטענבודן. / נעשה ע״י הגבאי ר׳
איצק גאלדשטיין שנת ת׳ק׳צ׳ג לפ״ק.

("This belongs to the Eternal Light Society of Matten-buden made for the *Gabbai* Itzig Goldstein the year [5]593" = 1833.) A large circular frame fills the remainder of the page. Within is a pen drawing of a man in top hat and frock coat approaching a seven-branched *menorah* with a lighted taper. Behind him is a cabinet labeled:

נר תמיד

("Eternal Light"), opened to reveal a flame. Page two is inscribed:

131.

132.

מי שברך אבתינו [כך!] אברהם יצחק ויעקב הוא / יברך את

("May he who blessed our forefathers Abraham, Isaac, and Jacob, bless. . . .") The names of the Society members are inscribed on the facing page within an arcade. This arcade forms the upper portion of a hall in which the members sit at their annual banquet. One of them holds a book open to the legend written on page two. The rabbi is at right, distinguished by his hat and throne. His is the first name on the list, Rabbi Yehiel Aryeh, the son of Rabbi Matityahu Hakohen. The book also contains a *piyyut,* a religious poem, written in the form of an alphabetical acrostic whose every line ends with the word *tamid* ("eternal"), and the hymn *Ma'oz Tzur* ("Rock of Ages") sung on Hanukkah.

The drawings in this book are vivid, yet crude. The artist obviously had difficulty rendering perspective, as can be seen from the representation of the room on the first page. From the contents of this rare book, it would appear that the Eternal Light Society was responsible for the maintenance of the *ner tamid* and for lighting the Hanukkah *menorah,* and that the Eternal Light was kept in a cabinet like the one illustrated on the frontispiece. A similar cabinet is part

of the Danzig collection (no. 98), and another minutes book, that of the Benevolent Society of Mattenbuden, is included in the exhibition.

132.

Tankard

> Pewter: engraved
> Danzig: 1811(?)
> Maker: Carl Wilhelm Juchanowitz
> Mark: Ostrich in an oval frame inscribed CARL WILH: IUCHANOWITA ..11, surmounted by a crown
> 8⅛ x 4½″ dm (20.6 x 11.4 cm)
> D 292

The plain body of this tankard tapers slightly towards the lid. The simple moldings of the cover and handle are the only ornamentation aside from two incised lines near the base of the spout. An engraved inscription reads:

שייך לחברה נר תמיד דק״ק מאטטענבודען / נעשה ע״י הגאבי
[כך!] ר' איצק ב״ר משה גאלדשטיין בשנת תקצב לפ״ק.

("Belongs to the Eternal Light Society of the h[oly] c[ongregation of] Mattenbuden. Made for the *Gabbai* Itzig b[en] Moshe Goldstein in the year [5]592" =1832.) The Eternal Light Society met for an annual banquet at which this tankard may have been used. For the Eternal Light Society, see nos. 98 and 131.

133.

Burial Society Mug

Silver: cast and engraved
Danzig: 1835
Maker: Carl Stumpf Widow and Son
Marks: Danzig city mark, Czihak² 532 (C. STUMPF Wᵂᵉ & SOHN.) and 541 (block letter W. in rectangular field, control mark of Gottlieb Ephraim Wulsten)
5½ x 3½" dm (14 x 8.9 cm)
D 295

The body of this vessel is a plain cylinder ornamented at top and bottom with narrow bands of floral design. The first words of the inscription engraved on the front form a circular frame for the concluding phrase:

זאת נעשה ע״י אלופי דח״ק מברייטעגגאס / בשנת / בל׳ע׳
ה׳מות׳ לנצ׳ח / לפק.

("This was made b[y the] officers of the Burial Society of Breitgas[se] in the year 'He will destroy death forever . . .' "; Is. 25:8 = [5]595 = 1835). A curved handle decorated with repoussé designs is attached to the side opposite the inscription.

Few objects in the Danzig collection can definitely be ascribed to the Breitgasse Synagogue, the oldest Jewish house of worship in Danzig. Another similar piece with an almost identical dedication is no. 134 and like this mug, it may originally have had a cover. Both vessels could have been used at the annual banquet held by members of the Burial Society. These are the only two pieces in the collection made by the firm of Carl Stumpf during the period when it was managed by his widow and son.

134.

Cylindrical Box

Silver: cast and engraved
Danzig: 1835

Maker: Carl Stumpf Widow and Son
Marks: Danzig city mark, Czihak² 532 (C. STUMPF Wᵂᵉ & SOHN.) and 541 (block letter W. in rectangular field, control mark of Gottlieb Ephraim Wulsten)
5⅜ x 3½" dm (13.7 x 8.9 cm)
D 73

The body of the box is a plain cylinder whose only ornaments are narrow bands of cast floral designs and an engraved inscription. The first words of the inscription form an arch enclosing a chronogram indicating the date of dedication:

זאת נעשה ע״י אלופי דח״ק מברייטגאס / בשנת זכ׳ור׳ כי׳
ע׳פ׳ר׳ / א׳נח׳נו׳ / לפ״ק.

("This was made b[y the] officers of the B[urial] S[ociety] of Breitgas[se] in the year '. . . He is mindful that we are dust' "; Ps. 103:14 = [5]595 = 1835.) From marks on the box, it appears to have originally had a handle similar in form to that of no. 133. On the plain cover with knob handle is a short German inscription, "Esrog Becher" ("*etrog* beaker").

From the character of the original Hebrew inscription, the signs of the missing handle, and the similarity to no. 133, we may conclude that this piece was originally a mug or tankard made for use at the Breitgasse Burial Society's annual banquet (see also no. 133). At some later date, the handle was removed; the mug was converted into an *etrog* holder; and the German inscription added.

135.

Printed Amulet for the Protection of a Mother and Newborn Son
Printed on paper; shellacked
Central Europe: late 18th-early 19th century
5 x 3⅝" (12.8 x 9.2 cm)
D 9
Inscriptions: in large letters,

מזל זכר טוב

("For good luck, male");

שדי קרע שטן

("Almighty, rend Satan");

לתמלמיי כמיללבד לתארוליב

(Acronym for: "You need not fear the terror by night, or the arrow that flies by day . . ." [Ps. 91:5]; "For He will order His angels to guard you wherever you go" [Ps. 91:11]; "No harm will befall you, no disease touch your tent"; [Ps. 91:10].)

136 a, b.

Printed Amulets for the Protection of a Mother and Newborn Daughter or Son
Printed on paper
Central Europe: late 18th-early 19th century
5 x 3⅝" (12.8 x 9.2 cm)
D 11
Inscriptions:

למזל טוב נקבה

("For good luck, female"); remainder as on no. 135.

137.

Circumcision Shield
Silver: engraved; niello
Europe: 18th-19th century
Marks: none
2¾ x 2⁵⁄₁₆" (7 x 5.9 cm)
D 156
Inscription:

ב״אי / א״מה / א״קב / וע״ה.

("P[raised are] Y[ou], L[ord] o[ur God], K[ing] o[f the universe] w[ho has] s[anctified our lives] t[hrough his commandments] c[ommanding] us r[egarding] c[ircumcision].")

138.

Curtain for the Circumcision Ceremony
Silk: embroidered with silk and metallic threads; stumpwork; couched work
Danzig(?): 1776
80⅛ x 49" (203 x 124.5 cm)
D 257
Inscriptions:

כתר תורה

("Crown of Torah");

ידידי אידל / יאקב חנה.

("The friends of Itel, Yakov, Hannah"). There follows the text of the circumcision ceremony and

בשנת תקלו לפק

("in the year [5]536" = 1776.)

139.

Mezuzah
Copper
Europe: 19th century
8¹⁵⁄₁₆ x 1½" (22.7 x 3.8 cm)
D 82

140.

Mezuzah
Tin
Europe: 19th century
6⅛ x 1" (15.5 x 2.5 cm)
D 83

141.

Mezuzah
Tin
Europe: 19th century
2⅞ x ½" (7.3 x 1.2 cm)
D 84
Inscription:

ש[די]

("A[lmighty]").

142.

Pair of Tefillin
Leather: painted; parchment
Europe: 19th century
2⅝ x 2⅝ x 2⅝" (7 x 7 x 7 cm)
D 291

143.

Heart-shaped Amulet
Silver: cast
Italy: 17th century
Maker: CK
Mark: CK
1⅝ x1⅛" (4 x 2.85 cm)
D 8
Inscription:

א״ מ״ / שלח רפאה [כך!] שלמה

("O[ur Father] o[ur King] send complete healing"; from the prayer, *Avinu malkenu*.)

144.

Heart-shaped Amulet
Silver: cast, repoussé, punched, engraved
Europe: 18th-19th century
Marks: none
3⁵⁄₁₆ x 3¹⁄₁₆" (8.4 x 7.8 cm)
D 5
Inscriptions:

שדי

("Almighty"; [written twice]); initial letters of the Ten Commandments [in Hebrew]. The round capsule affixed to this amulet held scraps of a *Maḥzor* for the High Holy days.

145 a, b.

Small Inscribed Plaque with Pendant Amulet Box
(a) **Inscribed Plaque**
Silver on copper
Europe: 19th-20th century
1⁷⁄₃₂ x 1¼" (3.1 x 3.14 cm)
D 7a
Inscription:

נ׳׳ומ׳׳כ׳׳יכ׳׳א׳׳ ה״ב חיים אליעזר ז״ל

("T[he] y[outh] Ḥayyim Eliezer of blessed memory.") The first seven letters have not been identified.

(b) **Oval Amulet Box**
Silver: engraved
Italy(?): 19th century
Marks: none
2¹⁄₁₆ x 1⅜ x ⁵⁄₁₆"

(5.2 x 3.46 x 0.75 cm)
D 7b
Inscription:

שדי

("Almighty"; written twice).

146.

Amulet
Silver: engraved; mirror glass;
turquoise
Asia Minor: 18th-19th century
Marks: none
3⅛ x2½" (8 x 6.5 cm)
D 12
Inscriptions:

וזה מעשה המנורה מקשה זהב עד יוכה
[כך!] עד פוחה [כך!] מקשה היא:

("Now this is how the lampstand
was made: it was hammered work of
gold, hammered from base to petal
. . .."; Num. 8:4.)

אל מול פני המנורה יאירו שבעת הנרות;
אנקתם פסתם פספסים

(". . . let the seven lamps give light at
the front of the lampstand [Num.
8:2] *Anaktam Pastam Paspasim* [Dio
Nsim]"; the 22-letter Divine name, a
kabbalistic formulation.)

147.

Kiddush Goblet
Silver: cast, engraved, punched
Berlin: 1817
Maker: Heinrich Wilhelm Ludwig
Wilm
Marks: Scheffler 13, 1435 (263)
7¼ x 3⅝" dm (18.4 x 9.2 cm)
D 68
Inscription:

זאת נדב ר" אברהם ב"ר"א בעבור בנו
ה"ב"ח מנחם מן הנמול ביום ב' ד'ר"ה
שנת ה"ת"ק"ע"ז.

("This was donated by . . . Abraham
b[en] A. on behalf of his son, the lad
. . . Menahem Mann circumcised on
the second day of R[osh] Ha[shanah]
5577" = September 24, 1816.)

148.

Kiddush Goblet
Silver: cast and engraved
Germany: after 1888
Marks: R 2; 800 and a man's profile
facing left
4½ x 2⁷/₁₆" dm (11.4 x 6.2 cm)
D 69

Inscription:

לזכרון / אמו מ" חיה טויבע ז"ל / מאת /
יצחק נייבורגער דנציג / תרפ"ב.

("To the memory of his mother . . .
Hayyah Toibe . . . by Isaac
Neuburger Danzig [5]682" = 1922.)

149.

Kiddush Goblet
Copper: cast and silver-plated
Danzig(?): 1873
7¾ x 3½" dm (19.7 x 8.9 cm)
D 67
Inscriptions: "5633"(= 1873); "W"
(sign of the Weinberg community).

150.

Kiddush Goblet
Silver: cast, repoussé, engraved
Warsaw: ca. 1847–50
Maker: Nowakowski
Marks: Lepszy 298 and 314
5⅞ x 2¾" dm (15 x 7 cm)
D 63
Inscriptions: "P.T."

ברוך אתה ה' אלקינו מלך העולם בורא פרי
הגפן:

("Praised are You, Lord our God,
King of the universe who creates the
fruit of the vine"; from prayer
service.)

151.

Spice Box
Silver: cast and filigree
Germany or Poland: 18th-19th
century
Marks: R̵ , Ⅎ
6¾ x 2" dm (17 x 5 cm)
D 194

152.

Spice Box
Silver: filigree and parcel-gilt
Eastern Europe: 18th-19th century
Marks: none
5⅜ x 2¾ x 2⅞" (14 x 7 x 7.2 cm)
D 196

153.

Spice Box
Brass: cast, cut-out, engraved
Near East: 19th-20th century
5⅞ x 2⅝" dm (15 x 6.7 cm)
D 198

154.

Spice Box
Brass: cast, cut-out, engraved
Near East: 19th century(?)
6⁹/₁₆ x 2⁵/₁₆" dm (16.6 x 5.9 cm)
D 199

155.

Shofar
Horn
Germany(?): 18th-19th century
12½ x 2⅜" (32 x 6 cm)
D 120

156.

Shofar
Horn: carved and engraved
Europe: 18th-19th century
11½ x 1¾" (29.2 x 4.5 cm)
D 119

157.

Shofar
Horn: carved and drilled
Europe: 19th century
16 x 2¾" (40.6 x 7 cm)
D 118

158.

Etrog Box
Silver: cast and engraved
Danzig: 1754–83
Maker: Abraham Schröder(?)
Marks: Danzig city mark; A.S. in a
rectangular field (perhaps Czihak²
477); R (perhaps Czihak² 448,
control mark of Wilhelm Raths)
4⅜ x 8" (11.1 x 20.3 cm)
D 72
Inscription:

שייך לח"ק תק"פא לפק

("This belongs to the B[urial]
S[ociety] [5]581" = 1821.)

159.

Etrog Box
Brass: cast
Danzig(?): 18th century
7¹/₁₆ x 9¼ x 5" (8 x 23.5 x 12.7 cm)
D 71
Inscription: "Esrog Behälter" ("Etrog
Box").

160.

Hanukkah Lamp
Brass: cast and engraved; white
metal: painted and gilt
France(?): early 19th century

15¼ x 14⅝ x 2½″
(38.7 x 37.2 x 6.4 cm)
D 208

161.
Hanukkah Menorah
Silver: cast and chased
Germany: 19th century
Marks: none
18⅜ x 17⅞ x 6″
(46.6 x 45.4 x 15.2 cm)
D 205
Inscription: "Gieldzinski dedit"
("Gieldzinski gave it").

162.
Hanukkah Menorah from the Danzig Synagogue
Brass: cast
Danzig(?): 1888–1910
62 x 44″ (156 x 112 cm)
D 215
Inscription: "Gewidmet von L. Gieldzinski" ("Dedicated by L. Gieldzinski").

163.
Hanukkah Menorah for the Synagogue
Brass: cast and engraved
Probably Poland: 18th century
28½ x 35″ (72 x 89 cm)
D 214

164.
Hanukkah Lamp
Brass: cast
Western Europe: 19th century
6 x 6⅜ x 2″ (15.2 x 16.2 x 5.1 cm)
D 216
Inscription:

כי נר מצוה ותורה אור.

("For the commandment is a lamp and the teaching is a light";
Prov. 6:23.)

165.
Hanukkah Menorah
Brass: cast, cut-out, engraved
Eastern Europe: perhaps late 18th century
14 x 11″ (36 x 28 cm)
D 210

166.
Hanukkah Menorah
Brass: cast
Eastern Europe: 20th century
13⅞ x 12½ x 4⅞″ dm

(35.3 x 31.2 x 12.4 cm)
D 203
Inscription: "W" (sign of the Weinberg community.)

167.
Hanukkah Lamp
Copper: repoussé and engraved
Europe: 18th-19th century
10 x 14¼ x 2½″
(25.4 x 36.2 x 6.3 cm)
D 209
Inscription:

אשר קדשנו / במצותיו וצונו / להדליק נר
של חנכה.

(". . . who has sanctified us through His commandments, commanding us to light Hanukkah candles.")

168.
Hanukkah Menorah
Brass: cast
Europe: 19th century
6½ x 6 x 3¹⁵⁄₁₆″
(16.5 x 15.2 x 10 cm)
D 102

169.
Hanukkah Menorah
Brass: cast
Europe: probably 20th century
11½ x 9½ x 5″
(29.2 x 24.1 x 12.7 cm)
D 204

170.
Purim Plate
Pewter: cast and engraved; niello
Danzig: ca. 1725; inscription probably 19th century
Maker: Gottfried Götz
Mark: Hintze[3] 329
6⁷⁄₁₆″ dm (16.3 cm)
D 239
Inscriptions:

שלח / מנות
lit. ("Sending Gifts"; i.e., Purim gifts)

מרדכי : אסתר
("Mordekhai: Esther")
On back: "F.H."

171.
Purim Plate
Pewter: cast and engraved; niello
Danzig: early 18th century; inscription probably 19th century
Maker: Johann Ludwig Böhm

Mark: Hintze[3] 301 (variation)
6⁷⁄₁₆″ dm (16.3 cm)
D 240
Inscriptions: "I.G."

מחצית / השקל

("Half a shekel").

172.
Megillah
Ink on parchment
Ashkenazi Europe: 18th-19th century
7⅞ x 83½″ (20.1 x 212.1 cm)
D 75

173.
Megillah
Ink on parchment
Ashkenazi Europe: 18th-19th century
15¾ x 61″ (40 x 155 cm)
D 78

174.
Megillah in Case
Ink on parchment; aluminum; wood; walrus
Ashkenazi Europe: late 18th-early 19th century
Case: 11 x 2⅛″ dm (28 x 5.4 cm)
Scroll: 4¼ x 67″ (10.7 x 170 cm)
D 77

175.
Megillah Case
Silver: engraved and parcel-gilt
Germany or Poland: ca. 1875
Marks: none
11½ x 2³⁄₁₆″ dm (29.5 x 5.5 cm)
D 80
Inscription: "Der Weinberger Gemeinde zu Danzig zum Andenken an Simon Becker geb: am 1, October 1793. gest: am 24, Juli 1875." ("To the Weinberg Congregation of Danzig in memory of Simon Becker b[orn]on October 1, 1793. d[ied] on July 24, 1875.")

176.
Megillah Case
Brass: cast, engraved, stamped
Europe: 19th century
10 x 2⅛″ dm (25.4 x 5.4 cm)
D 79
Inscription:

124

מגילת אסתר

("*Megillat* Esther").

177.

Seder Plate
Pewter: repoussé and engraved
Germany: 19th century
Marks: none
13⅜" dm (34 cm)
D 111
Inscription: Order of the Seder
service.

178.

Reader's Desk Cover
Velvet: embroidered with silk
threads; rope fringe
Danzig: 1929
53 x 61½" (134.6 x 156.2 cm)
D 275
Inscriptions:

ש" / תרפט לפ"ק / דאנציג

("The year [5]689 [= 1929],
Danzig");

חנוך בן יצחק עם אשתו שיינדיל בת ר' דוב
וידאווסקי.

("Ḥanokh ben Isaac with his wife
Sheindel the daughter of . . . Dov
Widowski.")

179.

Torah Curtain
Weave-patterned silk and metallic;
red velvet embroidered with silk and
metallic
Danzig: 1755
102 x 64½" (259 x 164 cm)
D 246
Inscriptions:

כתר תורה

("Crown of Torah");

יאקב / אליקום. בילא / רבקה

("Yakov/Eliakum/Bail'a/Rivka");

אלקי ידעתי כי אתה כחו לבב ומישרים /
תרצה אני כישר לבבי התנדבתי את / כל
אלה בבית אלקי יעקב / וסכת"י" ע"ל"
ח"ארון את הפרכת לפ"ק.

("I know also, God, that you try the
heart and have pleasure in the
upright. As for me, in the upright-
eousness of my heart I have willingly
offered all these things. [I Chr.
29:17] In the house of the God of
Jacob [variation on Is. 2:3, Micah
4:2] . . . and screen of the ark with a
curtain"; Ex. 40:3 = [5]515 = 1755.)

180.

Torah Curtain
Velvet; weave-patterned silk with
silver threads; gold lace ribbon with
gold foil and brass appliqués, gold
braid; silver ribbon; cut-out silver
appliqués, brass bells; linen
Danzig(?): 1777
69¼ x 46" (175 x 117 cm)
D 278
Inscriptions:

קדש לה'

("Holy to the Lord");

כתר תורה

("Crown of Torah");

ז"נ הרב / יהודה / בר יעקב / יארדן /
אשתו / הצנועה / מ' שרה / בת / אברהם
/ בשנת / תקלז / לפ"ק / מטוכל

("T[his was] d[onated by] Judah ben
Jacob Jordan [and] his modest wife
Sarah the daughter of Abraham in
the year [5]537" [= 1777] . . . [?].)

181.

Torah Curtain
Weave-patterned silk with silver
threads; stumpwork, couched work
with silk, silver and gold threads;
silver and gold foil sequins; woven
ribbon of silver threads and silver
foil, metallic fringe
Danzig: 2nd half of the 18th century
71 x 62¼" (108.3 x 158 cm)
D 244
Inscriptions: Ten Commandments
[5th commandment missing];

הירש / פעריל

("Hirsch/Pearl").

182.

Torah Curtain
Damask; silk brocade; silk ribbon;
metallic ribbon and stumpwork
Danzig(?): 1796-1853

82¼ x 56½" (209 x 143.5 cm)
D 258
Inscriptions:

כתר תורה

("Crown of Torah");

ז"נ מ"ר יוסף יעקב ע"א מרת רבקה
זצ"ל / בשנת ת"ק"נ"ו לפ"ק.

("T[his was] d[onated] by R[abbi]
Joseph Jacob w[ith his] w[ife] . . .
Rivkah of blessed memory in the
year [5]556" = 1796.)

ונתחדש בשנת תר"י"ג" לפ"ק / מן בנם /
חיים אלחנן ע"א אסתר עטיל

("and was restored in the year
[5]613 [= 1853] by their son
Ḥayyim Elḥanan w[ith his] w[ife]
Esther Ettel.")

183.

Torah Curtain
Embroidered silk; metallic braid; taffeta brocade; silver ribbon with
silver foil; silver braid and tassels;
stumpwork and couched work with
gold foil, silver foil, colored foil, silk
threads; heraldic appliqués, metal
buttons with applied sequins and
metallic thread; linen
Probably Danzig: 1809–19
68½ x 42½" (174 x 108 cm)
D 243
Inscriptions:

כתר תורה

("Crown of Torah");

זאת נדב / ר' זלמן ב"רמ עם אשתו מ' נוחה
/ ז'ק'ו'ף ב'י'ו'ת מ'ק'דש'ך' / לפק

("This was donated by Zalman b[en]
R[abbi] M[oshe] with his wife
Noḥah, 'Set up your sanctuary,'"
= [5]569 or [5]579 = 1809 or 1819.)

184

Torah Curtain
Weave-patterned silk with metallic
threads: embroidered with silk,
metallic threads and metallic foil;
metallic ribbon and fringe; stumpwork, heraldic appliqués
Danzig: 1815
71 x 43" (180.5 x 109.5 cm)
D 263
Inscriptions:

כתר תורה

("Crown of Torah"; repeated twice);

זאת |נ]דבו דאלופי חברה קדישה / בקק
דאנציג / בשנת תקעה / לפק.

("This was [don]ated by the heads of the Burial Society in the h[oly] c[ongregation of] Danzig in the year [5]575" = 1815.)

185.
Torah Curtain
Weave-patterned silk; velvet; metallic ribbons, braid, fringe, foil and threads; stumpwork; couched work; colored stones; heraldic appliqués
Danzig: 1824
78 x 54¾" (198.1 x 139 cm)
D 245
Inscriptions:

כתר תורה

("Crown of Torah");

התרני מ״ה איצק ב״ר משה עם אשתו /
הצנועה מרת חנה תחי׳ / שנת תקפד לפי״ק

("I was permitted by Itzig b[en] Moshe with his modest wife Hannah . . . the year [5]584" = 1824.)

186.
Torah Curtain
Embroidered silk: silk and metallic threads, sequins, stumpwork with metallic threads and foil, metal braid and bells
Danzig(?): 1825
83 x 57" (211 x 144.8 cm)
D 242
Inscription:

ז״נ / מרדכי קילה / לחו״ק וג׳״ח / ומשוש
חתן ע׳ל׳ כלה׳ / ישיש ע׳לי׳ך / אליהך.

("T[his was] d[onated by] Mordekhai Kilah to the B[urial] S[ociety] and B[enevolent] S[ociety] 'And as a bridegroom rejoices over his bride, so will your God rejoice over you' "; Is. 62:5 = [5]585 = 1825.)

187.
Torah Curtain with Valance
Velvet; weave-patterned silk; metallic braid and fringe; sequins; glass stones; metal letters and ornaments
Danzig: 1840–76
Curtain: 79 x 54" (200.8 x 137 cm)
Valance: 14 x 54" (35.5 x 137 cm)
D 247

Inscriptions:

גד בר״ם עם אשתו מירל [ה] / שנת / טוב
לישראל הוא לפק׳.

("Gad b[en] M. with his wife Mirel the year 'Surely God is good to Israel . . .' "; Ps. 73:1 = [5]600 = 1840.)

כתר תורה

("Crown of Torah");

מתנת קדש

("a sacred donation"; cf. Ex. 28:38); to the right,

מאת ה׳ ה׳ ר׳ יהודה ע׳ ה׳ עי׳ אשתו מ
חענא.

("From the R[evered] R[abbi] Yehudah z.l. by his wife Ḥena"); and at left,

ואחיו ההר ד׳ו׳ב׳ [?] אייערבאך / עם
אשתו מרת נוחח / בשנת תרלז.

("and his brother the R[evered] R[abbi] Dov Eierbach with his wife Noḥaḥ in the year [5]637" = 1877.)

188.
Torah Curtain
Velvet; metallic ribbons and threads; stumpwork; couched work
Danzig(?): 1877
86½ x 60" (219.2 x 152.4 cm)
D 249
Inscriptions:

כתר תורה

("Crown of Torah");

מנדבת הרב המופלג מה״ו חיים זצ״ל /
מ״ץ דקהלותינו נעשה זאת לעדת / החברא
והצבור

("From the donation of Rabbi Ḥayyim, the t[rue] t[eacher] of our congregation; this was done for the congregation of the Society and the Community.")

לזכר עולם יהיה צדיק / לפק

("The righteous will be for an everlasting memory" = [5]637 = 1877.)

189.
Torah Curtain
Weave-patterned silk; velvet; silk cannelé embroidered with silver threads, silver braid, fringe, and tassels, silk fringe
Danzig: 19th century

63 x 45" (160 x 114.3 cm)
D 251

190.
Torah Binder
Cotton: painted
Danzig or Schwersenz: 1796
8⅝ x 134½" (22 x 341.6 cm)
D 264
Inscription:

(ז״נ הילד ליב בזכ״ מנחם מאנוס יצו) ליב
בן במאנוס נולד במט יום א יד שבט (מזל
דלי) ת״ק״נ״ו״ ל׳ ה׳ יגדלהו לתורה
ולחופה ולמעשים טובינ[ם] אמן סלה

("T[his was] d[onated by] the child Leib son of . . . Menaḥem Manus . . . Leib son of . . . Manus, born w[ith] g[ood] f[ortune] on Sunday, the 14th of Shevat; sign of 'the Bucket' [= Aquarius] [5]556 = February 3, 1796; May the Lord raise him to Torah, and to *huppah,* and to go[od] deeds. Amen, Selah.")

191.
Torah Binder
Linen: painted
Danzig(?): 1845
8¼ x 128½" (21 x 326.5 cm)
D 265/66
Inscription:

(הנה אנכי שלח מלאך לפניך לשמר:כה
בדרך) אליעזר (המכונה ליזר) בן כה שלמה
שליט נולד במט (מאזנים) יו״ ו׳ ב דר״ה
ת״ר״ו״ השם יגדלהו לתורה (תורה צוה לנו
לנו משה כ״ת / וירד משה מן ההר ושני
לוחות בידו) ולחופה (ק״ש וק״ש / ק״ח
וק״כ) ולמעשים טובים א״ס (רץ כצבי
וגבור כארי)

(" 'I am sending an angel before you to guard you on the way' [Ex. 23:20]; Eli'ezer (called Leiser) son of . . . Shlomo . . . born w[ith] g[ood] f[ortune]; Libra; Friday, the second day of R[osh] Ha[-Shanah] [5]606 [October 2, 1845] May the Lord raise him to Torah; '. . . Moses charged us with the Teaching . . .' [Deut. 33:4]; C[rown of] T[orah]; 'Thereupon Moses . . . went down from the mountain bearing the two tablets of the Pact . . .' [Ex. 32:15] and to *huppah;* 'the s[ound of] m[irth] and g[ladness], the v[oice of] b[ridegroom] and b[ride] . . .' [Jer. 33:11] and to good deeds. A[men], S[elah]; 'Fleet as a stag, strong as a lion . . .' " [Mish. *Avot* 5:23].)

192.
Torah Mantle
Silk brocade; Beauvais embroidery with silk and metallic threads; colored stones
Neuteich: 1933
31 x 15″ (78.7 x 38.1 cm)
D 259
Inscriptions:

כ׳ ת׳

("C[rown of] T[orah]");

ת״ר / צ״ג

("[5]693" = 1933);

ז״נ ר׳ שלמה ב״ר זעליג ז״ל / ורעותו
גנענדיל ת״חי לבר / מצוה של בנם מאיר
נ״י / ביום כ׳ אדר נוייטייך / הערמאן

("T[his was] d[onated by] Shlomo b. Selig z.l. and his beloved wife Gnendel . . . for the Bar Mitzvah of their son Meir Hermann . . . on the 20th day of Adar, Neuteich [18 March].")

193.
Torah Mantle
Silk brocade; Beauvais embroidery with silk and metallic threads; colored stones
Neuteich: 1933
31 x 15″ (78.7 x 38.1 cm)
D 261
Inscriptions:

כ׳ ת׳

("C[rown of] T[orah]");

ת״ר / צ״ג

("[5]693" = 1933);

ז״נ ר׳ שלמה ב״ר זעליג ז״ל / ורעותו
גנענדיל ת״חי / לבר מצוה של בנם מאיר /
הערמאן / נ״י ביום כ׳ אדר נוייטייך

("T[his was] d[onated by] Shlomo b. Selig z.l. and his beloved wife Gnendel . . . for the Bar Mitzvah of their son Meir Hermann . . . on the 20th day of Adar, Neuteich [18 March].")

194.
Torah Mantle
Silk damask; silk cannelé; gold thread; metallic foil; silk thread;

metallic fringe; couched work; stumpwork
Germany or Poland: 18th-19th century
25½ x 19¼″ (65 x 48.5 cm)
D 255
Inscription:

כתר תורה / בענדיט אשא

("Crown of Torah / Bendit Asa [?]").

195.
Torah Mantle
Silk brocade; taffeta; couched work, stumpwork with silk and silver threads; glass stones
Germany or Poland: 19th century
24¾ x 18″ (63 x 45.5 cm)
D 253
Inscription:

כתר תורה / יוסף בר״ם ע״אמ נחה / כשנת
[כן!] תקצד לפק

("Crown of Torah; Yosef b[en] M. w[ith his] w[ife] Noḥah in the year [5]594" = 1834.)

196.
Torah Shield
Brass: cast, engraved, cut-out; silver: cast and engraved; niello
Italy and Germany: 18th-19th century
9⅞ x 6⅜″ (25.1 x 16.1 cm)
D 124
Inscriptions: abbreviated Ten Commandments;

שדי

("Almighty");

שבעות

("Shavuot").

197.
Torah Shield
Silver: cast, repoussé, parcel-gilt, filigree, engraved
Berlin: 1788–1802
Maker: son of Martin Friedrich Müller
Marks: Scheffler 11, 600 B (132)
11½ x 8″ (29.2 x 20.2 cm)
D 130
Inscriptions: abbreviated Ten Commandments and holy day names;

נעשה ע״י״ הגבאים ר״ איצק ב״ר״ משה
גאלדשטיין / ו״ר״ משה ליב דאנצגער שנת
תקץ.

("This was made for the *Gabbaim* Itzig b. Moses Goldstein and Moses Leib Danziger the year [5]590" = 1830.)

שייך לחברה / גמילות חסדים / ד״ק״ק״
מאטעננבודען / שנת תקץ לפי״ק״.

("This belongs to the Benevolent Society of the h[oly] c[ongregation] of Mattenbuden the year [5]590" = 1830.)

198.
Fragment of a Torah Shield
Silver: parcel-gilt, repoussé, cast
Berlin: 1788–1802
Maker: August Ferdinand Gentzmer
Marks: Scheffler 11, 30c, 1296 (219)
14⁵⁄₁₆ x 11⅝″ (36.5 x 29.5 cm)
D 141

199.
Torah Shield
Silver: cast, repoussé, parcel-gilt, engraved
Berlin: ca. 1815
Maker: Johann Carl Franz August Sonnabendt
Marks: Scheffler 12, 1614 (300)
11¾ x 8⅞″ (29.9 x 22.5 cm)
D 138
Inscriptions: abbreviated Ten Commandments and holy day names.

200.
Torah Shield
Silver: repoussé, cast, engraved, stamped, parcel-gilt
Berlin: 1821–50
Maker: Johann Christian Samuel Kessner
Marks: Scheffler 14, 1455 (264) and an indeterminate third mark
12 x 9½″ (30.5 x 24.1 cm)
D 135

201.
Torah Shield
Silver: cast, repoussé, parcel-gilt, engraved
Berlin: 1854–60
Maker: M
Marks: Scheffler 15, 21 and M
14 x 11⅛″ (35.5 x 28.3 cm)
D 145
Inscriptions: abbreviated Ten Commandments, holy day names and "E L."

202.
Torah Shield
Silver: cast, repoussé, parcel-gilt
Germany: after 1858
Mark: Scheffler 29
10⅝ x 8⅝″ (27 x 22 cm)
D 140
Inscriptions: abbreviated Ten Commandments and holy day names.

שייך / להמרומים / מ״ה איצק בר״ם / גאלדשטיין.

("This belongs to . . . Itzig b. M. Goldstein.")

203.
Torah Shield
Silver: cast, repoussé, parcel-gilt, engraved
Germany or Poland: 1841 (date of inscription)
Marks: none
8⅝ x 7 1/16″ (22 x 18 cm)
D 147
Inscriptions: abbreviated Ten Commandments and holy day names.

תרמא

"[5]641" = 1841) and "W" (sign of the Weinberg community).

204.
Torah Shield
Brass: cast, repoussé, engraved; glass stone
Germany or Poland: 19th century
15⅝ x 12¼″ (39.6 x 31.3 cm)
D 123
Inscription: abbreviated Ten Commandments.

205.
Torah Shield
Silver: cast, repoussé, parcel-gilt, engraved
Danzig: 1841–49
Maker: Carl August Winkelmann
Marks: Danzig city mark, Czihak[2] 544 and XLIX
9 x 7⅝″ (22.8 x 19.5 cm)
D 132
Inscriptions: abbreviated Ten Commandments and holy day names.

בשנת / ת״ר״ / לפ״ק.

("In the year [5]600" = 1840);

עם / אשתו / הצנועה / מ׳׳ מינדעל תי׳.

("with his modest wife Mindel . . .").

206.
Torah Shield
Silver: cast, engraved, stamped, repoussé, parcel-gilt
Danzig: before 1888 (date of inscription)
Maker: TK or TR
Marks: Czihak[2] 10, TR or TK and CSt (perhaps control mark of Carl Stumpf or Carl Moritz Stumpf)
10⅜ x 8″ (26.4 x 20.3 cm)
D 144
Inscriptions: "Zum Andenken an seinen Vater geschenkt von Marcus Goldstein."

ת״רמ״ה

("In memory of his father, donation of Marcus Goldstein [5]648" = 1888.) Inscription on back in circular frame: "TB," and

פסח

("Passover").

207.
Torah Shield
Silver: cast, cut-out, engraved, repoussé, parcel-gilt
Warsaw: early 19th century
Marks: none
8⅛ x 6¼″ (20.7 x 15.9 cm)
D 125
Inscriptions:

שנת / תק צ״דיק טית

("the year [5] 599" = 1839);

כתר תורה / כתר כהונה

("Crown of Torah; Crown of Priesthood");

ועשיתי ציץ / זהב טהור / ופתחת עליו / פתוחי חתם / קדש / ל״ר.

("You shall make a frontlet of pure gold and engrave on it the seal inscription: 'Holy to the Lord' "; Ex. 28:36.)

208.
Torah Shield
Silver: cast, parcel-gilt, engraved
Warsaw: 19th century
Maker: Mryngler(?)
Marks: Lepszy 298 and Mryngler
6½ x 7⅛″ (16.5 x 18.1 cm)
D 129
Inscription: abbreviated Ten Commandments.

209.
Torah Shield
Copper: repoussé, silver-plated, engraved; glass stones
Eastern Europe: 19th century
5½ x 3⅝″ (15 x 9.2 cm)
D 127
Inscription: the first ten letters of the Hebrew alphabet to represent the Ten Commandments.

210.
Two Dedicatory Plaques Suspended from a Metal Bar
Plaques: silver: cast and engraved
Bar: silver: cast, engraved, parcel-gilt
Danzig: 1836 (date of inscription)
Marks: none
3⅜ x 1⅛″ [width of plaque] (8.6 x 2.8 cm)
D 6
Inscription:

שלמה פרידלענדער / ע״א״ מ״ דברש / ת״י״ / בשנת תקצו / לפ״ק״.

("Shlomoh Friedländer w[ith his] w[ife] Dobrish . . . in the year [5] 596" = 1836.)

211.
Torah Crown
Brass: cast and repoussé
Italian(?): 19th century(?)
6⅝ x 5¾″ dm (16.8 x 14.6 cm)
D 56
Inscription: the first ten letters of the Hebrew alphabet engraved on Tablets of the Law.

212.
Torah Crown
Brass and white metal: cast and engraved
Prussia: late 19th-early 20th century
8 x 6 13/16″ dm (20.3 x 17.3 cm)
D 60
Inscription:

כתר תורה

("Crown of Torah").

213.
Torah Crown
Brass: repoussé and engraved; silver: engraved; glass stones
Eastern Europe: 19th century
7 x 9″ dm (17.8 x 22.8 cm)
D 57

Inscriptions:

כתר תורה

("Crown of Torah");

חברה קדישא

("Burial Society").

214.

Torah Crown
Wood: painted; metal appliqués;
glass stones; silver: cast and cut-out
Origin unknown: probably 19th
century
7⅞ x 3⅜" dm (20 x 8.5 cm)
D 55
Inscriptions:

י"קו"ק

(the Tetragrammaton);

כתר תורה

("Crown of Torah").

215.

Pair of Rimmonim
Silver: cast, cut-out, repoussé,
engraved, parcel-gilt; brass: cast
Berlin: 1788–1802
Maker: Casimir Ernst Burcky
Marks: Berlin city mark, Scheffler
30a, 1309a (220)
16¾ x 5¾" dm (42.5 x 14.5 cm)
D 178
Inscriptions:

את כלי הקדש האלה נדבו היורשים /
אשר נקבו בישמותם על פחי הכסף /
לב"ה"כנ" ד"ק"ק שאטלאנד יעא / בשנת
ת"ר"ה" לפ"ק".

("These sacred objects were donated
by the heirs who etched their names
on the silver, to the s[ynagogue] o[f
the] h[oly] c[ongregation of] Schottland . . . in the year [5] 605" =
1845.)

עבור נשמת היקר כ"ה" צבי הירש
העררמאן הלוי / ואשתו היקרה מ' אסתר /
זכרונם לא יסוף עד דור דורים.

("On behalf of the dear soul the
revered Rabbi Tzvi Hirsch Herr-
mann the Levite and his dear wife
Esther. Their memories will endure
over generations.")

216.

Pair of Rimmonim
Silver: cast, cut-out, repoussé,
engraved, parcel-gilt; brass: cast and
engraved

Berlin: 1788–1802
Maker: Casimir Ernst Burcky
Marks: Scheffler 11, 1309a (220)
14½ x 3¾" dm (36.8 x 9.5 cm)
D 179
Inscriptions:

נעשה מקופת החברה קדישא דביקור חולים
מ"ק"ק" ווינבערג על ידי הגבאי ר" סענדר
ב"ר"ם.

("This was made from the coffers of
the Burial Society and Visiting the
Sick Society o[f the] h[oly]
c[ongregation of] Weinberg by the
Gabbai Sender b[en] M.")

לפרט כ"תר ת"ור"ה" ע"ולה" ע"ל
ג"ב"יהן לפק.

("According to the count 'A Torah
Crown carried upon their backs'
[5]583" = 1823; Mish. *Avot* 4:17.)

217.

Pair of Rimmonim
Silver: cast, cut-out, parcel-gilt,
engraved
Berlin: 1788–1802
Marks: Scheffler 11, and an illegible
maker's mark
15¾ x 5⅛₁₆" dm (40 x 13.5 cm)
D 187

218.

Pair of Rimmonim
Silver: cast, cut-out, repoussé,
engraved, parcel-gilt;
brass: cast and engraved
Berlin: 1821–39
Maker: Johann Friedrich Wilhelm
Borcke
Marks: Berlin city mark, Scheffler
18, 1702 (330)
14½ x 3⁵⁄₁₆" dm (36.8 x 8.5 cm)
D 170
Inscriptions: "Danziger Wohl-
tätigkeits-Verein" ("Danzig
Benevolent Society"). "Durch den . . ."
("Through the . . .").

219.

Pair of Rimmonim
Silver: cast, repoussé, parcel-gilt,
cut-out, engraved
Germany: after 1858
Mark: Scheffler 29
14⅛ x 4" dm (35.8 x 10.2 cm)
D 171

220.

Pair of Rimmonim
Silver: cast, repoussé, cut-out,
engraved, parcel-gilt

Germany: 19th century
Marks: none
13 x 3½" dm (33 x 8.8 cm)
D 180

221.

Pair of Rimmonim
Silver: repoussé, cut-out, engraved,
parcel-gilt
Germany: 19th century
Marks: none
12 x 3⅝" dm (30.5 x 9.2 cm)
D 185
Inscription: "W" (sign of the
Weinberg community)

222.

Pair of Rimmonim
Silver: cast, repoussé, cut-out,
engraved, parcel-gilt
Germany: 19th century
Marks: none
20¹¹⁄₁₆ x 5⅞" dm (52.5 x 15 cm)
D 188

223.

Pair of Rimmonim
Silver: cast and cut-out; glass stones
Germany: late 19th-early 20th
century
Marks: none
8¼ x 2¾" dm (21 x 7 cm)
D 182

224.

Pair of Rimmonim
Silver: cast, parcel-gilt, cut-out,
filigree, engraved
Danzig: 1770–1820 with later
additions
Maker: uncertain
Marks: Danzig city mark, and
Czihak² 505 (control mark of
Johann Gottlieb Fischer)
19 x 3¾" dm (48.3 x 9.5 cm)
D 175
Inscriptions: "Dem Andenken ihrer
verstorbenen Eltern I.H. Italiener
gest. d. 2 Decbr. 1893. Friederike
Rosalie Italiener geb. Becker gest. d.
2 Octbr. 1886. gewidmet Danzig d.
2 December 1893." ("In memory of
their departed parents I.H. Italiener
who passed away December 2,
1893. Friederike Rosalie Italiener,
née Becker, who passed away October 2, 1886. dedicated Danzig
December 2, 1893."); "Heinrich,
Julius, Ludwig Italiener."

225.

Pair of Rimmonim
Silver: cast, parcel-gilt, cut-out, filigree
Danzig: 1829–31
Maker: L
Marks: L, Danzig city mark and Czihak² 535 (control mark of Johann Jakob Raths)
13½ x 3″ dm (34 x 7.6 cm)
D 172
Inscriptions:

שייך להחברה קדישא וב"ח דק"ק מאטטענבודען

("This belongs to the Burial Society and [Society for] V[isiting the] S[ick] o[f the] h[oly] c[ongregation of] Mattenbuden");

נעשה ע"י הגבאי ר' חיים אלחנן בר"יי פירשטענבערג בשנת תקצא לפ"ק

("Made for the *Gabbai* Ḥayyim Elḥanan b[en] Y.Y. Fürstenberg in the year [5]591" = 1831.)

226.

Torah Pointer
Silver: cast and engraved
Region of Orléans: 1819–25
Marks: R 6328 and two unreadable marks
11¼ x 1³⁄₁₆″ dm (28.7 x 3 cm)
D 22
Inscriptions:

איצק חנה / תקפה

("Itzig, Hannah / [5]585" = 1825.) "Zum Andenken an seinen Vater geschenkt von: Marcus Goldstein." ("In memory of his father donated by: Marcus Goldstein.")

ת"רמ"ח

("[5] 648" = 1888.)

227.

Torah Pointer
Silver: cast and engraved
Berlin: 1817–60
Maker: Johann August Gebhardt
Marks: Scheffler 1714 (336), an indeterminate Berlin city mark and one unintelligible mark
12 x 1⅜″ dm (30.5 x 3.5 cm)
D 34
Inscription:

שייך לח"ק / נעשה ע"י ר' שלמה י"ס"ט" ו"ר יוזפא ב"ר"מ / בשנת תק"פא לפק

("This belongs to the B[urial] S[ociety]. Made for . . . Solomon Y.S.T. and . . . Yuspa b[en] . . . M. in the year [5]581" = 1821.)

228.

Torah Pointer
Silver: cast, engraved, punched (?)
Berlin: 1821–50
Marks: Scheffler 14 and one unintelligible mark
11³⁄₁₆ x 1³⁄₁₆″ dm (28.3 x 3 cm)
D 36

229.

Torah Pointer
Silver: cast, punched, engraved
Germany: 1809–12
Mark: R 4424
10¾ x 1⅜″ dm (27.3 x 3.5 cm)
D 21
Inscription: "W" (sign of the Weinberg community).

230.

Torah Pointer
Silver: cast, cut-out, engraved
Germany: 1815 (date of inscription)
Marks: none
11 x 1⅜″ dm (27.9 x 3.5 cm)
D 41
Inscription:

ז"נ" ר' אהרון ב"ר"ס" מוויינבערג / בשנת תקעה לפ'ק / לחברה גמילת הריעים / ד'ק'ק' דאנציג

("T[his was] d[onated by] . . . Aaron b[en] . . . M. of Weinberg in the year [5]575"[= 1815] to the Mutual Assistance Society[?] of [the] h[oly] c[ongregation of] Danzig.")

231.

Torah Pointer
Silver: cast and engraved
Germany: 1817 (date of inscription)
Marks: unintelligible
11 x 1⅛″ dm (28 x 2.9 cm)
D 29
Inscription:

זאת נדבו / אלופי חברה קדישה / פה דנציג / ת"ק"ע"ז" לפ"ק

("This was donated by the leaders of the Burial Society here in Danzig [5]577" = 1817.)

232.

Torah Pointer
Silver: cast and engraved

Thorn(?): 18th century(?)
Marks: 10, and an unintelligible mark
13¼ x 1⁷⁄₁₆″ dm (33.7 x 3.7 cm)
D 35
Inscription:

ח"ק" ד"ק"ק" שאטטלאנד

("B[urial] S[ociety] of the h[oly] c[ongregation] of Schottland.")

233.

Torah Pointer
Silver: cast and parcel-gilt
Danzig: 18th-19th century
Maker: Gottfried Wendt
Marks: Danzig city mark, G W (perhaps Czihak² 435) and F(?)M.
6¼ x ¹⁵⁄₁₆″ dm (15.8 x 2.4 cm)
D 51

234.

Torah Pointer
Silver: cast, engraved, punched(?)
Danzig: ca. 1821–28
Maker: Theodor Gottlieb Schulz(?)
Marks: Czihak² 5 or 6, 𝒯𝒮 (529 ?), S (possibly Czihak² 525, control mark of Carl Benjamin Schultz)
11 x 1⁵⁄₁₆″ dm (27.9 x 3.5 cm)
D 40
Inscription: "E.L."

235.

Torah Pointer
Silver: cast and engraved
Danzig: 1822–28
Marks: S (possibly Czihak² 525, control mark of Carl Benjamin Schultz) and traces of another mark
10¼ x 1⁵⁄₁₆″ dm (26 x 3.3 cm)
D 30
Inscription:

זאת נדב ר" איצק ב"ר'ם' גאלדשטיין / להחברה קדישא וב"ח' מאטטענבודען / עבור נשמת אשתו הצנועה / מ" חנה ז"ל תקפו ל'פ'ק

("This was donated by Itzig b[en] M. Goldstein to the Burial Society and V[isiting the] S[ick Society] of Mattenbuden on behalf of the soul of his modest wife Hannah, z.l. [5]586" = 1826.)

236.

Torah Pointer
Brass: cast, openwork, engraved
Danzig: 1834 (date of inscription)

Marks: none
$10\frac{5}{8}$ x $1\frac{9}{16}$″ dm (27 x 4 cm)
D 16
Inscription:

שייך לקהל ד״ק״ק״ מאטענבודען תקצד לפ׳ק׳

("[This] belongs to t[he] h[oly] c[ongregation of] Mattenbuden [5]594" = 1834.)

237.
Torah Pointer
Silver: cast, cut-out, engraved
Danzig: early 19th century
Marks: Czihak[2] 5 and portions of two unintelligible marks
$11\frac{3}{4}$ x $1\frac{7}{16}$″ dm (30 x 3.7 cm)
D 28

238.
Torah Pointer
Silver: cast and engraved
Possibly Hungary: 19th century
Marks: none
$7\frac{11}{16}$ x $1\frac{1}{8}$″ dm (19.5 x 2.9 cm)
D 49
Inscription:

שניאור בר בן ציון / הכהן

("Shneour b[en] . . . Ben Zion the *kohen*.")

239.
Torah Pointer
Silver: cast, engraved, hammered, parcel-gilt; glass stones
Central Europe: 19th century
Marks: none
$12\frac{1}{4}$ x $1\frac{1}{2}$″ dm (31.1 x 3.8 cm)
D 39
Inscription: "W" (sign of Weinberg community).

240.
Torah Pointer
Walnut
Central Europe: 19th century
$9\frac{1}{4}$ x $\frac{7}{8}$″ [width of hand] (23.5 x 2.2 cm)
D 48

241.
Torah Pointer
Silver: cast, parcel-gilt, filigree; Mediterranean coral
Russia: 19th century
Marks: none
$9\frac{1}{2}$ x $1\frac{9}{16}$″ dm (24.1 x 3.9 cm)
D 46

242.
Pair of Rimmonim
Silver: cast, repoussé, cut-out, engraved
Eastern Europe: 19th century
Marks: M and two indecipherable marks
$16\frac{3}{8}$ x 5″ dm (41.5 x 12.7 cm)
D 189
Inscriptions:

כלי קדש לשרת בקדש / לעטרת תפארת תורתינו הקדושה

("Sacred objects to serve, in sanctity, the glory of our holy Torah.")
"Johanna Wollig/geb. Frank/Elkan Levinsohn/Ernestine Levinsohn geb. Wollig." ("Johanna Wollig née Frank, Elkan Levinsohn, Ernestine Levinsohn née Wollig.")

קנו מהונם לכבוד צורם וקונם / לקנין ולנחלה למשפחתם

("Take of their wealth in honor of their Rock and Creator, as an inheritance and a contract for their families.")
"Levin Wollig, Elkan Levinsohn, Ernestine Levinsohn geb. Wollig." ("Levin Wollig, Elkan Levinsohn, Ernestine Levinsohn née Wollig.")

243.
Torah Pointer
Silver: cast and engraved
Europe: before 1888
Marks: none
$11\frac{1}{4}$ x $1\frac{1}{4}$″ dm (28.5 x 3.2 cm)
D 26
Inscription:

שייך לקהל ברייטגאס

("[This] belongs to the community of Breitgasse.")

244.
Torah Pointer
Silver: cast and engraved
Europe: 19th century
Marks: none
$9\frac{1}{8}$ x $1\frac{3}{16}$″ dm (23.2 x 3 cm)
D 27

245.
Torah Pointer
Silver: cast and engraved
Europe: 19th century
Marks: none
$7\frac{3}{8}$ x $\frac{7}{8}$″ dm (18.8 x 2.2 cm)
D 32

246.
Torah Pointer
Silver: cast, engraved, hammered
Europe: 19th century
Marks: none
$11\frac{1}{2}$ x $1\frac{11}{16}$″ dm (29.2 x 4.3 cm)
D 38

247.
Torah Pointer
Silver: cast and engraved
Europe: 19th century
Marks: none
$11\frac{3}{8}$ x $1\frac{3}{4}$″ dm (28.9 x 4.5 cm)
D 42

248.
Torah Pointer
Brass: cast
Europe: 19th century
$7\frac{1}{8}$ x $\frac{5}{8}$″ dm (18.1 x 1.6 cm)
D 45

249.
Torah Pointer
Silver: cast, engraved, parcel-gilt
Europe: 19th century
Marks: none
$10\frac{5}{8}$ x $1\frac{1}{8}$″ dm (27 x 2.9 cm)
D 47
Inscription:

ח״ג

("Holiday").

250.
Torah Pointer
Silver: parcel-gilt, cast, engraved
Europe: probably 19th century
Marks: none
$9\frac{1}{4}$ x $1\frac{5}{16}$″ dm (23.5 x 3.3 cm)
D 18
Inscription: "W" (sign of the Weinberg community).

251.
Torah Pointer
Silver: cast, gilt, engraved
Europe: 19th-20th century
Marks: none
$11\frac{3}{16}$ x $1\frac{5}{16}$″ dm (28.5 x 3.4 cm)
D 20
Inscription: "I. Leburg."

252.
Eternal Light
Silver: cut-out and engraved
Eastern Europe: 18th century(?)

Marks: none
5½ x 5⅝″ dm (14 x 14.3 cm)
D 91

253

Eternal Light
Brass: cast and cut-out
Europe: 19th-20th century
4 x 3¹⁄₁₆″ dm (10.2 x 7.8 cm)
D 92

254

Reproduction of a Carpet Page from Isaac ben Israel's Bible (Leningrad, Public Library, Cod. II 53)
Hand-colored print on paper
7⁵⁄₁₆ x 7″ (21.2 x 17.8 cm)
D 13
This is a reproduction of a carpet page from Isaac ben Israel's quadripartite Bible written in Toledo before 1260. The page was cut from a printed book (see V. Stassof and D. Gunzburg, *L'Ornement Hébreu*, Berlin, 1905, pl. 1).

255.

Book Cover
Velvet; paper; wood; silver: cast, filigree, engraved; niello
Eastern Europe: late 19th century
6⅞ x 4⅞″ (17.5 x 12.5 cm)
D 167
Inscription:

סדור

("Siddur").

256.

Prayer Stand for Kaddish
Brass and copper: repoussé; glass stones; parchment; wood
Danzig: 18th-19th century
13 x 9⅞″ (33 x 25 cm)
D 106

257.

Candelabrum and Sheviti
Brass: cast, engraved, repoussé; wood
Danzig(?): 19th-20th century
21¼ x 17½ x 5¼″
(54 x 44.5 x 13.3 cm)
D 86
Inscriptions:

מזרח

("East");

דע לפני מי אתה עומד

("Know before whom you stand . . .";
var. on Mishnah *Avot* 3:1 and
Mishnah *Berakhot* 28b.)

258.

Memorial Lights Stand for a Synagogue
Brass: cast and repoussé; white metal: cast
Danzig(?): probably 19th century
49 x 16½″ dm (124.5 x 41.9 cm)
D 96

259.

Memorial Lights Stand for a Synagogue
Wood: carved and painted; tin
Danzig(?): 19th-20th century
11 x 16⅜″ dm (27.9 x 41.6 cm)
D 98

260.

Lamp for Memorial Candles
Brass: cast
Danzig: probably 20th century
9½ x 7″ (24.1 x 17.8 cm)
D 212

261.

Light Stand for Memorial Candles
Brass; wood
Poland: 19th century
13 x 24⅞ x 16⅛″
(33 x 63.2 x 41 cm)
D 99

262.

Memorial Plaque
Marble: engraved, painted, gilded
Danzig: 1918
63 x 46¾ x 1″ (160 x 118 x 2.5 cm)
D 284
Inscriptions: "1914 Im Weltkrieg 1918 starben aus unserer Gemeinde fürs Vaterland/Deine Toten Werden Leben. Jes. 2.19." ("1914 in World War I 1918 died from our community for the fatherland 'Oh, let Your dead revive' Is. 26:19.") Followed by 56 names of the dead.

ת.נ.צ.ב.ה

("M[ay their] s[ouls] be b[ound up] in [Eternal] life"; memorial prayer, *El mole' rahamim.*)

263 a,b.

Covered Urn and Basin
Copper: engraved
Danzig: 1819

Vessel: 15½ x 25 x 18¼″
(39.4 x 63.5 x 46.2 cm)
Urn: 31⅛ x 16½″ (79 x 42 cm)
D 301/303
Inscription on vessel:

נעשה / ע״י ר״ ליזר ברם גד״חק.

("Made f[or] Leiser b[en] M. G[abbai] of [the] B[urial] S[ociety].")
Inscription on urn: between the handles,

ז״נ / האלופים דח״ק / שנת תק״עט ל

("T[his was] d[onated by] the heads of the B[urial] S[ociety] the year [5] 579" = 1819.)

264.

Banner for the Synagogue
Beige striped silk with silk and metallic embroidery; silk brocade with metallic threads; velvet, metallic fringe and braid; glass stones; stumpwork with metallic threads and foil; wood
Danzig: 18th century
26¼ x 31½″ (66.7 x 80 cm)
D 272
Inscription:

זר [כך!] הדגל / לכבוד התורה.

("This is the flag in honor of the Torah.")

265 a,b

Pair of Plaques in form of Kohen's Blessing Hands
Brass: repoussé and engraved
Europe: 19th century(?)
15¾ x 4″ (14.5 x 10 cm)
D 287 a,b

266.

Chandelier
Brass: cast
Germany or Poland: 18th century
14⅝ x 12¼″ dm (37.2 x 31.1 cm)
D 95

267.

Pair of Wall Sconces
Brass: cast
Danzig(?): 19th century
11 x 6¾ x 26¾″ (28 x 17.5 x 68 cm)
D 332 a,b

268.

Pair of Wall Sconces
Brass: cast

Danzig(?): 19th century
10½ x 16½ x 15¾"
(27 x 41.5 x 40 cm)
D 333 a,b

269.
Pair of Wall Sconces
Brass: cast
Danzig(?): 19th century
13¾ x 21 x 16¼" (35 x 53 x 41 cm)
D 334 a,b

270.
Pair of Sconces
Silver: cast
Danzig: before 1910
Marks: Danzig city mark, B & R,
93 a: R**, 93b *R*
5 x 5½ x 10" (12.7 x 14 x 25.4 cm)
D 93 a,b

271.
Pair of Candlesticks
Brass
Probably Danzig: 19th century
6⅝ x 3⅛" dm (16.8 x 8 cm)
D 101 a,b

272.
Pair of Candlesticks
Brass on wood: partly silvered
Danzig(?): 19th century
30¹¹⁄₁₆ x 8 x 8½"
(78 x 20.3 x 21.6 cm)
D 103 a,b

273.
Pair of Candlesticks
White metal: cast; silver
Moscow(?): 18th-19th century
Mark: double-headed eagle in square
field (variation of Verzeichnis 449)
21¼ x 6¹¹⁄₁₆" dm (54 x 17 cm)
D 105 a,b

274.
Alms Dish
Silver: cast and engraved
Berlin: 1821-39
Maker: Johann Friedrich Wilhelm
Borcke
Marks: Scheffler 14, 18, 1702 (330)
6⅜ x 5⁷⁄₁₆" dm (16.2 x 13.8 cm)
D 226
Inscriptions:

("Congregation Schottland");

קהל שאטלאנד

נעשה עפ״י הגבאים ר׳ יוזפא ב״רב ור׳
וואלף מענדלסואן ב״צדק״ה ת״כ״ו״נ״נ״י
לפק

("Made for the *Gabbaim* Yuspa b. B.
and Wolf Mendelsohn 'You shall be
established through righteousness
. . . ' "; Is. 54:14 = [5]538 = 1878.)

275.
Alms Dish ?
Silver: cast and engraved; wood
Germany: early 19th century
Marks: 12, illegible second mark
4½ x 3⅛" dm (11.4 x 8 cm)
D 232
Inscription:

זאת נדב ר׳ איצק ב״ר״ם גאלדשטיין
להחברה קדישא וב״ח״ מאטענבודען
עבור נשמת אביו ר׳ משה ב״ר׳ מרדכי
ז״ל / תקפח לפ״ק

("This was donated by . . . Itzig
b[en] . . . M. Goldstein to the Burial
Society and [Society for] V[isiting
the] S[ick of] Mattenbuden in
memory of his father Moses b[en]
Mordekhai . . . [5]588" = 1828.)

276.
Alms Dish ?
Silver: cast and engraved
Danzig: 1713–56
Maker: Benjamin Berent
Marks: Czihak² 5, 430 and Ⓢ
1¼ x 5⁹⁄₁₆" dm (3.1 x 14.1 cm)
D 230
Inscription:

שייך להחברא קדישא ג״ח״ וב״ח״ דק״ק
האפנברוג לפרט ב״לע״ המי״ות״ לנצח

("Belongs to the Burial Society,
B[enevolent] S[ociety] and [the
Society for] V[isiting the] S[ick] of
the h[oly] c[ongregation of] Happen-
bruch; to the count 'He will destroy
death forever' "; Is. 25:8 =
[5]512 = 1752.)

277.
Alms Dish ?
Silver: cast and engraved; wood
Danzig (?): 1804 (date of inscrip-
tion)
Marks: none
6⅞ x 3⅛" dm (17.5 x 8 cm)
D 231

Inscription:

שייך לאלופי׳ דח״ק וג״ח דק״ק שאטלנד
לפרט תק״סד ל״פק

("Belongs to the heads of the B[urial]
S[ociety] and B[envolent] S[ociety] of
the h[oly] c[ongregation of] Schottland, to the count [5]564" = 1804.)

278.
Alms Box
Silver: cast and engraved
Danzig: 1809-13
Maker: Johann Gottlieb Ulrich
Marks: Czihak² 3, 526, 515
6⅜ x 3¹¹⁄₁₆" dm (16.2 x 9.4 cm)
D 223
Inscriptions:

שייך / לחברה גמולת [כך!] חסדים /
דמאטענבודען / פ״ה / דאנציג.

("Belongs to the Benevolent Society
of Mattenbuden here [in] Danzig");

לחסד ולרחמים / בעיניו ובעיני כל רואינו /
לפרט / ות׳גמלנ״ו חס״ד״י״י״ם״ / טובים /
לפק

(". . . favor and mercy both in your
sight and in the sight of all men by
the count and bestow loving kind-
ness on us" = [5]574 = 1814; from
the morning service);

ונעשה ע״י הגבאים / ר׳ אברהם ברוך
בר״ה / ור׳ איצק גאלדשטיין / תקעד.

("and made for the *Gabbaim*
Avraham Barukh b. H. and Itzig b.
M. Goldstein [5]574" = 1814.)

279.
Alms Dish
Silver: engraved
Danzig: 1814-19
Maker: MLITZ (?)
Marks: Czihak² 5, MLITZ, Czihak²
532 (control mark of Carl Stumpf)
¹⁵⁄₁₆ x 4⅞" dm (2.4 x 12.4 cm)
D 225
Inscription at center of dish in cir-
cular cartouche:

להעלות / נר תמיד / לפני ה׳.

(". . . to maintain lights regularly
. . . before the Lord . . ."; Lev.
24:2-3.) Inscription surrounding the
cartouche:

נעשה ע״י׳ הגבאי ר׳ אלחנן ב״ר״ם
מאנקעוויטש.

("Made for the *Gabbai* Elḥanan
b[en] R[eb] M[oshe] Mankewich.")

280.

Alms Dish ?
Silver: engraved
Danzig: 1822
Marks: Czihak² 2, 𝒯𝒮 (529 ?), S
(possibly Czihak² 525, control mark
of Carl Benjamin Schultz)
Maker: Theodor Gottlieb Schulz(?)
6⁵⁄₁₆ x 4⅝" dm (17.6 x 11.7 cm)
D 241
Inscription:

נעשה / יום א'' ב'' דח'''המ סוכות / ושייך
לבה''כנ נ''ל תק''פב / לפק.

("Made Sunday, the second day of
H[ol] HaM[oed] Sukkot and belongs
to the . . . s[ynagogue] [5]582"
= 1822.)

281.

Alms Dish
Silver: cast and engraved
Danzig: 1800–25 (?)
Marks: 𝒯𝒮 , 12, and one
unintelligible mark
1³⁄₁₆ x 4⅞" dm (2.2 x 12.4 cm)
D 235
Inscriptions:

שייך לחברה קדישה / וב'ח' דמב / שנת
תקפז לפק.

("Belongs to the Burial Society and
[Society for] V[isiting the] S[ick] of
M[atten] b[uden] the year [5]587"
= 1827.)

נעשה ע''י הגבאים ר'' אברהם ברוך בלוהם
ור'' איצק גאלדשטיין.

("Made for the *Gabbaim* Avraham
Barukh Bluhm and Itzig Goldstein.")

282.

Plaque with Star Appliqué
Wood; brass
Germany: 19th century
18½ x 9¼" (47 x 23.5 cm)
D 299

283.

Beaker
Pewter: engraved
Elbing: ca. 1737
Maker: Christian Kohlenberg
Mark: Hintze³ 457
4½ x 3⅝" dm (11.5 x 9.75 cm)
D 294

284.

Tankard
Pewter: engraved

Elbing: 1793 (date of inscription)
Maker: Johann Daniel Deveer
Marks: Hintze³ 462
9½ x 5⅝" (24.5 x 14.5 cm)
D 293
Inscription: "Vivat Es Leben Die
Zinn Gièszer Gesellen in
Elbing/Stiffter Diese Kanne Johann
David Schweitzer v. Tilsit/Daniel
Gottfried Deveer v. Elbing 1793."
("Long live the Members of the
Pewter Pourers Guild in Elbing/This
tankard was donated by Johann
David Schweitzer of Tilsit/Daniel
Gottfried Deveer of Elbing 1793.")

285.

Dish
Silver: cast and repoussé
Danzig: 1761
Maker: Simon Gottlieb Unger
Marks: Czihak² 5, 469, L (perhaps
461, control mark of Johann
Constantin Lange)
4 x 5¾ x 1¼" (10 x 15 x 3 cm)
D 233

286.

Dish
Pewter
Germany: 1763
Mark: Crowned rosette enclosing a
woman holding a standard(?) and
the date 1763; initials D. W.
5¾" dm (14.5 cm)
D 227

287.

Stand
Brass: cast, cut-out, engraved; iron
Near East: 19th century
8⅞ x 18¾" dm (22.5 x 47.6 cm)
D 114b

288.

Fragment of a Larger Object
Silver: cast, repoussé, cut-out,
parcel-gilt
Europe: 19th century(?)
Marks: none
4½ x 2" dm (11.4 x 5 cm)
D 200

Table of Concordance
of Danzig Catalogues

EXHIBITION NO.	CATALOGUE 1904	CATALOGUE 1933	JEWISH MUSEUM NO. D
1.	100	11	153
2.	98	13	152
3.	99	14	154
4 a-d.	99	14	157-60
5.			161
6.			250
7.		116	116
8.		120	268
9.	101	62	305
10.		121	280
11.		120	279
12.	75	86	81
13.	74	85	85
14.	1	1	1
15.	4	136	276
16.			277
17.	23	126	151
18.	18	54	54
19 a-c.	39		274, 273, 104 a,b
20.	90	2	2
21.	91	3	3
22.	92	4	4
23.			10
24.	77	109	94
25.			65
26.	45	64	64
27.			70
28.			F 4276
29.			66
30.	52	20	197
31.	49	17	191
32.	50	18	190
33.	48	16	193

EXHIBITION NO.	CATALOGUE 1904	CATALOGUE 1933	JEWISH MUSEUM NO. D
34.	47	15	192
35.	51	19	195
36.	57	117	117
37.		119	107
38.		10	269
39.			270
40.	56	33	74
41.	84	26	290
42.	84	26	201
43.	83	25	206
44.	86	28	202
45.	85	27	207
46.			211
47.			213
48.	62	76	76
49.	79	112	112
50.		113	113
51.	81	115	115
52.	80	114	114 a
53.			283
54.		102	248
55.	5	155	262
56.	10	160	267
57.			254
58.			256
59.			136
60.	19	122	122
61.			134
62.		147 a	150
63.		138 b	146
64.			139
65.		.144 a	148
66.		144 a	142
67.		146 a	133
68.		143 a	143
69.			126
70.		137 a	137

EXHIBITION NO.	CATALOGUE 1904	CATALOGUE 1933	JEWISH MUSEUM NO. D
71.	28	131	131
72.			149
73.		58	58
74.		138 c	61
75.			62
76.	15	53	53
77.	14	52	52
78.		59	59
79.		143 b	184 a,b
80.			173 a,b
81.			174 a,b
82.		146 b	181
83.	13	105	176
84.		108	183
85.			177 a,b
86.			186
87.			23
88.			24
89.		143 c	19
90.			25
91.		147 c	31
92.		147 c	37
93.		137 c	33
94.	30	43	43
95.		50	50
96.		47	17
97.	31	44	44
98.	42	90	90
99.	65	34	168
100.			289
101.	67	36	163
102.	66	35	169
103.			164
104.	39		165
105.		40	281
106.	69	39	282
107.	46	65	109

EXHIBITION NO.	CATALOGUE 1904	CATALOGUE 1933	JEWISH MUSEUM NO. D
108.		134	108
109.		89	89
110.		88	88
111.	76	87	87
112 a,b.		154	300, 302
113.	2	93	271
114.	126, 127		97 a,b
115.	118-123	68	100
116.	116	92	288
117.	107	163	217
118.			221
119.			220
120.			219
121.			222
122.			218
123.	104	161	238
124.			237
125.	98	13	162
126.			229
127.			224
128.			228
129.			236
130.	108	164	234
131.			166
132.			292
133.			295
134.			73
135.			9
136 a,b.			11
137.	98	13	156
138.		95	257
139.	71	82	82
140.	72	83	83
141.	73	84	84
142.	89	135	291
143.	96	8	8
144.	93	5	5

136

EXHIBITION NO.	CATALOGUE 1904	CATALOGUE 1933	JEWISH MUSEUM NO. D
145 a,b.	95	7	7 a,b
146.			12
147.			68
148.			69
149.			67
150.	44	63	63
151.	54	22	194
152.	55	23	196
153.	53	21	198
154.			199
155.			120
156.			119
157.	58	118	118
158.			72
159.			71
160.		31	208
161.			205
162.		32	215
163.			214
164.	88	30	216
165.			210
166.			203
167.	87	29	209
168.	40	67	102
169.			204
170.		166	239
171.		167	240
172.			75
173.			78
174.	63	77	77
175.			80
176.		79	79
177.			111
178.			275
179.		100	246
180.		103	278

EXHIBITION NO.	CATALOGUE 1904	CATALOGUE 1933	JEWISH MUSEUM NO. D
181.		98	244
182.			258
183.			243
184.			263
185.		99	245
186.			242
187.		101	247
188.			249
189.			251
190.	6	156	264
191.	7/8	157/158	265/66
192.			259
193.			261
194.			255
195.			253
196.	21	124	124
197.	27	130	130
198.		141 a	141
199.		138 b	138
200.			135
201.			145
202.			140
203.			147
204.	20	123	123
205.		132	132
206.			144
207.	22	125	125
208.	26	129	129
209.	24	127	127
210.	94	6	6
211.		56	56
212.		60	60
213.		57	57
214.	17	55	55
215 a,b.		142 b	178
216 a,b.		145 b	179

EXHIBITION NO.	CATALOGUE 1904	CATALOGUE 1933	JEWISH MUSEUM NO. D
217 a,b.			187
218.		144 b	170
219.			171
220.			180
221.			185
222.		107	188
223.			182
224.		147 b	175
225.		106	172
226.			22
227.		146 c	34
228.			36
229.			21
230.		138 d	41
231.		141 c	29
232.		140 c	35
233.	37	49	51
234.			40
235.			30
236.		48	16
237.			28
238.			49
239.			39
240.			48
241.	33	46	46
242.		141 b	189
243.			26
244.			27
245.			32
246.			38
247.			42
248.	32	45	45
249.	35	47	47
250.			18
251.			20
252.			91

EXHIBITION NO.	CATALOGUE 1904	CATALOGUE 1933	JEWISH MUSEUM NO. D
253.		91	92
254.	97		13
255.	70	38	167
256.		133	106
257.			86
258.	43	70	96
259.		73	98
260.			212
261.		71	99
262.			284
263.		154	301/303
264.			272
265.			287 a,b
266.		110	95
267 a,b.			332 a,b
268.			333 a,b
269.	124-125	148	334 a,b
270.			93 a,b
271.			101 a,b
272.		69	103 b
273.			105 a,b
274.			226
275.			232
276.			230
277.			231
278.			223
279.			225
280.			241
281.			235
282.			299
283.			294
284.			293
285.		168	233
286.			227
287.	80	114	114 b
288.			200

Bibliography
of Frequently Cited Sources

Beauty in Holiness   *Beauty in Holiness: Studies in Jewish Customs and Ceremonial Art,* ed. J. Gutmann, New York, 1970.

Berger, *Judaica*   Berger, M., W. Häusler, E. Lessing, *Judaica: Die Sammlung Berger,* Munich, 1979.

Barnett   Barnett, R. D., *Catalogue of The Jewish Museum London,* London, 1974.

Czihak   Czihak, E. von, *Die Edelschmiede-kunst früherer Zeiten in Preussen,* I, Leipzig, 1903; II, Leipzig, 1908.

Danzig, 1904   *Katalog der alten jüdischen Kultusge-genstände Gieldzinski-Stiftung in der Neuen Synagoge zu Danzig,* Danzig, 1904.

Danzig, 1933   *Sammlung jüdischer Kunstge-genstände der Synagogen-Gemeinde zu Danzig,* Danzig, 1933.

Hintze   Hintze, E., *Die Deutschen Zinn-giesser und ihre Marken,* I-VII, Leipzig, 1921-31.

Hintze, *Katalog*   Hintze, E., *Katalog der vom Verein "Jüdisches Museum in Breslau" . . . veranstalteten Ausstellung "Das Ju-dentum in der Geschichte Schlesiens,"* Breslau, 1929.

Kanof, *Ceremonial Art*   Kanof, A., *Ceremonial Art in the Judaic Tradition,* exhibition cata-logue, North Carolina Museum of Art, Raleigh, 1975.

Kayser-Schoenberger   Kayser, S. and Schoenberger, G., *Jewish Ceremonial Art,* 2nd ed., Philadelphia, 1959.

Lepszy   Lepszy, L., *Przemysł Złotniczy w Polsce,* Cracow, 1929.

Monumenta Judaica   Kölnisches Stadtmuseum, *Monu-menta Judaica. 2000 Jahre Ge-schichte und Kultur der Juden am Rhein,* exhibition catalogue, Col-ogne, 1963-64.

Narkiss, *Menorat ha-Hanukkah*   Narkiss, M., *Menorat ha-Hanuk-kah,* Jerusalem, 1939.

Parke-Bernet, *Feinberg Collection*   Parke-Bernet Galleries, New York, *The Charles E. Feinberg Collection of Valuable Judaica,* sales catalogue, November 29-30, 1967.

R   Rosenberg, M., *Der Goldschmiede Merkzeichen,* 3rd ed., I-III, Frankfurt-am-Main, 1922-25; IV, Berlin, 1928.

Scheffler   Scheffler, W., *Berliner Gold-schmiede: Daten, Werke, Zeichen,* Berlin, 1968.

Shachar, *The Jewish Year*   Shachar, I., *The Jewish Year,* Leiden, 1975.

Shachar, *Osef Feuchtwanger*   Shachar I., *Osef Feuchtwanger,* Jerusalem, 1971.

Synagoga   Historisches Museum Frankfurt am Main, *Synagoga Jüdische Altertümer Handschriften und Kultgeräte,* exhibition catalogue, Frankfurt-am-Main, 1961.

Verzeichnis   Slavisches Institut München, *Verzeichnis der Russischen Gold- und Silbermarken,* Munich-Autenried, 1971.

Color Photograph Credits

Malcolm Varon. Cat. Nos. 6, 11, 30, 31, 33, 45, 55, 61.

Black-and-White Photograph Credits

Ambur Hiken. Cat. Nos. 1, 2, 4, 5, 9, 10, 12, 14-21, 23-29, 32, 35-44, 46-51, 53, 54, 56, 57, 59, 60, 62-68.

Bob Zucker. Cat. Nos. 8, 13, 22.

Frank J. Darmstaedter. Cat. Nos. 6, 10, 39, 58, 86.

Wide World Photos, Inc. Pg. No. 11.

Black Star. Pg. Nos. 7, 8, 23, 30, 32.

Preis 20 P (in Polen 25 gr.)

JÜDISCHES GEMEINDEBLATT

Herausgegeben von der Synagogen-Gemeinde zu Danzig

Verantwortl. Schriftleitung: Dr. Curt Itzig, Gemeinde-
büro, Heumarkt 6, Telefon 22957. Verantwortlich für
den Inseratenteil sowie alleinige Inseraten-Annahme:
Freitag, 14. April 1939

Leo Salomon, Hundegasse 103², telefonisch erreichbar
unter 27903. Redaktionsschluß: Dienstag 16 Uhr. Druck:
Buchdruckerei u. Verlagsanstalt A. Fooken, Hopfengasse 71
XI. Jahrgang Nr. 30

Das Ende der Großen Synagoge.

Am 2. April 1933 fand in der Großen Synagoge an der Reitbahn ein Festgottesdienst aus
Anlaß des 50 jährigen Bestehens der Synagogen-Gemeinde statt. Fast auf den Tag sechs
Jahre danach findet der letzte Gottes-
dienst in diesem Hause statt. Der Sabbath nach Pessach vereint zum letzten Male die Danziger Juden an dieser Stätte, die ein Symbol ihres Auf-
stiegs, ihrer Einheit und ihrer Stärke
war. Mit der Gemeinde sinkt auch ihr
stolzer Tempel in den Schutt, seine
Zeit ist dahin, nachdem seine Träger
sich in alle Welt zerstreut haben.
·¹·ine Geschichte begann mit der Ge-
Jud·
schichte des einheitlichen Gemeinde
und sie endet mit ihr.

. Es leben nicht mehr viele unter
uns, die bei der Gründung der Ein-
heitsgemeinde im Jahre 1883 und der
Einweihung der Großen Synagoge am
15. September 1887, mit denen der
Name Gustav Davidsohns un-
trennbar verknüpft ist, zugegen
waren. Aber auch die, welche dieses
Gotteshaus bereits als etwas Fertiges
vorfanden, sahen zu ihm als dem
schwer errungenen Mittelpunkt des
Gemeindelebens auf, dessen Anlage
und Architektur bereits kennzeich-
nend waren für die Stellung der Juden in der Stadt Danzig. War es doch
der Wunsch der damaligen städtischen
Behörden der die Synagoge an diese
prominente Stelle der sich ausdeh-
nenden Stadt ins volle Licht der Oei-
fentlichkeit rückte; ihr Wunsch war
es, daß dieselbe Baufirma sie errich-
tete, die das Volkstagsgebäude, das
damalige Landeshaus erbaut hatte,
und ihr Wille ging dahin, sie architek-
tonisch weitergehend dem einheimi-
schen Baustil anzupassen, als dies sonst
irgendwo in deutschen Landen geschah. Wie die
Juden der Gesamtbevölkerung, so sollte ihre
Synagoge dem Stadtbild harmonisch eingeglie-
dert sein. Und so will es die geschichtliche

Konsequenz, daß in der Epoche der Ausgliede-
rung der Juden aus der Gesamtbevölkerung
auch diese Synagoge aus dem Stadtbild aus-
gemerzt wird.

Wen auch immer wir in all den Jahren ins
Innere dieses Gotteshauses führten, wenn er als
Fremder bei uns zu Besuch weilte, — er
drückte seine Bewunderung über die Weihe des
Inneren aus, über diese Vereinigung von Er-

habenheit und Schlichtheit, die für unsere Synagoge charakteristisch war. Es gab gewiß grö-
ßere Tempel, prächtigere Gotteshäuser, kost-
bareren Schmuck in Form und Material, aber
ihnen allen fehlte die Wärme, die
Innigkeit, die bei aller Größe von dem
einfachen Backstein und der reichen
Verwendung des Holzes ausging. Sanft
fiel das Licht durch die schönen Fen-
ster, der Raum atmete eine Stimmung
der Ruhe und der Sammlung, der sich
niemand entziehen konnte.

Hier hatten sie gestanden, die
Wortführer der Gemeinde, die Rabbi-
ner und Kantoren, und hatten in Rede
und Gebet die Andächtigen erei-
tert, aufgerichtet und getröstet. Hus-
man Werner war der ers' Rab-
biner gewesen, der von diese Kanzel
sprach; seine Rednergabe euchtete
denen, die den Ausgang des 19. Jahrhunderts in Danzig erlebt hatten, noch
lange in der Erinnerung nach. Der
jüngeren Generation verknüpfte sich
diese Kanzel vor allem mit der Ge-
stalt des Mannes, der am längsten,
18 Jahre hindurch der lebendige Mittelpunkt des Danziger Judentums gewesen war: Robert Kaelter. Wie
oft müssen wir heute, da die Auswan-
derung zur beherrschenden Aufgabe
geworden ist, gerade seiner und seiner Leistung in schweren Kriegs- und
Nachkriegszeiten gedenken.

Und in diesem Hause, dem großen
Versammlungshause der Danziger Juden, sprachen in den letzten Jahren
Führer des Judentums, ein Martin
Buber, ein Leo Baeck und andere
Männer, deren Wort entflammte und
klärte. Die edle Kunst synagogaler
Musik stellte sich an dieser Stätte in
den Dienst der Wohltätigkeit, und nicht zuletzt
war hier der Ort, wo unserer Toten in Kriegs-
und Friedenszeiten gedacht wurde.

Das alles wird nun nicht mehr sein. Die
Menschen, die in diesen Räumen sich versam-

Das Ende der Grossen Synagoge *(The End of the Great Synagogue).*

Dedication of the Langfuhr Synagogue in Danzig.

Jewish school children—
it was the custom for mothers to give cornucopias of candy on the first day of school in Danzig.

"All the News That's Fit to Print."

The New York Times.

Copyright, 1939, by The New York Times Company.

EXTRA

Partly cloudy at 3 somewhat warmer today. Tomorrow generally fair with moderate temperatures.

Temperatures Yesterday—Max. 67, Min. 61

VOL. LXXXVIII....No. 29,805.

NEW YORK, FRIDAY, SEPTEMBER 1, 1939.

THREE CENTS NEW YORK CITY | FOUR CENTS Elsewhere Except in 7th and 8th Postal Zones

GERMAN ARMY ATTACKS POLAND; CITIES BOMBED, PORT BLOCKADED; DANZIG IS ACCEPTED INTO REICH

BRITISH MOBILIZING

Navy Raised to Its Full Strength, Army and Air Reserves Called Up

PARLIAMENT IS CONVOKED

Midnight Meeting Is Held by Ministers—Negotiations Admitted Failure

By The Associated Press.

LONDON, Friday, Sept. 1.—The British Parliament was summoned to meet today at 5 P M [12 noon in New York].

British Call Up Forces

By FERDINAND KUHN Jr.
Special Cable to THE NEW YORK TIMES.

LONDON, Friday, Sept. 1.—All attempts to bring about direct negotiations between Germany and Poland appeared to have broken down tonight as Great Britain mobilized her fleet to full strength, stretched her other defenses, preparations close to the limit and began moving 3,000,000 school children and invalids from the crowded cities into the safety of the country-side.

Censorship was established everywhere after London had cut off for three hours from communication with the continent.

It was the peak of the crisis, but a day of rumors had not shifted the fundamental issue nor given a conclusive answer to the question of peace or war.

At midnight the British Government was not yet convinced that Germany really intended to attack Poland and provoke a world war.

Terms Called Smoke Screen

All that had happened during yesterday, including the sudden broadcasting of Chancellor Hitler's sixteen-point demands, was interpreted here as a smoke screen rather than the flash of guns.

Continued on Page Four

DALADIER SUMMONS CABINET TO CONFER

News of Attack on Poland Spurs Prompt Action—Military Move Thought Likely

By The Associated Press.

PARIS, Friday, Sept. 1.—Edouard Daladier, Premier and War Minister of France, informed that German troops crossed the Polish frontier today, summoned an urgent meeting of his Cabinet for 10:30 A M.

It was probable that Parliament would be called later.

Reports of the German invasion came from Berlin and from the Polish Embassy here. The Ministers were called to the Elysee Palace to meet with President Albert Lebrun.

Upon receipt of word of the German operations M. Daladier dashed to the War Ministry and called General Marie Gustave Gamelin, supreme commander of land and air forces, into consultation.

A little later Daladier summoned Foreign Minister Georges Bonnet.

The Polish Embassy said that Germans violated the Polish frontier at dawn at the same time it characterized German charges that Poles had crossed into Germany as "pure invention."

Continued on Page Four

Bulletins on Europe's Conflict

London Hears of Warsaw Bombing

LONDON, Friday, Sept. 1 (AP).—Reuters British news agency said it had learned from Polish sources in Paris that Warsaw was bombed today.

French Confirm Beginning of War

PARIS, Friday, Sept. 1 (AP).—The Havas news agency said today that official French dispatches from Germany indicated that "the Reich began hostilities on Poland this morning."

The agency also reported that the Polish Embassy here had announced that "Germany violated the Polish frontier at four points."

"German reports of pretended violation of German territory by Poland are pure invention, as is the fable of 'attack' by Polish insurgents on Gleiwitz," the embassy announcement said.

Attack on Entire Front Reported

LONDON, Friday, Sept. 1.—A Reuters dispatch from Paris said:

"The following is given with all reserve: According to unconfirmed reports received here, the Germans have begun an offensive with extreme violence on the whole Polish front."

First Wounded Brought Into Gleiwitz

GLEIWITZ, Germany, Friday, Sept. 1 (AP).—An army ambulance carrying wounded soldiers arrived at the emergency hospital here today at 9:10 A. M.

The men, carried in a wagon, were on stretchers. One had on a first aid field bandage. It could not be ascertained where the ambulance came from.

At about 9:30 a half-mile long truck train manned by the engineering corps drove through the heart of the city with pontoon bridge building material. In the tram were caterpillar tread, twenty-passenger motor vans.

Obviously the train had been on the road for a considerable time. All equipment was thickly covered with gray mud.

A scouting plane of the air force was patrolling an area over Gleiwitz.

Early today Gleiwitz residents reported that artillery fire

Continued on Page Four

BRITISH CHILDREN TAKEN FROM CITIES

3,000,000 Persons Are in First Evacuation Group, Which Is to Be Moved Today

By FREDERICK T. BIRCHALL
Special Cable to THE NEW YORK TIMES.

LONDON, Friday, Sept. 1.—The greatest mass movement of population at short notice in the history of Great Britain is under way. It is an evacuation, under government order, of little children, invalids, women and old men from non-safe areas.

From London, Birmingham, Manchester, Liverpool, Edinburgh, Glasgow and twenty-three other cities the great exodus is going on as this dispatch is being written. The numbers are stupendous. More than 3,000,000 of these helpless human beings are being taken out of danger of German bombs.

Nothing like it has ever been attempted anywhere; yet it is going on without mishap so far, indeed, without serious confusion.

Even everywhere were men whose whether in the aristocratic West End or the proletarian East Side, but one that this correspondent

Continued on Page Five

Soviet Ratifies Reich Non-Aggression Pact; Gibes at British and French Amuse Deputies

By G. E. R. GEDYE

MOSCOW, Aug. 31.—With Premier and Foreign Commissar Vyacheslaff M. Molotoff, working under high pressure—as routinely applied without any previous indication and contrasting to sharply with earlier delaying tactics this week as to suggest German insistence that the matter be finally settled—the Supreme Soviet [Parliament] tonight unanimously ratified the Russo-German non-aggression pact.

Ratification, which was first foreshadowed at midday, was preceded by a speech by Mr. Molotoff in which he delivered the definition of Soviet obligations to refrain from participating on the side of Great Britain and France in any war against Germany, in veiled language against German collaboration.

HOSTILITIES BEGUN

Warsaw Reports German Offensive Moving on Three Objectives

ROOSEVELT WARNS NAVY

Also Notifies Army Leaders of Warfare—Envoys Tell of Bombing of 4 Cities

By JERZY SZAPIRO
Wireless to THE NEW YORK TIMES.

WARSAW, Poland, Friday, Sept. 1.—War began at 5 o'clock this morning with German planes attacking Gdynia, Cracow and Katowice.

At Gdynia three bombs exploded in the sea.

The regular German Army started an offensive in the direction of Dzialdowa in Upper Silesia and Czestochowa. The German plan apparently is to cut off Western Poland along the line of Dzialdowa-Lodz-Czestochowa.

The offensive is developing, from East Prussia, toward Rhine and northwards from Slovakia.

At 5 o'clock an attempt was made to bombard Warsaw. The planes, however, did not reach even the suburbs.

A military attack on the garrison at Westerplatte in the Danzig area was repulsed.

The Foreign Office at 8:45 A. M. issued a communiqué saying that military action had begun in Westerplatte in the Danzig area as well as in Bie-known near Gdynia, and at Czestochowa, Chojnice and Lawa.

Hostilities have begun and Poland has been attacked, said the communiqué.

Three cities in Upper Silesia suffered artillery bombardment, particulars of which are lacking, it was said.

While this dispatch was being telephoned, the air-raid sirens sounded in Warsaw.

Danzig Fighting Reported

WARSAW, Poland, Friday, Sept. 1 (AP).—It was reported today that Tczew and Czestochowa were bombed by German airplanes early this morning.

There was no official confirmation of the bombing.

Fighting was reported at Danzig and attacked Polish defenses near Mlawa, bordering the southern part of East Prussia.

There was no announcement of the damage resulting from the bombing. Mist and clouds were overhanging the city. A light drizzle apparently afforded momentary protection against air raids. Warsaw went to work as usual.

Roosevelt Warns Navy

WASHINGTON, Friday, Sept. 1 (AP).—President Roosevelt directed today that all naval ships and army commands be notified at once by radio of German-Polish hostilities. The White House issued the following announcement:

"The President received word at 2:50 A. M. Eastern standard time

Continued on Page Five

FREE CITY IS SEIZED

Forster Notifies Hitler of Order Putting Danzig Into the Reich

ACCEPTED BY CHANCELLOR

Poles Ready, Made Their Preparations After Hostilities Appeared Inevitable

Special Cable to THE NEW YORK TIMES.

DANZIG, Friday, Sept. 1.—By a decree issued early this morning Albert Forster, Nazi Chief of State, proclaimed the annexation of the Free City to the Reich, thus settling by a fell stroke the original point of contention in the international crisis.

In a telegram to Chancellor Hitler Herr Forster explained his action as necessary to remove "the pressing necessity of our people and State." Herr Forster also issued a proclamation to the people of Danzig saying the hour awaited for twenty years had arrived because "our Fuehrer, Adolf Hitler, has freed us."

[A New York Times dispatch from Berlin this morning said Herr Hitler telegraphed Herr Forster today thanking him and all Danzigers, and stating:

"The law for reannexation is in effect immediately."

The Chancellor stated, furthermore, that Herr Forster was appointed head of the civil administration of the Danzig area.]

In a front-article decree Herr Forster declared the Constitution of Danzig no longer valid. He declared himself sole administrator of the Danzig part of the German Reich, and he declared that until the Reich's legal system had been introduced by command of Herr Hitler all laws except the Constitution remained in effect. Then Herr Forster immediately wired Herr Hitler of his action, begged the Chancellor to give his approval of the move and through Reich law complete the annexation.

The German flag is now flying everywhere over Danzig. Herr Forster and, and 11 church bells resound in the event. "Soldiers of God," he declared, "that He gave the Fuehrer the strength and the possibility to free also us from the evil Versailles treaty."

Hitler Accepts Danzig

By The Associated Press.

BERLIN, Friday, Sept. 1.—The German official news agency, D. N. B., announced today that Albert Forster, Nazi Chief of State in Danzig, had proclaimed the reunion of the Free City with the Reich.

Herr Hitler today accepted the Free City of Danzig into the Reich. "I acknowledge your proclamation of the return of the Free City of Danzig to the Reich," Herr Hitler's telegram said. "I thank you, Gauleiter Forster, and all Danzig men and women, for your loyalty where you have displayed for so many years.

"Greater Germany welcomes you with joy in her heart.

"The hour of reunion will be awaited forthwith. I appoint you, Herr Forster, chief of the civil administration in the Danzig territory."

Forster's telegram to Herr Hitler read:

"My Fuehrer:

I have just signed and then put into effect the following basic law concerning the reunion of Danzig with the German Reich.

The basic State law of the Free State of Danzig and the reunion of Danzig with the German Reich is effective Sept. 1, 1939.

To lift the immediate distress of the people and State of the Free City of Danzig, I decree the following basic State law:

ARTICLE I
The Constitution of the Free City of Danzig has been suspended all effective immediately.

ARTICLE II
All legal and administrative power is in the hands of the civil administration by the head of State.

ARTICLE III
The Free City of Danzig with its territory and its peoples form

Continued on Page Five

Hitler Acts Against Poland

The port of Gdynia, north of Danzig (toward top of map), was blockaded this morning. At Gleiwitz (shown by cross) artillery fire was heard after a Polish-German skirmish had been reported there. Cracow, to the east, was among Polish cities said to have been bombed.

Hitler Tells the Reichstag 'Bomb Will Be Met by Bomb'

Chancellor Vows 'Fight Until Resolution' Against Poland—Gives Order of Succession As Goering, Hess, Then Senate to Choose

Chancellor Adolf Hitler of Germany, in a world broadcast this morning, opened "a fight until the resolution of the situation" against Poland, announcing that "from now on bomb will be met by bomb."

At the same time he announced, to the any eventuality, that if anything "happened" to him, Field Marshal Hermann Goering was to be in charge; if to Marshal Goering, Rudolph Hess; if to Herr Hess, the Senate, which he proposes to appoint, will select a successor.

The Chancellor, after attempting to narrow the conflict with Poland by assuring the Western powers that he had no designs on their frontiers, by assuring the neutrality of the nations to whom he was bound, acknowledging the friendliness of Italy and the new relations with Russia, issued a defy to Poland's allies.

Says He Will Carry on

"I shall carry on the fight regardless of against whom I may come," he declared.

At the same time he held the door open for Poland to capitulate to his demands, declaring that he did not intend to make war against unarmed children. He said that if a solution did not come from the Reich, and the provincial capitals, would be accepted by the German people.

The scene opened in the Kroll Opera House in Berlin was carried over armed waves to most of the nations of the world. From Berlin back up, had been arranged with the major networks of the United States, and, according to the announcer F., the German broadcasting system, over the Italian, Hungarian, Spanish, Norwegian, Swedish, Danish, Yugoslav, British and French national networks.

The comment to the Reichstag, opened by Herr Hitler himself, had been met and only a few hours before in the morning. Most of the members

Continued on Page Three

HITLER GIVES WORD

In a Proclamation He Accuses Warsaw of Appeal to Arms

FOREIGNERS ARE WARNED

They Remain in Poland at Own Risk—Nazis to Shoot at Any Planes Flying Over Reich

By OTTO D. TOLISCHUS
Special Cable to THE NEW YORK TIMES.

BERLIN, Friday, Sept. 1.—Charging that Germany had been attacked, Chancellor Hitler at 5:11 o'clock this morning issued a proclamation to the army declaring that from now on force will be met with force and railing on the armed forces "to fulfill their duty to the end.

The text of the proclamation reads:

To the defense forces
The Polish nation refused my efforts for a peaceful regulation of neighborly relations; instead it has appealed to weapons.

Germans in Poland are persecuted with a bloody terror and are driven from their homes. The series of border violations, which are unbearable to a great power, prove that the Poles no longer are willing to respect the German frontier. In order to put an end to this frantic activity no other means is left to me now than to meet force with force.

"Battle for Honor"

German defense forces will carry on the battle for the honor of the living rights of the re-...ened German people with determination.

I expect every German soldier, in view of the great tradition of eternal German soldiery to do his duty until the end.

Remember always in all situations you are the representative of National Socialist Greater Germany!

Long live our people and our Reich!

Berlin, Sept. 1, 1939.
ADOLF HITLER.

The commander-in-chief of the air force issued a decree effective immediately prohibiting the passage of any airplane over German territory excepting those of the Reich air force or of the government.

This morning the naval authorities ordered all German merchant ships in the Baltic Sea not to run to Danzig or Polish ports.

Anti-air raid defense were mobilized throughout the country early this morning.

A formal declaration of war against Poland had not yet been declared up to 8 o'clock [3 A M New York time], but a formal declaration from Herr Hitler

Reichstag Will Meet Today

Foreign correspondents at an official conference at the Reich Press Ministry at 3:30 o'clock [9:30 A M New York time] were told that they would receive every opportunity to facilitate the transmission of dispatches. Wireless stations have been instructed to speed up communications and the Ministry is installing additional batteries of telephones.

The Reichstag has been summoned to meet at 10 o'clock [4 A M New York time] to receive a more formal declaration from Herr Hitler.

SUMMARY OF SPEECH

A summary of Herr Hitler's speech was translated as follows:

"Whereupon we have been suffering under the burden of the Versailles. During war and visited atrocities on Germans, especially women and children, rolling many of them."

Continued on Page Three

The New York Times, September 1, 1939.